D0082741

AMERICAN HUNGERS

20|21

AMERICAN HUNGERS

The Problem of Poverty

in U.S. Literature, 1840–1945

Gavin Jones

PRINCETON UNIVERSITY PRESS

PRINCETON AND OXFORD

Library of Congress Cataloging-in-Publication Data

Jones, Gavin Roger, 1968-

American hungers : the problem of poverty in U.S. literature,

1840–1945 / by Gavin Jones.

p.   cm.   — (20/21)

Includes bibliographical references and index.

ISBN 978-0-691-12753–8 (alk. paper)

1. American literature—19th century—History and criticism.

2. Poverty in literature. 3. American literature—20th century—

History and criticism. 4. Social classes in literature. 5. Literature

and society—United States—History. I. Title.

PS217.P67J66 2007

810.9'355—dc22   2007008406

British Library Cataloging-in-Publication Data is available

This book has been composed in Helvetica Neue Light

Printed on acid-free paper. ∞

press.princeton.edu

Printed in the United States of America

10 9 8 7 6 5 4 3 2 1

To the memory of my mother,

MAUREEN JONES

You can philosophize, gentle reader . . . on the evils of amalgamation. Want is a more powerful philosopher and teacher.

—Harriet E. Wilson, *Our Nig*

CONTENTS

LIST OF ILLUSTRATIONS ▮▮▮▮▮▮▮▮▮▮

ACKNOWLEDGMENTS

FOR A NUMBER of important conversations early on, I am indebted to Daniel Aaron, Hugh McNeal, Peter McNeal, Elaine Scarry, Jeffrey Dolven, Sudhir Venkatesh, Samuel Otter, and the late Ian MacKillop. This project originated in Harvard's Society of Fellows, and grew in Stanford's Humanities Center; I am grateful for the collegial environment and the financial support of both institutions. Additional help toward production and research costs has been provided by Gordon and Dailey Pattee, and by Stanford's Office of the Vice Provost for Undergraduate Education. My thinking has been disciplined and energized by the following scholars, all of whom read and commented generously on chapter drafts: Denise Gigante, Arnold Rampersad, Shelley Fisher Fishkin, David Riggs, Lori Merish, Robert Ferguson, Maria Farland, Lee Mitchell, Tobias Gregory, and Bruce Simon. My colleagues Robert Polhemus, Seth Lerer, and Sianne Ngai offered encouragement at crucial times. Amanda Glesmann has been simply inspirational in helping to select and present the illustrations (thanks also to Davey Hubay for some sharp photography), while William Clayton assisted me diligently in the late stages of bibliographical research. A single conversation with Jay Fliegelman is worth a year of thinking on your own; this book has benefited immeasurably from many such conversations. Special thanks go to Walter Michaels for his intellectual generosity and his unwavering belief in the project. I am grateful to the anonymous readers for Princeton University Press, who offered helpful suggestions, and to Hanne Winarsky for her commitment and her skill in piloting the book through the publication process. Gordon Hutner and Paul Giles gave timely advice to publish sections of the developing manuscript. Accordingly, an earlier version of the introduction appeared as "Poverty and the Limits of Literary Criticism" in *American Literary History,* vol. 15.4 (Winter 2003), pp. 765–92, published by Oxford University Press;

and an earlier version of my discussion of Edith Wharton in Part III appeared as "Poverty, Gender, and Literary Criticism: Reassessing Edith Wharton's *The House of Mirth*" in *Comparative American Studies,* vol. 1.2 (Summer 2003), pp. 153–77, copyright Sage Publications. Both are reprinted here with permission. Finally, this book would not have been possible without the love and support of my family. My children, Eli and Hazel, have adorably distracted me throughout, while Judy Richardson has helped me get through all the difficult bits, and has filled the margins of writing with much more besides.

PREFACE

THE PURPOSE of this book is to redress the neglect of poverty as a category of critical discourse in the study of American literature and culture. Despite its prominence as a subject in the social sciences, poverty has remained unfocused in literary studies that privilege the cultural identity of the marginalized. It has been de-emphasized in accounts of the class consciousness of workers, and obscured by critical methodologies designed to deconstruct such monolithic ideas as "the poor." Scholars have largely overlooked the complexity of poverty as a subject of representation that runs throughout U.S. literature, rather than a subject that congregates in a particular literary period, movement, or genre, or that preoccupies a single writer. There may no longer be the "poverty of theory" in American studies scholarship that Robert Sklar noted in 1975.[1] But there has been little theory of poverty, and thus virtually no critical and theoretical framework to situate literary works that have grappled with the ethical, cultural, and linguistic difficulties of poverty as a substantive category of social being.

American Hungers is not an exhaustive literary history of writing about poverty in the United States (an undertaking far beyond the scope of a single study) but an attempt to revise our critical idiom by offering fresh ways to view both established and less established texts. Recent scholarship has made powerful cases for the work of previously neglected writers, as pressing concerns with race, ethnicity, gender, and (to a lesser extent) class have recovered a vast range of material. Yet too often analyses of writing by or about the socially marginalized have referenced poverty with little sense of the ideological battles surrounding it; *poverty* has remained a vaguely descriptive term and not a dynamic category that develops structurally and thematically across textual space. What is needed now, I believe, is an unlocalized critical language that helps us see how poverty, as a fused social and cultural concern, operates in literary texts in complex ways that move beyond the perspectives of discrete classes, races, or genders, and that shape the contours of both mainstream and minority traditions of writing.

To confront poverty in an American context is in many ways a shocking act. Attempts to understand the persistence of poverty have remained remarkably controversial aspects of American intellectual and social history, just as they continue to unsettle national ideologies and to disrupt conventional ways in which we think of class and cultural identity. The political contradictions of poverty necessitate close linguistic analysis. Thus, I chart the development of poverty as a literary polemic through case studies of selected authors and texts, all of which powerfully animate—and are animated by—important historical and cultural contexts in which awareness of poverty developed. The three parts of this book treat specific texts within three historical periods marked by downturns and depressions that heightened public and political consciousness of economic inequality. Herman Melville's prolonged literary treatment of poverty, which ranged from *Redburn* (1849) to *The Confidence-Man* (1857), is situated within the literary and social discourse on poverty emerging from a turbulent economy of recurrent slumps between 1837 and 1858. Theodore Dreiser's *Sister Carrie* (1900) and Edith Wharton's *The House of Mirth* (1905) are considered in light of a prominent pseudosociological discourse of pauperism that flowed from the deep economic crisis of the mid-1890s, and in light of the issues of gender and poverty that featured in women's cross-class representation of the female poor. James Agee's *Let Us Now Praise Famous Men* (1941) and Richard Wright's *Black Boy* (1945) are analyzed in relation to documentary expressions of the peculiar cultural and ideological crisis of the Great Depression, and in relation to the sociological discussion of black "delinquency" from the late 1930s and early 1940s—a period when it became most apparent that the legacies of slavery had condemned African Americans to disproportionately high levels of want. From the perspective of literary history, I work to appreciate the subject of poverty transhistorically, unhooked from particular literary movements or genres, while also recognizing how poverty is always intertwined with conventional literary categories such as naturalism, documentary realism, and autobiography.

Poverty, as a term and a concern, emerges with remarkable frequency in American literature. What I choose to emphasize here are texts that offer especially self-conscious theorizations of poverty as a material, social, cultural, and psychological condition that impacts the practice of literary representation. Each of our textual case studies attempts to uncover a particular problematic that emerges when poverty is isolated as a category that both relates to and differs from broader issues of race, social class, and gender. In Melville, we explore the foundations and the limits of a cultural analysis that balances the social causes of poverty with its ideological, behavioral, and linguistic effects. In Dreiser, we confront the problems of maintaining such an approach in light of the troubling persistence of poverty among allegedly mobile, white, male Americans. In Wharton, we treat the feminization of poverty—the special ways it seems to affect women economically and psychologically. In Agee, we consider the ethical dilemmas of treating poverty as an aesthetic category of representation. And in Wright, we realize the difference race makes in the experience of poverty by African Americans and, implicitly, by other minority groups—a point we return to in the conclusion. This book uncovers historical developments in the form and content of poverty discourse, whereby moral and cultural approaches to poverty in the antebellum era merged into biological and social explanations in the Progressive age, and then into psychological and subjective responses during the Great Depression. But we will also see how the nature of poverty as a subject tends to destabilize straightforward historical narrative, as moral and biological explanations of poverty return to complicate the very moments when progressive socioeconomic explanations were developing.

Recent literary critics, historians, and sociologists have suggested that prevalent racial explanations and representations of social difference in the United States have traditionally stood in for the nation's "extremely impoverished political language of class."[2] A major argument of this book is that, in literature at least, this language is not impoverished at all—indeed, it is poverty itself that provides this language. What I describe here is a polemics of poverty that was firmly established by the 1840s and reached a kind of apotheosis in the Depression years. Though partially eclipsed by debates over slavery in the antebellum era, this contentious discourse comprehended economic inequality in ways largely independent of race, even as it defined poverty as a condition with cultural ramifications never quite reducible to a socioeconomic view of class. We can isolate a national debate over poverty, I suggest, despite the fact that many of the concepts and institutional responses we encounter in this study developed in similar and earlier forms in European countries. That poverty seems to fit more naturally in other national situations is, ironically, at the heart of my thesis. The peculiar pressures on the term *poverty* in the United States, pressures that make cultural and personal explanations dominate public policy, have also yielded a sophisticated literary strain in which the ideological subversiveness of persistent want translates into epistemological and formal dilemmas of a textual kind.

American Hungers attempts to combine creative literature and social discourse, and thus to inhabit ground between literary (or cultural) criticism and the history of social thought. It strives to show how the problem of poverty engenders literary aesthetics and cultural explorations in largely unrecognized ways, while recovering the social and historical work of that representation. This cultural history of poverty matters now precisely because so many of the dominant opinions and legislative policies regarding income inequity repeat beliefs that were formulated, debated, and frequently challenged in past generations. This book uncovers the literary and cultural foundations of the poverty problems that confront us today, in a nation that is peculiarly one of tremendous wealth and significant poverty—a nation haunted by widespread hunger and malnutrition, growing socioeconomic inequality, and an increasing institutional abandonment of the chronically disadvantaged.[3] By knowing the past we can better understand the present, if only to realize how stuck we are in past ways of seeing and treating poverty.

AMERICAN HUNGERS

INTRODUCTION

The Problem of Poverty in

Literary Criticism

"THIS association of poverty with progress is the great enigma of our times," wrote the social reformer Henry George toward the end of the nineteenth century, "the central fact from which spring industrial, social, and political difficulties that perplex the world, and with which statesmanship and philanthropy and education grapple in vain." For George, the persistence of poverty in the wealthy nations of the industrialized world posed problems that were ideological as much as material—problems with the power to destroy the progressive notions underpinning "civilization" itself. If George was discussing a crisis that afflicted Western nations at large, then the paradox of want amid wealth seemed especially intense in an American context where political institutions of theoretical equality were based on "a state of most glaring social inequality." Echoing George in the *New York Times* at the beginning of the twenty-first century, the economist Paul Krugman has described the contemporary era as a new Gilded Age in which wealth and income have shifted dramatically toward a super-rich elite, leaving the United States—despite its economic achievements—with "more poverty and lower life expectancy than any other major advanced nation." For Krugman, as for George, the prominence of poverty in an American context poses more than just a social problem. It augurs the collapse of democracy itself as a political and social ideal.[1]

The presence of poverty within the developed nations of the industrialized world has always tended to antagonize the liberal assumptions of freedom and universality that underpin a market economy. Hence the long tradition in Western social thought of rationalizing poverty by describing the poor as inherently disordered and degraded.[2] In the United States, with its pronounced ideologies of social fluidity and equality of opportunity, difficult questions have surrounded the masses of people who lack the material resources for decent living, and who seem unable to rise freely on an economic scale. Doctrines of individualism have tended to downplay poverty as a problem of social structure by rooting its causes in the flawed character or in the immoral behavior of individuals. The nation's legacy of institutional racism, and the disproportionate rates of poverty among the nonwhite population, have worked to highlight cultural categories, such as race, over social categories, such as class, in explanations of economic inequality. According to Adolph Reed, Jr., in an analysis of the 2004 presidential election results, "the language of cultural divide has come to mask the class dynamics in American politics. Culture has swallowed or displaced class as an analytical category in American political debate, across the ideological spectrum." When poverty attracts the attention of legislators, as it did during the welfare reforms of the mid-1990s, its origins are consistently traced to alleged dysfunctions in family structure and lifestyle, or a refusal to conform to correct behavioral values.[3] Media projections of a predominantly dark underclass have further encouraged popular perceptions that poverty emerges from factors subcultural and ethnic rather than external and economic.[4] Despite the strong interest of sociologists in the poor, and despite periodic moments of public consciousness of the nation's neediest, the subject of poverty has remained a partial blind spot in the broader culture, unable to be seen directly or for long.[5] The deep economic inequities exposed by Hurricane Katrina in 2005 have made little lasting impact on public attitudes, recent research has shown, with poverty and inequality remaining the nation's "dirty little secret."[6]

The literary expression at the heart of my study is significant, first and foremost, because it highlights poverty as a crucial political problem, verging on a national catastrophe. Our writers may be drawn more to the polemics of poverty than to its potential solutions, yet the debate in which they engage is an essential prerequisite to social understanding and action—a making visible of a social situation that Barbara Ehrenreich describes as virtually hidden in the national culture, and largely absent from its political rhetoric.[7] Literary analysis can also help to fill what sociologists have described as a significant "absence of a historical context in the analysis and dialogue about poverty in this country" by engaging integrally with intellectual and social history, and by offering access to groups of people who—in the words of the Depression writer Meridel Le Sueur—"leave no statistics, no record, obituary or remembrance." Literature can shed light too on a topic that has tended to resist rigorous philosophical analysis, and has remained far less parsed, in literary theory and criticism, than companion categories such as desire and consumption.[8] (Even those Western philosophers who purport to offer a "philosophy of the poor," argues Jacques Rancière, merely reduce the poor to shells of impotence, passivity, and fatigue, whose real purpose is to sanction the intellectual privilege that makes philosophy possible.)[9] My aim is to let this literature open up the complexities and contradictions of poverty as we go along, yet some important coordinates can help us to map something like an initial theory of poverty, or at least an initial framework of ideas, that can in turn help us to locate the distinctiveness of this contentious category, and thus to understand why—despite its powers of political, historical, and philosophical illumination—poverty has been too overlooked in literary criticism.

This book is concerned with literature as an acknowledgment of poverty as a specific state of social being, defined by its *socioeconomic suffering*—a term that emerges from broader sociological and anthropological theories of "social suffering" as a cultural process.[10] I choose the narrower term *socioeconomic suffering* because it gets at the peculiar dialectics of poverty as a category—its position between material and nonmaterial, objective and subjective criteria. As a condition of *socioeconomic* suffering, poverty is primarily material and economic. It rests on levels of possession and power, and is physical at its extreme, returning ultimately to the body as the site that bears the marks, the damage, of being poor. In this regard, poverty loses its urgency if it is not at least potentially absolute, if it is not defined by the lack—or by the threat of the lack—of the resources necessary for subsistence, for life itself, or for health and well-being. We can thus attempt to look at poverty objectively as a line, a threshold of human welfare. But if poverty is ultimately marked on the body, as hunger or as physical suffering, then it is always as much subjective as it is objective. "'Tis not always poverty to be poor," remarks the narrator of Herman Melville's sketch, "The Two Temples."[11] Here poverty, as a socioeconomic level, becomes impoverishment specifically when it is experienced, by an individual or a group, as a kind of suffering. The materiality of need thus opens into the nonmaterial areas of psychology, emotion, and culture, with poverty moving away from the absolute and the objective toward the relative, the ideological, and the ethical. The suffering of poverty is sharpened by socioeconomic inequality, and is thus always pressured relatively by the context of wealth, and warped in the United States by ideological forces that work to internalize indigence as shame or blame.[12] And poverty is an ethical dilemma, more than simply a static "social condition," because it provokes controversial questions of distributive justice—whether, for example, disadvantaged individuals are *unfairly* kept from social opportunities—which themselves return to the difficulties of defining a socioeconomic minimum and evaluating what is necessary for a level of decent living.[13] Any definition of what it means to be poor is doubly difficult because it combines shifting economic criteria (the problem of where to draw the line, or where to stop drawing it) with much broader community judgments on what constitutes an acceptable standard of living, and who is responsible, ultimately, for those people who fall beneath it.[14]

Literature reveals how poverty is established, defined, and understood in discourse, as a psychological and cultural problem that depends fundamentally on the language used to describe it. This is why creative writers have responded so productively to poverty. The problems that poverty raises, whether ideologically, ethically, or linguistically, have fueled a network of signifying practices—a history of writing and thinking about poverty that remains central to any understanding of the history of socioeconomic inequality. We can think of poverty as a *discourse* in more Foucauldian terms: a system of thought that materially disciplines and disempowers the poor. Yet *polemics* is a better term because it more accurately captures a degree of contestation and instability in discussions of poverty. Hence poverty gains significance as a social problem that posits a relation and, frequently, a contradiction between the discursive—understood qualitatively as psychology, culture, politics, and so on—and the material: limited quantities of resources and opportunities, for example, or physiological facts of hunger and malnutrition. It is instructive in this regard to think of poverty alongside the category of *desire* because both seem to return to a fundamental "lack," yet they are not terms that perfectly collapse into one another. Though theories of desire differ, literary critics have been particularly drawn to its essential resistance to fulfillment, which explains subjectivity as constituted in an impossible desire to return to an original oneness, and explains language itself, whose very premise is "based on the foreclosure of satisfaction."[15] Poverty may presuppose desire, yet it is a socioeconomically bounded form of desire based on the *possibility,* not the foreclosure, of satisfaction—a possibility of being materially unpoor, which helps shape the suffering of poverty in the context of greater levels of wealth, making this suffering seem so problematic and, for some at least, so unjust. For many of the writers in this study, poverty is also intertwined with questions of selfhood, being, and language, yet always in a struggle against a universal, metaphysical understanding of *lack,* and toward an understanding of *need* as a specific kind of suffering that is at once materially bounded, socially inscribed, and psychologically registered.

This dialectical relationship between the material and the discursive defines the theoretical parameters of the literary debate over poverty—its particular thematics—and engenders further dialectical relations between necessity and contingency, location and mobility, enslavement and freedom, domination and exploitation, as we shall see throughout this book. Poverty is such a polemical subject in part because any balance between its socioeconomic and its psychocultural dimensions is always on the verge of being upset, especially in an overweighting toward nonmaterial characteristics that can easily seem the cause of need. And there has been an imbalance, or a series of biases, in recent critical discourse as well—a failure, put simply, to harmonize the competing claims of "class" and "cultural identity" in a way necessary to illuminate poverty as a category or a concept. This imbalance is particularly significant, I suggest, because it tends to mirror trends within the mainstream political discourses that the institution of academic criticism often purports to oppose.

Of course, this blindness toward poverty in literary criticism is far from total. Robert Bremner's groundbreaking study, *From the Depths* (1956), offers a history of social and creative writing on the poor, ranging from the "discovery" of poverty as a chronic condition in the 1840s to the growing substitution of environmental for individualistic explanations of poverty by literary realists and social analysts at the turn of the century. Yet Bremner's study remains a broad overview with little in-depth textual analysis. Benedict Giamo's *On the Bowery* (1989) and Keith Gandal's *The Virtues of the Vicious* (1997) offer excellent introductions to the varieties of poverty writing in the Gilded Age, and to the middle-class fascination with the alternative subculture of the poor. Both of these studies expand the thesis outlined by Bremner: that the literature of naturalism, with its predominant interest in the underprivileged and the downwardly mobile, necessarily follows the more enlightened view of the poor—as victims of their physical environment—found within turn-of-the-century social science and Progressive reform. Discussion of poverty is dotted throughout criticism of literary naturalism. Yet even Jennifer Fleissner's *Women, Compulsion, Modernity* (2004)—one of the best recent reevaluations of the genre—depends on a formalist mode of analysis whereby the poverty of characters becomes determined by the force of narrative modes, such as "sentimentalism" or the "plot of decline," more than by an authorial engagement with poverty as a social dilemma.[16] In addition to this genre-based containment of poverty, book-length studies have targeted individual authors, such as Erskine Caldwell, or specific literary archetypes, such as the southern poor white, which Sylvia Jenkins Cook traces into the literature of the 1930s.[17] There has, of course, been specific attention to poverty in British literature, prompted in part by Gertrude Himmelfarb's exhaustive analyses of poverty as a dilemma within social philosophy from mid-eighteenth-century thinkers to the late Victorians.[18] In a broader, North American context, Roxanne Rimstead's *Remnants of Nation* (2001) is an interesting analysis of writing about poverty by Canadian women that does much to unpack poverty as a distinctive narrative category. Yet Rimstead tends to entrench the distinction between a politically oppositional discourse in which poor subjects speak their own experience of poverty, and a "dominant discourse" that necessarily blames or erases the poor through discursive marginalization or symbolic violence.[19]

Most typical is the way that poverty enters as a subcategory, or as an occasional series of references, within studies of writing by women or by racial/ethnic minorities, and within studies of social class in literature. Stacy Morgan's *Rethinking Social Realism* (2004), for example, shows how African American writers and graphic artists confronted the psychological strain of poverty, as a disruption to radicalized working-class consciousness, alongside their more pervasive consideration of racial injustice (Morgan is one of the few literary scholars who makes *poverty* an entry in her index).[20] Amy Lang's *The Syntax of Class* (2003) refers throughout to the power of poverty to determine the class positions of characters, yet the book remains mostly interested in the ways that social class, as a broader category of identity, interacts with gender and, to a lesser extent, with race. Lang's study adds to a strong critical focus on domesticity as the locus of U.S. class consciousness, which tends to emphasize how the middle class anxiously constructed itself against representations of the working classes. Within this literature on class, however, the referencing of poverty has often remained vague and has refused to coalesce into a focused and specific analysis, as we shall see. Critics have tended to discuss representations of human subjects understood to be poor without explicitly targeting or debating poverty as a distinct form of socioeconomic suffering (a point that can apply to primary texts as well). Why has an overwhelming concern with the socially marginalized emerged without a sufficient framework in which to situate an explicit discussion of material deprivation? The answers, I suggest, lie both within the characteristics of contemporary critical methodologies, and within the nature and difficulty of poverty itself as a category.

The obvious reason for the neglect of poverty lies in the notorious downgrading of class as a category of literary analysis, which reflects the silencing of working-class consciousness and the masking of class segregation in American society.[21] In their unusually statistical analysis of the breadth of articles that have appeared in *American Quarterly* since its inception in 1949, Larry Griffin and Maria Tempenis conclude that there is a long-standing bias in American studies toward the multicultural questions of gender, race, and ethnicity at the expense of analyses of social class—an emphasis on questions of identity and representation rather than on those of social structural position. Griffin and Tempenis argue that disciplinary borders within American-studies scholarship have hampered engagement with social-science methodologies that have maintained an emphasis on socioeconomics.[22] Writing in the early 1990s, John Carlos Rowe makes a similar point. Methodologies divide social theorists, who have emphasized changing class divisions since World War II, and postmodern critical theorists for whom the concept of class has become almost an embarrassment in its maintenance of rigid Marxist distinctions.[23] If the 1980s saw an explosion of interest in race and gender (ironically, Rowe's own book, *At Emerson's Tomb,* analyzes the politics of classic American literature almost solely from the perspectives of race and gender), then the 1990s saw the emergence of the nation as a category that some critics describe as threatening to displace class altogether from the front line of critical analysis.[24] The theoretical and critical movement now to decenter the nation itself in an effort to think "transnationally" may have originated from social theories of globalized capital, yet the greatest influence on literary scholarship has been work that stresses not global inequity but the international flow of cultural commodities and ethnic identities.[25] Rimstead has even argued that postcolonial modes of criticism have tended to place perceptions of poverty *outside* the developed world.[26] At the very least, the theoretical unsettling of the nation as a unit of analysis can act to distract attention from the social experience of class difference, and can neutralize awareness of the state as the domain of welfare and the regulator of social resources by which economic inequities get maintained or reduced.[27]

Rowe makes a convincing case for the inevitable clash between poststructuralist theory and traditional notions of social class. But the most powerful force sidelining class has surely been the persistent concern, among literary scholars, with the question of cultural identity, seen most recently in transnational work that looks like multiculturalism on a global scale. An overwhelming interest in oppressed subject positions has tended to evade the problem of economic inequality by centering social marginalization on the cultural identity of the marginalized.[28] Of course the study of cultural identity is by no means monolithic. The school of postpositivist realism, associated with scholars such as Satya Mohanty, for example, rejects overly essentialist views of identity and considers class location in its complex account of social experience. Yet class can still seem buried, at times, in a mode of analysis that stresses domination over exploitation, and that inevitably works to affirm the cultural identities of minorities by according them "epistemic privilege."[29] Even modes of minority criticism that do keep class more squarely in the picture tend to emphasize the affirmative and self-emancipating power of collective class consciousness over the suffering of economic deprivation.[30]

In his attempt to reintroduce social class into the canon debate that raged in the late 1980s and early 1990s, John Guillory argued that the reduction of political questions to the realm of the cultural explains why class is often left out of the discussion: "For while it is easy enough to conceive of a self-affirmative racial or sexual identity, it makes very little sense to posit an affirmative lower-class identity, as such an identity would have to be grounded in the experience of deprivation per se."[31] Guillory is one of a number of scholars who have attempted to understand the difference of class, as a category of analysis, and to argue forcefully for its importance. In this regard, work that bemoans the absence of class discourse in the United States becomes the discourse itself. (The concluding point of Griffin and Tempenis's analysis of *American Quarterly* is not that class has become any less important in recent years, but that class analysis has always been practiced at a constant, if rather low, level.) There has, if anything, been a resurgence of interest in class in recent years, as critics have offered to rethink class theoretically, to expand our knowledge of how middle-class writers represented inequality, and to revise the canon by establishing the aesthetic range and ideological complexity of neglected writings by left-wing intellectuals and by members of the working class. There has been strong critical interest in cross-class representation, in the depiction of work, in the proletarian novel, and in "panic fiction"—just some of the areas in which class issues naturally feature. To explain the neglect of poverty, then, we need to analyze not only the downplaying of class within critical debates but also the ways that class typically gets included and discussed.

Guillory's use of the term *lower class* is revealing in this regard as it points to a conceptual slipperiness in class analysis, whereby the terms *class* and *poverty* tend to blur into one another, as if to be poor and to be working class were one and the same thing.[32] The term *poverty* has always had an uncertain position in class analysis, going back even to Marx himself, who famously described the Lumpenproletariat ("ragged poor") in images of residue and waste—a counterrevolutionary conception that later thinkers such as Frantz Fanon have sought to revise.[33] Rimstead has speculated that this negative designation of the poor in Marxist theory, which results from poverty being defined "more by consumption than by production, more by deprivation and need than by labor or political agency," helps to explain some of the differences between poverty narratives (as she characterizes them) and working-class writing, and to explain the relative neglect of poverty in class-based discourse as a whole.[34] The category of poverty certainly remains ambiguous in traditional Marxist thought, varying between the one-dimensional oppression and domination of the "naturally arising poor," and the revolutionary potential of the "artificially impoverished," exploited proletariat.[35] Poverty is always implicit, at some level, within class discourse, just as Raymond Williams describes how "the massive historical and immediate experience of class domination and subordination" has inspired Marxian analysis of the materiality of cultural production.[36] Yet this *implicitness* of poverty is really the problem: class analysis often fails to focus sharply on what poverty means as a social category. One of the most comprehensive studies of nineteenth-century American class discourse, Martin J. Burke's *The Conundrum of Class* (1995), for example, charts the controversies surrounding the categorization of class in the United States, but almost entirely ignores the specific discourse on poverty that had developed fully by the 1840s.[37] Even the boldest of recent efforts to reposition social class within critical theory, such as Rowe's essay "The Writing Class," passes over issues of economic injustice and dispossession to arrive at an analysis of the technological and philosophical implications of the new global economy of representation. Class analysis has, in this way, targeted the system of capitalist production and consumption, rather than considering the individuals and groups who have remained partly excluded from it.

This last point is true of perhaps the most prevalent concern in recent literary studies of class, the concern with middle-class identity and with the feminized domesticity through which it has often been understood. This perennial interest in the middle class, driven powerfully by scholars of nineteenth-century women's writing, has coalesced recently into studies of panic literature, particularly the writing that emerged from the economic slumps at midcentury. Analysis of panic literature tends to follow Ann Fabian's thesis that, by undermining confidence in the capitalist system itself, financial panics provoked conservative literary responses that sought to resolve the ideological contradictions of the market. The recent critical interest in the literature of middle-class fears of economic instability has inevitably made poverty seem less a specific, analyzable social state than a potential and somewhat vague threat (or at best a momentary slump), while the poor themselves become the negative symbols of moral degradation against which middle-class identity is defined.[38] Even when we turn to analyses that *have* emphasized the lower social classes rather than the middle-class lens through which they are seen—hence the rise of what John Russo and Sherry Lee Linkon term the "New Working-Class Studies"—various critical trends still conspire to cloud analysis of poverty as a category.[39] These trends can be broadly termed the *affirmative,* the *deconstructive,* and the *composite.*

Affirmative methods of class criticism (we will return later to the deconstructive and composite methods) have tended to highlight the culture of the working class, rather than the socioeconomic situation of the poor. For example, Michael Denning's *Mechanic Accents* (1987), an analysis of the nineteenth-century dime novel, follows the lead of new labor historians by stressing not class structure but class formation—the social, cultural, and linguistic ways that class relations get signified and represented.[40] The working class becomes a complex "identity," formed in response to material conditions and socioeconomic power relations, but by no means reducible to questions of exploitation and inequality alone.[41] Denning's *The Cultural Front* (1996) is a painstaking investigation of the impact of the labor movement on the culture of the 1930s, yet again any consideration of social hardship is displaced by the aesthetic and intellectual effects of a class consciousness based broadly on the rise of an inclusive popular front. Indeed, Denning seeks explicitly to overturn the belief that the leftward turn in the 1930s emerged from the poverty of the Depression (or from the rise of fascism in Europe), rooting it instead in the combination of new union organization and a burgeoning culture industry. When Denning highlights the representation of urban social conditions, found within the era's "Ghetto Pastorals," he turns more to the ethnic and racial concerns of this literature than to its confrontation with poverty and lack.[42]

Running against the complex forces that Stanley Aronowitz identifies as silencing questions of working-class identity in the United States, a dominant strain of recent criticism has sought to establish the importance of class not as a response to socioeconomic suffering but as an ideological perception and historical experience shaped positively from what George Lipsitz terms "organizational learning, social contestation, and political mobilization."[43] The emphasis on class as a form of cultural identity and/or political agency can be seen clearly in recent reevaluations of the proletarian literature of the 1930s. Barbara Foley's *Radical Representations* (1993), for example, suggests how economic deprivation penetrates the subject matter of proletarian fiction, though her central concern is with the representation of class consciousness, in the politically affirmative sense of class as an instrument for socialist revolution—a partial reprising of earlier traditions of Marxist criticism.[44] Criticism that views literature as evidence for the history of political consciousness, moreover, tends to avoid the kind of close textual analysis necessary to understand the ambiguity, instability, and controversy of poverty as a category. Though Foley undermines overly simplistic accounts of the political dogmatism and stylistic naïveté of proletarian fiction, she explicitly refrains from "detailed readings of individual texts" in an effort to "offer omnibus analyses generalizing about the relation of generic to doctrinal politics in a broad range of novels."[45] A number of recent books that direct attention to the nation's overlooked history of left-wing writing (particularly from the 1930s) tend to base their reevaluations on the diversity or the technical complexity of a writer's literary production rather than on an engagement with a single topic such as poverty—a topic that can, after all, make a writer seem reductively materialist or overly propagandistic.[46]

Supplementing this concern with proletarian fiction, an interest in the category of work has also grown in recent literary criticism. Occasionally such criticism stresses the impoverishing impact of exploitative labor practices, yet this emphasis on work has often deflected direct analysis of poverty.[47] Laura Hapke's *Labor's Text* (2001) is by far the most exhaustive examination of representations of the worker in American literature, and it too makes occasional reference to the working poor and to the inequalities of class that, according to Hapke, get minimized by multiculturalists. Yet Hapke is primarily concerned with the cultural perception of the working class as an identity, founded on labor as a behavior, and with the political agency of the worker.[48] In terms of themes, Hapke is drawn most powerfully to the ideology of upward social mobility that she describes as haunting labor writing. Ironically, though, Hapke herself is most critical of a writer such as Upton Sinclair who represents the damage of poverty and "casts doubt on workers' ability to climb out of the mire." The flip side of a desire to see the working class as having intelligence and political agency is a frustration with writers who depict individuals limited by their socioeconomic environment—writers who thus themselves come to seem constrained by their middle-class condescension.[49] Hence an awareness of the negative effects of poverty can get partially obscured in criticism that valorizes working-class consciousness, or that surveys labor writing.

The overall point here is that a certain branch of class studies has itself shifted away from a consideration of socioeconomics, toward an interest in the complexities of social and cultural identity construction. Guillory's point that class cannot be affirmed as an identity, in the same way as race and gender, is only partly true. When class arrives with a degree of political agency, it can be (and indeed has been) affirmed as a category of identity. Prominent reevaluators of class, such as Wai Chee Dimock, have thus emphasized historical evidence that working-class women in antebellum America enjoyed income, cultural pursuits, and communal happiness not typically associated with brutalizing industrial conditions.[50] But to view class in this way, as something that transcends socioeconomic suffering, is also to imply the reverse: there are elements of exploitation and deprivation that resist a cultural perspective—what Guillory himself describes as the institutional powers that restrict access to the channels for representing social identity.[51] There are undoubtedly avenues along which poverty, as a specific category, can be affirmed as a positive good. Lawrence Buell, for example, has called for critics to take seriously the long tradition of "voluntary simplicity discourse" that runs through American literature, whereby downward mobility represents moral virtue in the context of capitalist materialism. Walter Benn Michaels has identified a similar trend in Michael Hardt and Antonio Negri's *Empire* (2000): a desire to reclaim the poor for the Left by ontologizing poverty as a desirable identity.[52] Yet as an enforced situation of economic disadvantage, poverty resists the affirmative pull of working-class consciousness, middle-class self-privation, or ontological theory. To interpret class as a cultural or social identity that operates beyond poverty only leaves questions of "need," "deprivation," and "social necessity" untheorized and excluded.

Not all analyses of the working class tend to view class as an affirmative entity. Critics such as Guillory and Rita Felski perhaps go too far in reducing working-class status *to* poverty, making it inevitably the realm of material deprivation and limited infrastructural resources, radically isolated from an implicitly middle-class norm.[53] No absolute relation links low income to illiteracy, for example, while environmental barriers are always potentially surmountable and unstable. Alongside the recent trend that characterizes class as a positive formation, a powerful countertrend has sought to deconstruct overly rigid assumptions of class consciousness. Ironically, though, this poststructuralist reevaluation of class has only again reinforced the displacement of poverty as a category of social discourse.

    Wai Chee Dimock and Michael T. Gilmore's edited collection, *Rethinking Class* (1994), remains an influential attempt to work against the subordination of class within literary studies. Most of the essays in *Rethinking Class* are concerned with the complexities of middle-class identity construction, just as the collection as a whole strives to understand class as a relational structure not necessarily tied to a privileged view of working-class experience and agency. *Rethinking Class* is directed against an orthodox Marxist account of class as the determinant of historical change. Far from a primary force, class thus becomes, at times, a "second-degree register," an "epiphenomenon," virtually an abstract social relation lacking "causal ground." When class *is* targeted centrally, it becomes valued as "a theoretical enterprise" rather than "an empirical description of social groups." This rejection of "class essentialism" has yielded a version of class not as a stable material fact but as a polymorphous, unstable, and contradictory cultural arena.[54]

Recent considerations of the difference between class and categories such as race and gender have repeatedly argued that class does not share in the anti-essentialist project of race and gender studies—the move to reveal the socially constructed nature of allegedly natural or biological features.[55] Class only makes sense *as* a social relation, these arguments run, and thus does not require demystification but instead necessitates an understanding of its hierarchical and dynamic structure. Ironically, though, such efforts to establish the social uniqueness of class tend to re-essentialize race and gender as epistemologically different "experiential realities" (Foley), as forces that "often mark identity inescapably" (Felski). And arguments for the *contingency* of class as a social relation (Lang) stress its capacity to be transcended (again making race and gender seem insurmountable absolutes), thus sanctioning the normalcy of mobility as a way to think about how class operates.[56]

Class analysis, then, has been drawn in recent years to the relational and contingent aspects of class as a category. Panic fiction generates criticism in part because it highlights the instability and unpredictability of the market. The recent interest in cross-class contact is another example of a critical approach that harbors a poststructuralist view of class as mobility and change. Michael Trask's *Cruising Modernism* (2003), for example, employs queer theory to argue that American modernist literature is rooted in the irregular sexual desire that the upper classes felt toward lower-class transients. Rather than simply being overlooked, poverty gets explicitly displaced by the historical thesis that, in the early twentieth century, fundamental class relations broke down into a pleasure economy based on desire and surplus wealth, as a consumer culture of choice supposedly replaced a pain economy rooted in subsistence. Contingency outstrips necessity, distinct classes become fluid groups, and the very categories that might cohere into a definition of poverty—irregularity, casual labor, insecurity, for example—become linked instead to the risky pleasures of working-class consumerism and erotic sexuality.[57]

Current critical methodologies are finely geared to break down essences, to dissolve race, gender, nation, and class as stable absolutes, to emphasize instead that individuals are more complex and hybrid than the categories into which we want to place them. Such criticism reveals rich potential by liberating class from material certitudes and from economic determinism. But in this effort to highlight instability and uncertainty, what happens to the specificity of socioeconomic need? How do we treat the question of whether individuals may be restricted in crucial ways by their material resources, or lack access to the tools of social movement? Whether we see class as different from a category such as race because the former is less stable, or whether we view class and race as essentially similar because they are equally the performative product of unstable situations and behaviors, the contingency and indeterminacy of class is in both cases presupposed. The result is a neglect of the aspects of class that can harm individuals physically and intellectually, frustrate them emotionally, and, most importantly, hinder in some form their social agency and political liberty.[58] In other words, any definition of poverty as a state of material necessity comes to seem pure determinism from a perspective that views the possibility of social transition as the inevitability of categorical disintegration.[59] To argue that class is at heart a temporal category of change and movement can work to nebulize the issue of poverty, dissolving it into categorical indistinctness and impermanence. There may be a crucial clash, then, between poverty as a condition of relative and unhealthy material lack and these dominant trends in literary analysis. Poverty is not something that can be affirmed in the same way as other cultural identities, including, to an extent, the identity of being working class. But then should poverty be de-essentialized, in the same way that race and gender get de-essentialized, when the concern with economic justice that underscores poverty returns to social amenities that are *essential* to a decent quality of life, whether or not the measure of poverty is absolute (based on resources judged essential to subsistence) or relative (based on what a community believes is essential for decent living, in comparison with broader levels of wealth)? Thus understood, the notion of poverty puts pressure on quantification more than deconstruction.

The clash of poverty with affirmative *and* deconstructive critical methodologies begins to account for its insignificance in critical discourse. This double clash clarifies why "[t]he issue of poverty is rarely center stage even in inquiries about class conflict in proletarian fiction and working-class writing," as Rimstead argues in her study of poverty narratives by Canadian women, "or in new radical fields of inquiry such as feminism, postcolonialism, and multiculturalism, all of which are concerned with social justice."[60] But there is another major reason why the topic of poverty may have been partially obscured: the emergence of a composite form of critical analysis, outlined by Griffin and Tempenis, whereby class becomes inextricably connected to multicultural concerns.[61] Even Rimstead's analysis, unusual in its direct treatment of poverty, privileges the specific realm of women's writing about the poor, as if the subject of poverty can only become visible when combined with a nonsocioeconomic category such as gender.

Cora Kaplan has described the recent critical interest in gender, race, and ethnicity as a productive, nonreductive recontextualizing of class. There are definite ways in which this composite style of analysis has sharpened the focus on poverty. The historian Mark Pittenger's compelling essay on Progressive Era cross-class representation, for example, demonstrates how the categories of class, race, and culture conspired in popular and academic writing to produce an ambivalent view of the poor as more vital and alive on the one hand, yet a revolting, degenerate threat to civilized order on the other.[62] More typical, though, is the tendency for composite analyses to overwhelm the socioeconomic, and particularly the category of socioeconomic *need,* even as they seek to raise the prominence of class. We have already seen how Trask's attempt to merge class studies and sexuality studies shifts economic relations into erotic instability and bodily desire. The scholarly interest in female domesticity, as Dimock and Gilmore have pointed out, likewise makes class present only as it is negotiated and determined by an implicitly bourgeois power of gender.[63] I will offer two brief examples of this broader trend: Paula Rabinowitz's *Labor and Desire* (1991), which uncovers a neglected tradition of radical writing by women in the 1930s, and Cora Kaplan's own special issue of *PMLA,* "Rereading Class" (2000).

According to Rabinowitz, a focus on the effects of hunger on the body—or rather, a focus on the virile masculine transcendence of that hunger—is central to conventional proletarian literature and criticism, helping to shape a radical class consciousness that has repressed gender as a political category. The concept of economic lack becomes explicitly male, and is thus naturally displaced from a study that prioritizes femaleness as mobilized desire and bodily plentitude. Rather than balancing gender and class as "mutually sustaining discourses," Rabinowitz discovers the difference of female writing in its argument that embodied sexuality, not economic relations, determines history.[64] She thus suppresses the concern with female bodies among male proletarians such as Michael Gold and Jack Conroy, and she downplays the way female writers, such as Meridel Le Sueur, stress the universally destructive power of poverty and hunger on the bodies and minds of both the male and the female poor.[65] Kaplan's *PMLA* issue, on the other hand, maintains diverse perspectives on class, with essays by Peter Hitchcock and Cynthia Ward offering different ways to theorize the sensate substance of class as a lived socioeconomic experience.[66] The two essays in this issue that treat mainstream works of American literature, however, return to remarkably similar and predictable arguments. Eric Schocket bases his reading of Rebecca Harding Davis's "Life in the Iron Mills" (1861) on the assumption that Davis's era was unable to account for class segmentation in terms of class itself, for it supposedly lacked an adequate language to talk about economic exploitation. Hence Davis turns to racial discourse to explain the dependency of the working class, yet she is most interested, argues Schocket, in freeing her workers from the deterministic markers of blackness by establishing the unimpeachable agency, potentiality, and privilege of pure whiteness. Jennie Kassanoff's reading of Edith Wharton's *The House of Mirth* (1905) similarly argues for a concealed meaning in Wharton's novel that is less class based than racial. Far from a victim of her social environment, Lily Bart allegedly represents Wharton's racial ideal, an absolute, immutable, Anglo-Saxon whiteness—an essentialist answer to the cultural vulnerabilities of class and gender. Questionably taking the racial part for the whole, both of these essays displace class almost wholly into racial questions of whiteness.[67]

Schocket and Kassanoff illustrate the degree to which class studies has come to share in the efforts of whiteness studies to decenter an "unraced" white norm.[68] Matt Wray and Annalee Newitz's edited volume, *White Trash* (1997), may contain essays that stress how whites also suffer from poverty, thus bringing to the fore class lines that cut across racial identities. Yet the book's introduction clearly reveals the controlling motive of the project: to show how whites (or at least, poor whites) can be considered a racial minority too, and thus be included in a racially based multiculturalism. The isolation of "white trash" as an analytic category has privileged racial associations over the socioeconomic dynamics of class marginalization. Studies of the working classes can similarly verge on giving race an enabling priority in its capacity to generate class sensibility. Eric Lott's brilliant *Love and Theft* (1993), for example, argues that the racial transgressions of blackface minstrelsy "made possible the formation of a self-consciously white working class," with race actively signifying a class-conscious public sphere. Just as gender can overwhelm class and entirely displace poverty in a feminist analysis such as Rabinowitz's *Labor and Desire,* so too does class consciousness become a function of racial ideology rather than of economic forces in Lott's work. Downplayed in Lott's account of the making of the American working class are the "pressures from below" identified by the labor historian Jonathan Glickstein—the pressures of increasing relative poverty, and of the perceived threat to socioeconomic well-being posed by "various groups of low-status 'others.'"[69] If the affirmative strain within class studies has emphasized political agency instead of the trauma of poverty, and if the deconstructive theory of class has stressed uncertainty instead of the concrete limitations of need, then the composite kind of class analysis returns us full circle to the forces that have always acted to unsettle socioeconomic awareness of the lower classes—the forces that work to emphasize, above all else, the cultural categories of race and gender.

There is a powerful need for a specific and complex analysis of poverty within the discussion of social class in studies of American literature. Yet the neglect of poverty as a critical keyword cannot be laid entirely at the doorstep of recent critical trends. This categorical blind spot may have deeper causes that lie in the very effort to view "the poor" as an analyzable social group that remains partially distinct from the working class. The problem here is not that poverty has been refused the special attention it needs, even within discourses of class, but that it has already been subject to a wealth of cultural analysis that, ironically, has placed it culturally off limits. I refer here to the "culture of poverty" thesis that developed with the emergence of poverty as a political issue in the late 1950s and early 1960s. Michael Harrington's *The Other America* (1962) stressed poverty as "a way of life," a type of personality, a "fatal, futile universe, an America within America with a twisted spirit." In his contemporaneous studies of Mexican and Puerto Rican communities, Oscar Lewis argued that the chronically poor develop a unique subculture, beyond regional, racial, and national distinctions, a way of life that inspires a system of values and behavioral patterns—some positive but many pathological in kind—passed on from generation to generation. Similar beliefs have a long history in American social and political thought, returning to nineteenth-century theories of chronic, character-based "pauperism" and to the moral distinction between the deserving and the undeserving poor.[70] Such ideas gained theoretical definition among mid-twentieth-century leftists and liberals who attempted to grapple with the elusive nonmaterial results of economic situations, and to expose poverty as a crisis in need of urgent political action.[71] Recent scholars have emphasized how Lewis's ideas were clearly within a Marxist tradition that traced the origins of the culture of poverty to the mode of capitalist production, especially its power to destroy traditional community structures.[72] Whatever the merits of Lewis's original thesis, it has clearly been co-opted by other agendas, with a cultural concept that Lewis applied to a minority of the poor—and, indeed, de-emphasized in a U.S. context—being applied much more broadly.[73] Crucial to Lewis's thesis was the belief that the culture of poverty can gain an *autonomy* from its economic causes, and thus become much more difficult to cure than material need itself.

To say that the poor possess a self-perpetuating culture is to imply that poverty is not fundamentally a product of economic and political forces, thus making the poor seem morally culpable for their financial status. As Michael Katz suggests, cultural explanations of poverty place moral blame on the poor by emphasizing their passivity and disorganization, effectively rationalizing schemes to limit welfare and other forms of economic redistribution.[74] Ironically, the very category that seems to resist arguments that it can be deconstructed as a mere attitude or socially constructed belief also reveals the ease with which it can register such invidious forces of identity imposition, particularly when cultural patterns are seen not as a response to but as an active cause of socioeconomic situations.[75] There is thus a marked difference between a cultural approach to poverty and a cultural approach to race and ethnicity. Criticism has been directed recently at the idealistic treatment of culture in a certain type of multiculturalist thought—culture as an autonomous and collective domain abstracted from its socioeconomic contexts.[76] If the debate concerns the socioeconomic specifically, then the recourse to culture becomes more questionable still, more of an obvious distraction from the social and political roots of domination and exploitation. And if the cultural context becomes problematic in this way then we are left with a void, at least from the perspective of literary criticism that has become so culturally concerned.

Sociological theories of poverty may be missing, to some extent, from literary studies. Yet social theory is also haunted by the cultural determinism it developed not so long ago, one that continues to taint poverty as a category because this determinism has stayed alive in legislative debates and in popular ideologies. How do we isolate poverty while resisting the pitfalls of that isolation, namely a rigid definition of "the poor" as a class in themselves, and a treatment of poverty as something like an ethnic affiliation with a transhistorical integrity that is tangled in alleged cultural and psychological pathology? (The idea of an "underclass" is similarly controversial in suggesting the unreachability and permanence of the poor, who are made to appear outside of politics and social structure altogether.)[77] Defining the poor as a powerless mass in which individual agency has collapsed tends to cement a class hegemony that—unlike similar impositions of gender or racial identity—allows little room for a countering affirmation by the victimized group itself. To paraphrase Katz, dangers emerge from any reduction of the poor to islands of despair and isolation, unable to surmount environmental forces and disconnected from the working class as a whole.[78]

Knowledge of how the category of poverty has been used and abused historically, returns us to the rationale behind the poststructuralist decentering of a determinism within class analysis. Yet if our concern lies with the significant numbers of people who have lived in conditions of relatively painful material deprivation and restricted social resources throughout U.S. history, then it remains essential to retain a definition of poverty, however complex and contentious it may be, rather than theorizing it into inconsistency and ambivalence. Substantial questions emerge if we see poverty both from a linguistic-ideological perspective and from a socially referential perspective, as a category that has always suffered from attempts to root its causes in cultural pathology and moral failure, or from attempts to dismiss it as the register of such oppressive usage. The term *poverty* may seem particularly ripe for deconstruction but we need at least to address the stakes of arguments that implicitly deprive it of shape altogether, especially if the understanding and redressing of material inequities are pressing concerns. Despite an engagement of social theory with poststructuralist ideas, the reigning sociological tendency is to treat poverty not as an unstable construct but as a quantifiable term for complex social forces, an analyzable condition defined by a network of shifting factors such as income level, unemployment, homelessness, hunger, and access to educational and health-care facilities.[79] Its significance always relative within a context of economic inequality, poverty has usefully described a dynamic, contextual, and flexible social state that people move into and out of from many positions.[80] It is a term whose definitional difficulties never outweigh the consequences of abandoning it altogether.[81]

There is a strong need for a critical language that can recognize the links between *and* the separation of poverty and class. According to census data, poverty affects large numbers of the working class: no inverse relation links work and want.[82] Poverty is not inevitably associated with a single, lower-class group, however, but is cross-class in nature—a condition that can affect individuals from all walks of life.[83] To some extent, poverty is not the problem of a marginalized underclass but a widely experienced condition, not just for the nation's legion of low-paid workers but even for suburban couples who seem to embody middle-class values.[84] And there are aspects of poverty, as a category, that move it partly beyond a conventional class structure altogether. The clearest example here is the relationship between poverty and race. On the one hand, poverty is far from an exclusively nonwhite problem. In relative terms, African Americans and nonwhite Hispanics are much more likely than whites to become poor, and much less likely to transition out of poverty, yet in absolute terms most poor Americans are white.[85] A number of prominent sociologists have used such evidence to criticize cultural perspectives that deflect attention from the truly significant socioeconomic and political causes of want. An extreme position holds that the focus on race in particular has acted to divide and pacify the working class, thus delegitimating poverty as a political question.[86] But mainstream considerations of social disadvantage and exclusion in the United States have always been so culturally based in part because poverty rates *do* correspond to conventional categories of cultural identity. The fact that poverty disproportionately affects African Americans, Hispanics, and—increasingly—women, shows how socioeconomic forces have gone hand in hand with structures of racism and sexism throughout American history. The critique of American exceptionalism should teach us to be wary of claims that the United States differs from comparable countries in its failure to attach poverty so explicitly to issues of an industrialized working class. But we need to appreciate, as well, the pressures that have always existed here to unhouse poverty from a purely structural class perspective, and to associate it strongly with groups who seem to be marginalized primarily on grounds of their cultural identities.[87]

We have arrived at a more politicized restatement of the dialectical challenge of poverty—in this case the challenge of developing a critical language capable of recognizing both the cultural (racial, ethnic, gendered) and the socioeconomic (class) dynamics of the category. Many of the challenges of this approach stem from the difficulty of extricating poverty, as a category of literary and social discourse, from competing and traditionally overwhelming categories, such as race and class. *American Hungers* attempts to hold on to a definition of poverty, founded in material disadvantage, without slipping into the parallel, if more nebulous, discourse of personal failure, which Martha Banta describes as the imagination of frustration beyond the "facts of material achievement and tangible social position." We strive to see the category of poverty explicitly, in its own light, and not simply as the negative state that highlights the frustrations and paradoxes of an American ideology of success.[88] The nonmaterial questions of "spiritual poverty" and "voluntary simplicity"—often associated with the middle classes—are engaged without losing sight of the privileged relation between poverty and the economically neediest. And we attempt to understand the psychological and cultural experience of socioeconomic suffering—what Ehrenreich has eloquently described as a "repetitive injury of the spirit"—without slipping into cultural causality.[89] Perhaps the greatest challenge of all is to recognize the aesthetic dimension of poverty, the complex ways that it has catalyzed the forms and content of literary expression, without merely dismissing this aesthetic as an act of internal "colonization" or as a repressive, bourgeois appropriation of the poor—a justifiable anxiety that emerged with early Marxist intellectuals and has been a persistent concern of critics on the Left.[90] Writing about the poor always has the potential for a troubling power dynamic in which states of structural inferiority and social barriers that threaten literacy are brought, ironically, into the literary sphere. Writing in the 1890s, William Dean Howells noted how the virtual institution of inequality in a nation "that means equality if it means anything" causes a crisis of literary representation whereby poverty seems unreal, or is distanced by a recourse to the picturesque that treats with callous indifference the ruin and misery of the poor.[91] The writers who interest us here are not those who practiced uncritically such modes of "neutralizing the disinherited" but those who confronted head-on the tensions involved in producing discursive richness from analyses of poorness, particularly within an American cultural and political context.[92]

We have seen some of the problems that make poverty such a difficult topic from the perspective of literary theory, the problems of affirming poverty as a cultural identity, and of breaking it down as something more than socioeconomic, something cultural and hence unstable. Opposing tendencies—to view culture affirmatively on the one hand, and to undermine apparently hegemonic social categories on the other—may have combined to hinder analysis of literature as a forum in which poverty can be investigated as a social and historical problem that demands critical definition. I hope to demonstrate how the very forces that seem to remove poverty from the realm of viable literary criticism actually brought into being a materially concerned, polemical mode of discourse with rich potential for literary study and cultural theory, and with equal relevance to the history of social thought by illuminating the contentious cultural and psychological dynamics of poverty easily overlooked in structural sociology. Poverty possesses this potential precisely because it has provoked a self-conscious struggle with the political, intellectual, and cultural problems surrounding its acceptance as an integral social condition and as a subject of literary representation. Rather than challenging poststructuralist interpretations of identity, in other words, poverty provokes epistemological and ideological dilemmas of its own.

ONE ▰▰▰▰▰▰▰▰▰▰▰▰▰▰▰

Beggaring Description:

Herman Melville and Antebellum

Poverty Discourse

The native American poor never lose their delicacy or pride; hence, though unreduced to the physical degradation of the European pauper, they yet suffer more in mind than the poor of any other people in the world. Those peculiar social sensibilities nourished by our own peculiar political principles, while they enhance the true dignity of a prosperous American, do but minister to the added wretchedness of the unfortunate. — Herman Melville, "Poor Man's Pudding"

THE VIEW expressed by J. Hector St. John de Crèvecoeur in *Letters from an American Farmer* (1782), that the New World was the regenerative home for those individuals made "countryless" by their poverty, received radical revision in the years leading up to the Civil War. David Rothman has shown how antebellum Americans differed from their forebears in seeing poverty as a dangerous social problem in need of urgent reform—a response to the economic instability of the antebellum decades, and to the newfound visibility of homelessness, which grew quickly after 1820 and became epidemic during the depression of 1857.[1] Apparently woven into the social fabric of the nation, poverty came to seem a chronic rather than a temporary condition, well illustrated by the Maule family in Nathaniel

Hawthorne's *The House of the Seven Gables* (1851): "generally poverty-stricken; always plebeian and obscure; working with unsuccessful diligence at handicrafts . . . living here and there about the town, in hired tenements, and coming finally to the alms house, as the natural home of their old age."[2] Debates raged over the social and personal causes of need, and over the relative merits of institutional versus "outdoor" solutions. The question of charity became the subject of intense political and philosophical evaluation. Which is all to say that a complex, prominent public discourse of poverty had developed fully by the late 1840s, a discourse partly distinct from an emerging awareness of the working class as a sociopolitical group. The literary output of the 1840s and 1850s naturally shared in this public discussion of poverty. Urban mystery novels, melodramatic plays, sentimental domestic novels, and "panic fictions" all expressed interest in poverty as a social state that demanded rationalization, especially when it threatened incursions into middle-class security. Within this vast literature on poverty, writers such as Henry David Thoreau and Rebecca Harding Davis developed complex approaches to socioeconomic suffering. Their works challenge the scholarly view that a cultural and psychological view of the poor—a view worthy of aesthetic contemplation— only grew at the end of the nineteenth century among Progressives and naturalists.[3] And there emerged in these antebellum years a writer whose work remains somewhat unique for its sustained development of a dynamic, balanced, yet critical response to the contentious cultural questions that always seem to inform debates over socioeconomic inequality. That writer was Herman Melville.

To isolate the single theme of poverty in Melville's writing might appear to work reductively against the tenor of Melville criticism, which has reflected the multiplicity of literary analysis—with the added twist that Melville is often described as preempting the concerns and even the methodology of the mode of criticism itself, whether deconstructive, identity driven, or, most recently, transnational.[4] There has been close attention to questions of socioeconomic class in Melville's writing—most influentially by C.L.R. James in *Mariners, Renegades, and Castaways* (1953) and by Michael Rogin in *Subversive Genealogy* (1983)—and to issues of work.[5] The most resilient (some might say most successful) readings of Melville have perhaps been in the areas of religious-philosophical study, gender and sexuality, imperialism, and most prominently race, with important readings of Melville's racialized thinking appearing in the 1990s from critics such as Eric Sundquist and Samuel Otter. With Otter, I argue "for a Melville fascinated with the rhetorical structures and ideological functions of antebellum discourse"—the discourse not of race but of poverty, which sought to grade the bodily and mental meanings of social inequality and to find in economic need an issue that questioned national coherence and defined cultural difference.[6] The aim of my argument is not to displace race or gender with a class-based analysis. A narrowly socioeconomic approach is equally inadequate to the complexity of poverty, at least as Melville describes it operating both within and beyond a working-class perspective. By recognizing in poverty a degree of categorical autonomy, we will see instead how the concerns with identity and difference that drive literary criticism are themselves transformed by participating in a heated discourse that could seem confusingly cultural, biological, and social all at once.

Critics have begun to uncover how poverty was a central category for Melville—hence Carol Colatrella's work on poverty in relation to penitentiary reform, and Susan Ryan's insightful study of the antebellum culture of benevolence, *The Grammar of Good Intentions* (2003).[7] Ironically, though, Ryan's recent book suggests why the *complexity* of poverty often gets reduced even in analyses that appear to emphasize socioeconomic inequality. Ryan argues that the discourse of benevolence served above all as a means of constructing white national identity for antebellum Americans. Need itself came to seem an implicitly nonwhite condition, according to Ryan, and discussions of injustice, of reform—of doing good at large—became inevitably and pervasively racialized. Ryan's approach illustrates the ease with which race is offered as the Rosetta stone of the period, a default mode of analysis that seems fundamentally inadequate when forced to translate a social category, such as benevolence or poverty, that by definition reached beyond any single racial or cultural group.[8] Ryan's chapter on Melville makes a case for this writer on the grounds that he sought to undermine such purportedly racist associations of need with blackness by stressing the instability of racial masquerade in *The Confidence-Man* (1857) and "Benito Cereno" (1856)—an argument that raises problems not in what it emphasizes but in what it neglects to stress. To focus solely on the brief "Black Guinea" episode in *The Confidence-Man,* to the exclusion of the novel's parade of nonblack representatives of alleged need (the man with the weed, the unfortunate husband of Goneril, the soldier of fortune, the cosmopolitan, Charlemont, the crazy beggar, China Aster, the ragged peddler boy, and so on); and to highlight "Benito Cenero" to the exclusion of Melville's dealing with benevolence and poverty beyond the context of slavery (three major novels, *Redburn, Pierre,* and *Israel Potter,* and a host of sketches such as "Poor Man's Pudding and Rich Man's Crumbs," "The Paradise of Bachelors and the Tartarus of Maids," "Cock-A-Doodle-Doo!," "The Two Temples," and "Jimmy Rose"): this emphasis not only misses the remarkably multicultural, multiracial thrust behind Melville's analysis of social need but it also obscures an antebellum discourse of poverty that must remain largely unappreciated if reduced to an albeit anxious construction of whiteness.[9]

Paradigms of Poverty and Pauperism

Antebellum Americans may have emphasized the social causes of poverty but conventional opinions that dire economic circumstances stemmed primarily from the faults of the individual, or were an inevitable result of providence, persisted throughout the nineteenth century and would last into the twentieth.[10] Antebellum debates over socioeconomic inequality included diverse viewpoints, representing a range of class interests, yet despite this complexity an important distinction was consistently drawn between *poverty* on the one hand and *pauperism* on the other. The values ascribed to poverty were various. For some observers, particularly those identified with elite social backgrounds, the apprehension of want was a necessary force that built moral character and spurred self-improvement. For others—those who sought to speak for the interests of labor—poverty was most often a stressful possibility that degraded the worker.[11] The values ascribed to pauperism, however, were the subject of much broader consensus over the negative effects of public or private relief.[12] The relativity of poverty, marked by a belief that individuals could move into and out of it from various positions, confronted pauperism as a catastrophic, irreversible, intransigent location defined by *dependence* as more of a behavioral than a fiscal situation—a mark of character not class. According to the minister Charles Burroughs in 1835, poverty was an unavoidable evil brought on by misfortune not fault; pauperism, however, was a direct consequence of willful error, shameless indolence, and vicious habit. An allegedly irredeemable pauper class was described as enjoying a way of life that could be passed from generation to generation. William Ellery Channing spoke of the "fatal inheritance of beggary," while the founder of the New York Association for Improving the Condition of the Poor, Robert Hartley, expressed fear that the poor "love to clan together in some out-of-the-way place, are content to live in filth and disorder with a bare subsistence, provided they can drink, and smoke, and gossip, and enjoy their balls, and wakes, and frolics, without molestation." In his first annual report (1854) as head of New York's Children's Aid Society, Charles Loring Brace expressed his era's anxiety that the permanently poor were forming a separate class with dangerous cultural and behavioral characteristics.[13]

This focus on the poor had transatlantic parallels, of course, with poverty itself often seeming a preeminently English condition.[14] The British Poor Law Commission *Report* of 1834 was clearly influential on American discourse, feeding beliefs that public outdoor relief actively demoralized its able-bodied recipients.[15] A little later in the century, Henry Mayhew's *London Labour and the London Poor* (1849–62) made one of the era's strongest cases for the cultural causes of need among London's desperately poor street people, thus sidestepping the increasingly apparent social contradictions of capitalism.[16] This blaming of poverty on behavior or moral failure was inevitably heightened in an American context, when the United States was so self-consciously vaunted as the very solution to such old world problems as hunger and want, and even to social stratification itself. Many Americans assumed a national quarantine against poverty, provided by the Constitution and the Declaration of Independence. The construction of pauperism as a psychosocial condition can be understood, then, as a means to explain those who clashed with what the labor historian Jonathan Glickstein describes as the ante-bellum era's exceptionalistic coupling of "paeans to national economic growth with persistent references to extraordinary social fluidity and unrivaled popular access to the burgeoning economic opportunities."[17] In this respect, the "dependency" of pauperism had its unrecognized flip side. The values underpinning the social state were themselves dependent on an image of the needy, which provided an ex-ample of how *not* to be—an example that allowed ideologies of independence to float by excluding the extremely poor from assumptions of social normalcy. As we shall see when we turn to the literary engagement with poverty, the construction of pauperism may have been a function too of middle-class vulnerability amid a turbulent economic climate that saw major panics and slumps in 1837–43, 1855, and again in 1857–58. In the words of Kenneth Kusmer, the public displays of pov-erty in midcentury America were another reminder "that economic mobility was a two-way street, that—in a society with no safety net—losing everything and slip-ping into homelessness was far from impossible, even for the middle class."[18] The fear of falling down the social scale necessitated a reassuring vision of the poor as alien and irreclaimably inferior. Hence too a vision of persistent poverty as an in-ternally generated disease—a cultural and moral condition into which the middle classes supposedly need not worry about slipping, or at least could escape through hard work and moral rectitude.

The antebellum discourse of poverty was inevitably intertwined with that of race and slavery. Southern defenders of slavery and radical northern critics of wage labor alike described the capitalistic system of the North as more enslaving than even the chattel slavery of the South. They pointed to the North's brutal exploita-tion of the worker and its whiplike fear of starvation.[19] Frederick Douglass's 1845 *Narrative* suggests that an awareness of different levels of wealth and poverty ex-isted within the context of slavery too, even if the privations of the slave always transcended any relativistic appreciation of the qualities of comfort (as Douglass describes it, slaves "find less difficulty from the want of beds, than from the want of time to sleep").[20] The intertwining of poverty and race was furthered by the recognition that free African Americans were disproportionately visible among the American poor. Witness Charles Dickens's account of the Five Points neighbor-hood of New York City, published in *American Notes* (1842) and echoed in George Foster's *New York by Gas-Light* (1850). Dickens described American poverty as either hidden from view or else falling squarely on the shoulders of the free African Americans who could seem its natural and unquestioned victims.[21] Yet the poor as a group were remarkably multicultural, as Kusmer suggests in his history of home-lessness in the United States. Native-born migrants from depressed farming areas as well as immigrants flocked to the notorious slums of New York City, where home-lessness came to affect an increasingly impoverished working class.[22] The dis-course of poverty, moreover—at least that which predominated in the antebellum

North—was always about much more than the racial identities of either the poor or their nonpoor analysts. Glickstein has identified an important strand within the mid-nineteenth-century discourse of labor that reached self-consciousness not through the racist ideology of whiteness but through socioeconomic pressures of impending poverty.[23] Discussions of the degenerate "dependency" ascribed to the state of pauperism were always informed by the context of race slavery, which offered models of domination that colored the perception of chronic need. But this alleged collapse of social autonomy and economic agency required most translation when it affected individuals irrespective of racial or national background. The crucial belief was not that the poor came from other cultures but that poverty had become itself a dysfunctional culture, with multicultural reach.

A dominant viewpoint can be detected in antebellum discussions of poverty, one that—despite the period's erratic economy and despite efforts to indict the social system as the cause of want—still lauded the autonomy of, and the opportunity available to, free laborers.[24] Many Americans believed their case differed substantially from Europe's because the potential to eradicate poverty still existed in the United States, argues Rothman. There was also a competing sense that American poverty was a particular enigma, a puzzling paradox, heightened by perceptions of the nation's scarcity of labor and vast availability of land.[25] According to Joseph Tuckerman, a pioneering social worker in Jacksonian Boston, poverty was a "very dark and difficult subject," full of great and embarrassing moral problems; it presented an intellectual labyrinth that few could follow to its termination. In language close to Tuckerman's, Charles Burroughs believed the subject to be "enveloped in the thickest darkness, and encumbered with inextricable difficulties." Walter Channing too thought poverty complex and baffling. There was only so much, in other words, that the discourse of pauperism could explain away. Beyond it lay ideological manifestations of the heightened *danger* that Charles Loring Brace ascribed to poverty in the United States. Prefiguring apocalyptic reactions to the Depression of the 1930s, chronic poverty—especially among the white, native-born population—seemed to jar with national ideals of freedom, equality, and self-improvement to such an extent that it silenced conventional discourse. Hence Channing's desire "to speak another language, if other language can be found" to comprehend the mysteries of impoverishment—a desire that relates ideological complexities to the problems of linguistic representation.[26]

Walter Channing's *An Address on the Prevention of Pauperism* (1843) illustrates in depth how the problems that poverty presented, in an American context, gained this linguistic relevance. The brand of chronic poverty described as pauperism "has no voice in its deep and ever pressing want and misery to make the inquiry" into its own social causes, writes Channing (28), thus predicting more recent philosophical speculation that need is by nature "powerless to enforce its right."[27] The trouble is not simply that the poor lack access to the channels of political representation, and thus need a mouthpiece like Channing to make their voices heard.

Fig. 1.1. "Lodging Houses for Homeless Boys—As They Were." Illustration for Charles Loring Brace, *The Dangerous Classes of New York and Twenty Years' Work among Them* (New York, 1872). This opening image of Brace's book displays the suffering of poverty viscerally in the contortions of bodily form, even as vision itself is threatened by the encroaching abyss.

The problem is more profound because the poor seem to lack language altogether. They live not in a culture of poverty but in *cultural poverty;* they lack the moral, intellectual, and spiritual qualities that make sympathetic communication possible (19, 42, 45).[28] Channing is in large part constructing the poor as a voiceless, powerless, degenerate mass. His efforts to understand the cultural and psychological effects of material lack result in elitist horror at those who contravene fiscal and behavioral norms. But Channing's kind of dilemma is in some ways less significant than its degree. His shock at confronting poverty leaves his own expressive mechanisms in tatters. If the poor inhabit an abyss of consciousness, then Channing's own contact with that abyss negates the very cultural and psychological mechanisms that make representation possible. The "lack" becomes, in effect, the observer's—a linguistic lack whereby mainstream political discourse flounders before extremes of human suffering that necessarily destroy the intellectual processes of comprehension and communication. "Who knows the depths of poverty,—of those forms of it which may 'die, and make no sign?'" (20), asks Channing, expressing an inability to signify that is as much his as it is the poor individuals he purports to represent.

Literary Uses and Abuses of Poverty

The linguistic difficulties encountered by Channing in the face of poverty are important but they were not pervasive. If the antebellum years witnessed the "discovery" of poverty as a literary theme, then most of its exponents resorted not to epistemological and linguistic crises but to tried and tested conventions that made representing the poor more of a reflex than a dilemma.[29] Fredric Jameson has detected narrative paradigms within European Victorian literature that implicitly managed middle-class anxieties over the lower classes. Sentimentalism encoded the sweetness and simplicity of poverty as a utopian refuge from class, while melodrama represented fear of the Lumpenproletariat, the terror and villainy of the mob.[30] On American shores, the sensationalistic novels of George Lippard and Ned Buntline refigured English and continental literary models that stressed vice over the structural causes of slum life. As Michael Denning has argued, Lippard's *Monks of Monk Hall* (1844) is more concerned with the seduction of women than with the exploitation of workers.[31] In Buntline's *Mysteries and Miseries of New York* (1848), poverty is described repeatedly as a state of extreme material need and intense social suffering that forces women into "the hot-house of vice" (1:104). Yet the occasional awareness of poverty's roots in the socioeconomic system collapses beneath a fascination with "crime and depravity," and with the moral "pollution and infamy" that controls and dominates the lives of Buntline's characters (3:28, 1:47). In similar fashion, Foster's journalistic *New York by Gas-*

Light is dimly aware of how poverty pressures individuals into vice, but is obsessed with "the orgies of pauperism, the haunts of theft and murder, the scenes of drunkenness and beastly debauch" of New York's "lower stratum" (69)—particularly the prostitution that becomes "a mother and nurse of every vice that afflicts and degrades humanity" (92).[32]

The female-authored, sentimental, domestic novels that became best sellers in their time, and have received extensive attention since the pioneering works of critics such as Nina Baym and Jane Tompkins, also presented a somewhat conventionalized view of the poor. As Amy Lang argues in her masterful reading of Maria Cummins's *The Lamplighter* (1854), poverty is associated with moral viciousness and depravity, and becomes one of the extreme coordinates—the other being not "famine" but "fashion," an equally unacceptable state of wealthy hypocrisy—against which the middle class defined itself by seeking to deny the structure of class altogether. Material deprivation becomes an implicitly masculine danger to social harmony and to the private sphere of the home, continues Lang, a dangerous distortion cured by recourse to a gendered language of natural, female self-possession that transcends social injustice through the universal power of sentimentality.[33] Fanny Fern's semi-autobiographical novel *Ruth Hall* (1855) represents the eponymous heroine's descent into a poverty caused primarily by the immorality of individuals—indifferent relatives, "rapacious landlords," and greedy Jewish shopkeepers (90)—and her rise into financial independence through moral rectitude and hard work. Ruth's success as a writer depends, fittingly, on the essential trait of this literary sentimentalism: a reputation for sympathetic identification with the worthy poor, which emerges from Ruth's readers' knowledge of the writer's own struggle with poverty (165, 179). If sensationalistic "city mystery" novels understood poverty as a moral abyss, a virtually unchangeable condition of depravity, then works such as *Ruth Hall* represented poverty as a temporal condition that characters fall into or are empowered to rise out of—what David Morris describes as less a condition, or a state of being, than an event within a larger plot.[34]

The era's "panic fictions," which arose in response to middle-class financial vulnerability during economic cycles of boom and bust, also identified economic failure as a temporary bankruptcy that resulted from irresponsible financial speculation. According to Mary Templin, novels such as Anna Bartlett Warner's *Dollars and Cents* (1852) and Hannah Farnham Sawyer Lee's *Elinor Fulton* (1837) partially challenged the doctrine of separate spheres by stressing the material basis and economic underpinnings of middle-class domestic identity. Yet poverty again remains merely a coordinate against which middle-class fears are assuaged and faith in capitalism is restored. If the discourse of sympathy became the medium for understanding and resolving the contradictions of the market, then Joseph Fichtelberg has demonstrated how this discourse began to break down in the 1850s and 1860s, in the face of increasing feelings that economic insecurity had

Fig. 1.2. "Thanksgiving Day, 1860—The Two Great Classes of Society." Wood engraving based on a sketch by Winslow Homer, *Harper's Weekly*, December 1, 1860. Sterling and Francine Clark Art Institute, Williamstown, Massachusetts. The playwright who occupies the center of Homer's image of material inequality looks to the poor not the rich, and seems caught bodily in an ambivalent repulsion from and attraction to their plight.

become permanent following yet another panic in 1857. Reading "bankruptcy fictions" such as Van Buren Denslow's *Owned and Disowned* (1857), Augustine Duganne's *The Tenant-House* (1857), and Azel Roe's *How Could He Help It?* (1860), Fichtelberg shows how the hardening of middle-class consciousness brought a negative view of the poor as vicious, weak, and degraded, existing beyond the bounds of sentimental exchange—the diseased source of panic itself.[35]

In addition to narrative fiction, the era's popular sentimental and melodramatic plays were important sites for awareness of poverty. This dramatic tradition undoubtedly encouraged compassion for the poor and the homeless, but often in ways that punctured radical intervention. Dion Boucicault's *The Poor of New York* (1857), for example, follows a group of wealthy New Yorkers who have been temporarily reduced to poverty either by the whims of the financial markets (the play is set largely during the financial Panic of 1857) or by the underhand dealings of corrupt bankers. In a remarkable scene that addresses the meaning of poverty directly, the play's hero, Mark Livingstone, attracts a small crowd of followers with his words of wisdom:

> The poor!—whom do you call the poor? Do you know them? do you see them? they are more frequently found under a black coat than under a red shirt. The poor man is the clerk with a family, forced to maintain a decent suit of clothes, paid for out of the hunger of his children. The poor man is the artist who is obliged to pledge the tools of his trade to buy medicines for his sick wife. The lawyer who, craving for employment, buttons up his thin paletot to hide his shirtless breast. These needy wretches are poorer than the poor, for they are obliged to conceal their poverty with the false mask of content—smoking a cigar to disguise their hunger—they drag from their pockets their last quarter, to cast it with studied carelessness, to the beggar, whose mattress at home is lined with gold. These are the most miserable of the Poor of New York. (13)

Boucicault's play illustrates how discussions of poverty often tended to resist attachment to a single social class in a situation where fear of falling down the social scale was a pressing one for all. According to Livingstone, there are two forms of poverty, that of the lower classes and that of the middle classes. In the former case, poverty becomes a form of spiritual richness that contains the seeds of its own negation, a blessed state that purifies honesty and opens the heart to generosity and nobility—a condition inevitably soiled by false gold.[36] Following a Christian compression of poverty and piety, the lower-class poor are by definition not really poor. Those truly in need are the struggling middle classes who lack the cultural consolations of lower-class poverty, those who feel a painful disjunction between their apparent status and their fiscal indigence. They suffer mentally, forced into subtle acts of masking in which cigars and coats disguise their actual bankruptcy. In Livingstone's symbolic economy, signifiers are inherently ironic: to seem rich is to be poor; to seem poor is to be rich. Only by deep acts of reading, suggests

Boucicault, can we see through the social surface to the paradoxical truths that shift the problem of poverty away from the economic underclass toward the psychological stress of fluctuating finances.

Attention to poverty was clearly widespread in the antebellum era, ranging from the works of New England patricians such as James Russell Lowell, who expressed Christian recoil at the inequities of capitalism in his poem "A Parable" (1848), to southern humorists such as Augustus Baldwin Longstreet, who helped pioneer the poor white southern character in *Georgia Scenes* (1835). Occasionally, this literature of southern humor approaches a complex analysis of poverty as a socioeconomic problem with damaging cultural and educational consequences. The severely limited cultural literacy of George Washington Harris's character Sut Lovingood, for example, develops into a countercultural, dialect-driven attack on the system of educational privilege and on the agents of implicitly northern, "civilized" values. Within this southern tradition, however, social critique easily dissolves into a fascination with the allegedly grotesque comedy and vicious behavior of the poor white—qualities that root the causes of poverty in the moral and intellectual degradation of the individual.[37] Popular sentimentalized and sensationalistic representations of the poor in the North muted the social contradictions of poverty in similar ways. Yet we can still locate texts in which the ethical and literary *tensions* of approaching poverty are fully on display—texts such as Henry David Thoreau's classic study of self-reliance, *Walden* (1854), and Rebecca Harding Davis's experiment in protorealism, "Life in the Iron Mills" (1861).

The Ambivalence of Thoreau and Davis

If Boucicault's *The Poor of New York* romantically evades the idea that poverty might be a chronic, endemic social dilemma, then it also illustrates an attitude with broader scope in antebellum America. The tendency to treat poverty less economically than spiritually merged pre-industrial, Christian approaches to the poor with an effort to analyze the inner life of an increasingly commercial middle class. Walter Channing believed that the true misery of poverty lay in its remove from moral, intellectual, and spiritual culture; education could cure poverty by revealing to man "his spiritual, his highest nature." For Ralph Waldo Emerson, wealth and poverty were primarily spiritual conditions: without true genius, the affluent remain poor, while poverty itself could be a blessed good to mankind.[38] With transcendental thinkers, the debate over poverty centered on the spiritual dearth that could affect all people, irrespective of social class. The "seemingly wealthy" can be the "most terribly impoverished class of all," argues Thoreau in *Walden,* because the complexity of civilization, the frantic effort to obtain gross luxuries, alienates man from the spiritual necessities of life, from the true appreciation of intellectual and moral culture (16, 33–34, 103). Against the bankrupt principles of the new commercial class, Thoreau famously sets another idea of poverty, a *voluntary* poverty that enables true philosophical wisdom (14). "Cultivate poverty like a garden herb, like sage," he writes with characteristic pun (328).

Thoreau's *Walden* warrants attention here because it raises to a heightened level of philosophical self-consciousness a point shared by the era's more popular responses to the poor—the point that poverty as a social state could catalyze literary creation. Rather than causing linguistic crisis, Thoreau's version of voluntary poverty functions to liberate aesthetic interest and energy. Poverty embodies the principle of organic form, represented in the farms of "poor farmers" that stand "like a fungus in a muck-heap," exuding the sense of an aesthetic order that has grown naturally, unconsciously, from the free and honest labors of vigorous men (196–97). The "most unpretending, humble log huts and cottages of the poor" are inherently picturesque to Thoreau because the lives of their inhabitants are "agreeable to the imagination" (47): they embody an independence and simplicity, a refining of existence to the "most significant and vital experiences," a living of life "near the bone where it is sweetest" (329). Only by freeing himself from material possession can Thoreau gain a true appreciation of value in the landscape, an ideal spiritual state in which "I had been a rich man without any damage to my poverty" (82).

Lawrence Buell has argued that it is perhaps too easy to dismiss Thoreau's gospel of voluntary simplicity as merely a "bourgeois mystification of individual autonomy complicit with capitalism."[39] Buell outlines some of the ways that the counterculture of self-imposed moral and economic restraint, advocated by Thoreau and still alive today, can provide an important antimaterialist critique. But the complexity of *Walden* lies not on one side or the other—not in its resistance to *or* in its complicity with dominant attitudes toward poverty and wealth—but in the ambivalence that emerges from Thoreau's discovery of aesthetic virtue in socioeconomic lowliness. In a pioneering article, Thomas Woodson observes that if poverty is an inspiration to Thoreau's imagination in one sense, then it threatens his capacity to create when approached directly.[40] This ambivalence becomes particularly pointed when Thoreau's ideal, voluntary poverty runs against a degenerate destitution ascribed to the real world. The cultural poverty of the "degraded rich" (35) is easy for Thoreau to explain: they become spiritually poor because they are tempted by luxury. But how to explain the spiritual poverty of the "degraded poor" (34), who lack similar incentives to remain in conditions akin to those of miserable savages (35)? Thoreau offers two explanations, the first of which is cultural: "Often the poor man is not so cold and hungry as he is dirty and ragged and gross. It is partly his taste, and not merely his misfortune. If you give him money, he will perhaps buy more rags with it" (75). Echoing Emerson, Thoreau attacks conventional philanthropy because it perpetuates such misery and dependence (76,

152).[41] The second explanation lies somewhere between the cultural and the bio-logical. Thoreau tries to help the allegedly shiftless and ignorant Irish immigrant John Field by educating him in the proper methods of economy, fishing, and farm-ing (Field earns a pittance from digging a field—"bogging"—for a neighboring farmer), but Thoreau's advice falls on barren ground:

> Poor John Field!—I trust he does not read this, unless he will improve by it,—thinking to live by some derivative old country mode in this primitive new country,—to catch perch with shiners. It is good bait sometimes, I allow. With his horizon all his own, yet he is a poor man, born to be poor, with his inherited Irish poverty or poor life, his Adam's grandmother and boggy ways, not to rise in this world, he nor his posterity, till their wading webbed bog-trotting feet get *talaria* to their heels. (208–209)

Supplementing his ignorance, Field suffers from a colonial inheritance: raised in a culture of poverty, he brings its seemingly inescapable patterns to the New World.[42] Disturbingly, Thoreau's cultural prejudice verges on racial absolutism. The Irishman is figured as a genetic throwback, kept in his primitive condition by webbed feet that only a miracle can change (*talaria* are the winged sandals worn by Roman gods). Figurative though this language may be, it captures Thoreau's frustration that the culture of the poor might be a response to their social situation rather than an effort to transcend it. His anger emerges from the seemingly fixed values of the poor who adhere to ways of life that directly contravene the belief that poverty can be anything like an ideal state. Thoreau's uncultured wealthy are "poor," yet at least they have the potential of changing their lives, of becoming spiritually rich by adopt-ing the voluntary poverty that *Walden* expounds. The uncultured poor, however, are destitute in a double sense because they lack even this potential for choice and regeneration, so absolute is their degenerate lifestyle. By ending the "Econ-omy" section of *Walden* with a passage from Thomas Carew's masque, *Coelum Britannicum* (1634), which gains the title "The Pretensions of Poverty," Thoreau fur-ther lambastes the "lazy or pedantic virtue" and the "Falsely exalted passive forti-tude" claimed by the poor, valuing instead the excessive bravery, magnanimity, and magnificence of Herculean heroes.[43]

The prevalence in the 1840s and 1850s of melodramatic works like Boucicault's may have led Keith Gandal to describe poverty writing before Jacob Riis as itself impoverished. Thoreau's *Walden* demonstrates a preexisting strain of poverty writ-ing in the United States, one in which a cultural concern with the poor developed into a self-conscious exploration of the linguistic and literary possibilities and prob-lems of representing indigence. Yet for all its concern with depicting abject need, and for all its opposition to the degraded materialism of commercial culture, *Walden* still taps a little too unselfconsciously into assumptions common to literary genres that sought to evade rather than to confront socioeconomic suffering. Hence Thoreau's emphasis on poverty as a sign of preexisting cultural degeneracy is juxtaposed with his belief in poverty as a moral and spiritual virtue whose values negate the social lack in which it is founded. Which is to say that even the most complex and enlightened approaches to poverty from the mid-nineteenth century tend to get troubled when the *causes* of chronic poverty are faced. The same can be said of Davis's "Life in the Iron Mills," a text that sits between antebellum religious sentimentalism and postbellum social realism, and indeed demonstrates an ethical equivocation over poverty that continued throughout the nineteenth century and into the twentieth.

Predicting the work of Charlotte Perkins Gilman and others at the end of the nineteenth century, Davis's social critique is undoubtedly sharpened by a concern with gender. The effective rediscovery of "Life in the Iron Mills" by the Feminist Press, and Tillie Olsen's biographical introduction to the 1972 reprinting, have steered critics toward assumptions that Davis's representations of hunger, starvation, and thwarted lives all refer to the special condition of women in American society. Indeed, criticism of Davis's tale has tended to follow the trends, outlined in my introduction, that have distracted attention from poverty as a fundamental category. The dominant interpretation that "Life in the Iron Mills" is about gender (Pfaelzer, Hapke) has been supplemented by arguments that it really concerns the racial construction of white identity (Schocket), or that it represents a philosophical deconstruction of categories such as personhood (Seltzer) or class (Dimock). Even Lang's compelling argument that Davis's tale illustrates how class differs from the seemingly more "natural" categories of race and gender, returns to the premise that class is defined by its *contingency*—a premise unable to account for those characters in the story whose class position seems far from uncertain or incidental.[44] Davis's story is certainly remarkable for its focus on class, though its central subject is not the working class in general but a subset, the working poor—a multiracial group described repeatedly as "the lowest" (39).[45] The story deserves critical attention for its resistance to the mainstream melodramatic or sentimental methods of rationalizing inequality. It flags instead the representational and structural problems that emerge from a confrontation with individuals who no longer possess the right or the might to rise up the social scale.

Like *Walden,* "Life in the Iron Mills" exposes the cultural contradictions that surround poverty as a recognized category, contradictions that appear when the narrator attempts to describe the working poor:

> Masses of men, with dull, besotted faces bent to the ground, sharpened here and there by pain or cunning; skin and muscle and flesh begrimed with smoke and ashes; stooping all night over boiling caldrons of metal, lairled by day in dens of drunkenness and infamy; breathing from infancy to death an air saturated with fog and grease and soot, vileness for soul and body. What do you make of a case like that, amateur psychologist? You call it an altogether serious thing to be alive: to these men it is a drunken jest, a joke,—horrible to angels, perhaps, to them commonplace enough. (12)

Davis puts definitional pressure on poverty by tracing its suffering to the physical and environmental conditions of population density, pollution, and exploitative labor practices. This impoverished situation marks individuals physically, with the biblical phrase "grind the faces of the poor" (Isaiah 3:15) providing the subtext of the sharpened features that register a literal wasting of the flesh, echoed in Hugh Wolfe's disease of "consumption" (24). The narrator's appeal to the "amateur psychologist" transcends conventional moral outrage at poverty. Explored instead are the objective causes of emotional frustration and depression, the chronic and extreme impact of material environment on bodily and mental welfare (hence the argument that Davis predicts naturalism's concern with a self determined by brutalizing socioeconomic forces).[46] The molding of the unprotected mind in infancy, and the consistent maintenance of these impoverished conditions until death, inevitably brings a protective shift in social ethics. Living in a separate social environment, the poor develop an integral value system, a "cunning" that is antagonistic to mainstream norms. But there is always some uncertainty over cause and effect in this passage: the dullness and besotted quality of the faces *precedes* the description of their material situation as bent to the ground (an echo of the unnatural stooping of the labor process). The "begriming" of poverty marks muscle as well as skin. It seeps *into* the body, just as class can seem an essentialized "order of being" to Wolfe (27)—an ontology, more than a response to social situation, that emphasizes morality and behavior at least as much as economics.

The above passage captures the pattern of Davis's tale as a whole, a pattern we will encounter again in the poverty discourse of the Gilded Age and the Great Depression. On the one hand, Davis places the causes of poverty in the socioeconomic environment, which stunts the intellectual and spiritual growth of characters yet still produces cultural rituals of survival and expression. The psychological and behavioral responses of Davis's iron workers stem directly from the social, political, and material contexts of inequality and exploitation.[47] Hence the "korl woman," the rough sculpture that Wolfe hews from industrial waste, represents the dumbness, cultural lack, and spiritual hunger of Wolfe's neediness (64). Yet the irony of the korl woman—the irony that the cultural effects of poverty only reveal a deeper poverty of culture—illustrates the ethical twist at the center of the tale. There is only a narrow sense in which culture maintains a nonpejorative significance as rational adaptation to material conditions, as an organized and purposeful community structure beyond the "pathological" and "negative" qualities of social alienation. The reason for this is crucial: the idea of culture in the sociological sense, which leaves room for something akin to an ethnographic explanation of behaviors and mindsets, is infiltrated by an opposing sense of culture as the cause and not the effect of material conditions (just as the "culture of poverty" thesis has itself shifted in recent decades from political Left to Right, from an effort to understand the nonmaterial effects of poverty to an implication that lifestyle is the cause of need). The ethnic Welsh, for example, seem to have adapted in special ways to their poverty, having developed a dysfunctional mindset with the power to transfer between generations, just like the hereditary qualities commonly associated with race.

Here poverty becomes a trait of identity, with class status coming to seem natural rather than contingent. The story may hold harsh criticism for the powerful characters who refuse to accept their communal obligations to those who lack the basic necessities to ensure their social freedom. But those who fail to rise also seem themselves to blame for their cultural values and psychological patterns, thus deflecting an analysis of causes *away* from the economic structure. This is the source of the hopeless atmosphere of the story, in which the poor lie entirely beyond social reform or revolution, in an alienated state only touchable by a Christian millennium.[48] The working poor no longer share in national ideologies of individual entitlement and mobility. As Upton Sinclair would write a half century later in his novel of industrial exploitation, *The Jungle* (1906), these workers have "made terms with degradations and despair" (367). In Davis's story, this spiritual degradation reinforces a kind of "guilt," played out finally in Wolfe's decision to shoulder the burden of his alleged crime (56). Wolfe may show glimpses of potential, yet his dwarfed brain is finally incapable of attaining anything like "class consciousness." Even the most idealized of Christian reformers is unable to reach Wolfe because the reformer's words are "toned to suit another class of culture"— a cultural class that seems essentially different from those who live in "poverty" and "hunger" (49).

Thoreau's *Walden* and Davis's "Life in the Iron Mills" are balanced on an ethical pivot, whereby the recognition of rigid social stratification, and the desire to understand the social and cultural effects of poverty, are always about to tip into the implication that the poor are morally complicit with their conditions. By representing causes of poverty that have sprung free from their socioeconomic base, both texts tap into a discourse of poverty that seems to move out of class altogether, or at least to move out of purely socioeconomic considerations. Poverty gains a determining power of its own, based on psychological and cultural values that ensure its capacity to entrap and become self-perpetuating. It was exactly this slope toward cultural causality—a slope always steep in an American context—that Herman Melville confronted in an interlinked series of novels, stories, and sketches in which he balances a transnational with a national analysis of the causes and consequences of inequality and want. Scholars of literary realism tend to assume that prevalent sensationalistic and picturesque depictions of poverty went unchallenged until the late-nineteenth-century writings of Stephen Crane and Theodore Dreiser.[49] Melville had already experimented with poverty writing in ways that anticipated the cultural radicalism of "critical realists" and that reappeared in the documentary, modernist, and sociological developments of the 1930s.

Redburn *and* Israel Potter:

Transatlantic Counterparts

Wellingborough Redburn, the first-person narrator of Melville's semi-autobiographical fourth novel, *Redburn* (1849), is shocked at seeing white beggars on the streets of Liverpool. Redburn's democratic idealism encodes racial assumptions that remove whites from the category of America's poor. He is struck in England by "the absence of negroes; who in the large towns in the 'free states' of America, almost always form a considerable portion of the destitute," reminding Redburn that he is not in his native land, where "to be a born American citizen seems a guarantee against pauperism" (201–202). At least some of Melville's readers would surely have picked up on the irony of such comments. During the depression of 1837–43, for example, complaints were frequently made that hordes of beggars, many of them white and native born, thronged the New York streets—"almost as thick as the hogs are," wrote Buntline in the appendix to *The Mysteries and Miseries of New York.*[50] The main irony lies in the fact that Redburn himself suffers from a type of poverty, though one different in kind to the beggary he inevitably encounters on Merseyside. Melville may seek ways in his fiction to undermine any natural association of blackness and need, as Susan Ryan argues, yet he does so not by destabilizing assumptions about race but by positioning need in a comparative analysis of different states of social alienation.[51] *Redburn* marks the beginning of Melville's relativistic interest in poverty as a multicultural condition transcending racial and national boundaries, a social category that, as we shall see, becomes partly divorced from both black and working-class contexts.

Redburn suffers from a brand of poverty common to his era, which we saw in Boucicault's *The Poor of New York*—a sudden falling on hard times that follows the bankruptcy and death of Redburn's father, an event that clearly echoes Melville's own family situation in early youth.[52] Redburn is sent on a voyage to Liverpool to find his fortune, but poverty cannot be so easily shaken off:

> Talk not of the bitterness of middle-age and after life; a boy can feel all that, and much more, when upon his young soul the mildew has fallen; and the fruit, which for others is only blasted after ripeness, with him is nipped in the first blossom and bud. And never again can such blights be made good; they strike in too deep, and leave such a scar that the air of Paradise might not erase it. And it is a hard and cruel thing thus in early youth to taste beforehand the pangs which should be reserved for the stout time of manhood, when the gristle has become bone, and we stand up and fight out our lives, as a thing tried before and foreseen; for then we are veterans used to sieges and battles, and not green recruits, recoiling at the first shock of the encounter. (11)

In an antebellum economy defined by the panic of boom and bust, it was not difficult to find observations of bankrupts "crippled and enervated by the wounds and bruises they suffer, [who] go halting and maimed all their lives long, with nerves shattered by anxiety."[53] What emerges from this early moment in *Redburn* is the categorical complexity of poverty for Melville—a complexity that will expand to dominate a major phase of his literary career. Melville's biblical imagery establishes poverty as primarily a spiritual crisis, an early loss of innocence that moves the victim beyond religious redemption into secular suffering. The reference to military combat further defines poverty as a physical wounding and a psychological trauma. (Recent sociologists have similarly compared poverty to the hopelessness, anger, and depression that follow military combat.)[54] If the era's panic fictions sought to conserve middle-class identity amid financial insecurity by claiming the virtue of feminized sentiment,[55] then *Redburn* emphasizes the *permanence* of poverty as a psychosocial syndrome marked by shame and confusion. And if a degree of sexual voyeurism could inform the middle-class gaze on the poor subject, then Melville reverses the equation by interiorizing poverty as a sexual dysfunction with ideological significance. The ideals of the self-made man invert to become the unmaking of manhood itself. Poverty is thus cross-class in kind—it is established relatively through the act of falling down the social scale—yet poverty also moves beyond an economic definition of class altogether because it stays with Redburn, as an indelible mental scarring, irrespective of his station in life. Poverty thus powers a discrete syndrome with describable and lasting behavioral patterns. But it also irritates the process of description when the insanity, caused by sudden and unappeasable hunger, develops into a blinding state of existential crisis that endangers Redburn's powers of articulation (26, 36). At once spiritual, physical, psychosexual, and ideological, poverty thus has linguistic significance too. An "uncongenial" (10) network of intensely dysphoric feelings and psychological breakdowns works at times to disable the progress of conventional narrative.

Redburn's subsequent journey to and from Liverpool further complicates poverty by shifting it from an individual to a community problem, and by establishing it as a subject for political economy. Redburn is given Adam Smith's *Wealth of Nations* (1776) to read on his voyage, in the hope that it will teach him "the true way to retrieve the poverty of [his] family" (86). Smith's work may seem dry as crackers and cheese, offering Redburn little profit for his pains (87), yet Smith's ideas resound throughout *Redburn,* particularly Smith's relativistic belief that the standard of living of the poor would always be improving within a free and progressive economy, though the structure of inequality would stay the same.[56] It is never enough, for Redburn, "to regard as a special advance, that unavoidable, and merely participative progress, which any one class makes in sharing the general movement of the race" (139). The sections dealing with sailor life lead Redburn to realize that social stratification is a structural prerequisite of "civilization" itself, that sailors are forced into their position by the need of a commercial class for muddy wheels upon which the coach of luxury must roll (139). Any rise in living standards can never escape the absolute stigma of being relatively poor, the degrading effects of exploitation and prejudice.[57] These ironic early sections of the book, in which a naïve and condescending Redburn becomes victimized by the impoverished sailors he attempts to educate, also allow Melville to explore how lowly class status can transcend passive victimization to fuel a countercultural consciousness that directly inverts the values of civil society. Far from the genteel reification of a "magical" middle-class status defined against an inferior proletariat, for which Laura Hapke has argued, *Redburn* marks the beginning of Melville's relativistic appreciation of the cultural values of the poor—an appreciation that gets tested during Redburn's shocking encounters on the streets of Liverpool.[58]

"Poverty, poverty, poverty, in almost endless vistas: and want and woe staggered arm in arm along these miserable streets" (201), exclaims Redburn, whose initial reactions follow a series of established patterns, from Malthusian repulsion at the purportedly vicious and revolutionary potential of the dangerous classes (191), to the kind of epistemological and linguistic crisis that confronted Walter Channing. Redburn's encounter with a starving woman and her children resists representation because the poor are themselves voiceless, while their poverty is so pronounced that it outstrips the sympathetic cognition that would enable description (180–85).[59] If Redburn's response to the poor seems conventional and unsurprising in several ways—he considers professional beggary "dishonorable to civilization and humanity," for example—his fascination with the "marvelous and almost incredible shifts and stratagems" of the beggars themselves, their "art in attracting charity" (186), is a wholly different matter:

> I remember one cripple, a young man rather decently clad, who sat huddled up against the wall, holding a painted board on his knees. It was a picture intending to represent the man himself caught in the machinery of some factory, and whirled about among spindles and cogs, with his limbs mangled and bloody. This person said nothing, but sat silently exhibiting his board. Next him, leaning upright against the wall, was a tall, pallid man, with a white bandage round his brow, and his face cadaverous as a corpse. He, too, said nothing, but with one finger silently pointed down to the square of flagging at his feet, which was nicely swept, and stained blue, and bore this inscription in chalk:—
>
> > "*I have had no food for three days;
> > My wife and children are dying.*"
>
> Further on lay a man with one sleeve of his ragged coat removed, showing an unsightly sore; and above it a label with some writing.
>
> In some places, for the distance of many rods, the whole line of flagging immediately at the base of the wall, would be completely covered with inscriptions, the beggars standing over them in silence. (186–87)

Despite the silence of these beggars, they are far from voiceless. The unsightly horrors of social disablement may be beyond direct verbal expression, but they can be represented allusively by pictures and texts that claim authenticity and authority in their attempt to transcend communicative breakdown with the outside world. There is no direct link here between low income and illiteracy. The elements of "dependence" that were thought to place the needy beyond expression altogether, cocooning them in a bubble of speechlessness, effectively speak back by colonizing a segment of the public sphere. These inscriptions represent a kind of vernacular poetry, a pavement aesthetic that emerges from social conditions many writers considered inherently antagonistic to intellectual culture. Though ephemeral in kind, destined to be obliterated imminently by a thousand wayfarers' feet, these signs and inscriptions reveal not just subjectivity but the *control* of that subjectivity—the effort and care of self-presentation that strives to find a language adequate to the acknowledgment of lack. The beggars' silence becomes itself a rhetorical gesture of power, a demand for consideration that challenges the observer to trust the expression of need and thus to concede that the urgency of this need entitles the poor to fiscal relief.[60]

If Dickens discovered among the worst squalor of New York's Five Points an African American creativity epitomized by the "break-down" of a black dancer called Juba, then Redburn hears a similar voice of cultural resilience on the streets of Liverpool, embodied in the sailor ballad singers who sing their verses and thereafter beg passersby to purchase printed copy. Ann Fabian has identified a genre of autobiographical publications by individuals whose social status, as criminals and tramps, for example, would seem to place them beyond the realm of letters—including the narrative of Israel Potter, the source of Melville's 1855 novel of that name.[61] Redburn discovers a similar collection of writer tramps who turn the details of their poverty into saleable material. They do so both in written form, and in a manipulation of the body that, in one peculiar case, combines a creative density of expression—an ability to reproduce itself in multiple layers of sound—with a similarly reproductive physical performance, whereby the singer's arm "somehow swung vertically round and round in the air, as if it revolved on a pivot" (190). Just as the ballad singer composes and prints his own verses for sale, so too does his body become a machine that manufactures representation of his injuries, and that alludes ironically to the idealized "invisible hand" of laissez-faire economics, through which the free practice of self-interest will supposedly promote the general welfare of society as a whole. This "naturally unaccountable," seemingly automatic feat makes cultural capital from the physical condition that produced the ballad singer's original impoverishment, "since he said that in falling from a frigate's mast-head to the deck, he had met with an injury, which had resulted in making his wonderful arm what it was" (190). His texts and their performance allow survival in a world of want by turning the conditions of poverty against themselves, recycling destitution into the raw material of creativity. Both poet and machine, artist and manufacturer, this ballad singer lives entirely off himself.

Redburn's education in poverty is thus twofold. He realizes that individuals are brought into destitution by economic and social forces, while also recognizing that the poor can, to an extent, survive within poverty through their cultural resources. On Redburn's return voyage he encounters a group of emigrants, traveling as steerage passengers to the United States, who are forced into starvation and disease by the rigid social hierarchy of the ship. Yet at the heart of this incommunicable misery we have a young accordion player called Carlo, who—like the ballad singers of Liverpool—can convert lowliness into gain by manipulating a sexualized aesthetics of poverty. Carlo uses his romantic and implicitly homoerotic identity as a street-urchin musician to manufacture a wealth of pleasure for his sentimental audience, capitalizing on the intertwining of sexual desire and charitable giving (247, 250). These final episodes repeat the novel's broader ambivalence toward the poor, which reflects a vacillation between a Rousseauian sense of compassion as an equalizing enabler of communication between social classes, and something much more akin to a Nietzschean sense of sympathy as a danger that can overwhelm the self with an unbearable flood of suffering, effectively destroying rational judgment.[62] Refiguring the trauma of collapsed fortune that scars Redburn's American youth, any interest in the creative and cultural rituals that arise from social disadvantage always confronts the capacity of poverty to undo creativity with its moments of unspeakable suffering that transcend comprehension and representation. Poverty may provide the preconditions of sympathy and hence of communal belonging.[63] Yet this sympathy is also socioeconomically bounded when poverty is recognized as a reality that gnaws into the "vital beings" of the poor (290)—a state of suffering with the power to damage, if not actually destroy, subjectivity itself.[64]

Melville would again contrast British and American social states in *Israel Potter: His Fifty Years of Exile* (1855), a work based in part on Henry Trumbull's *Life and Remarkable Adventures of Israel R. Potter* (1824), the story of how a hero of the American Revolution eventually becomes a homeless exile and impoverished peddler in London. Walter Bezanson comments that "American readers of Trumbull, at least, must have been baffled that so energetic a Yankee as Potter could get trapped in London for more than forty years." The final chapters of Melville's novel seek to explain just such a point.[65] Following a picaresque series of bizarre adventures in Europe, with Benjamin Franklin in Paris and with Paul Jones aboard the *Bon Homme Richard,* Potter finds work as a brick maker in a remarkable episode that explores the self-perpetuating mechanisms of industrial poverty. Moving beyond biblical tropes for understanding poverty, the act of labor becomes a complex combination of the physical and economic with the cultural and psychological. The reckless gesture of slapping clay into molds is translated into a "reckless sort of half jolly despair," a nihilistic mindset that maintains the laborer in his fiscal and physical hardships, teaching him "to slap, with similar heedlessness, his own sadder fortunes, as of still less vital consideration" (155).[66] Davis's "Life in the Iron Mills" also describes harsh labor conditions feeding "reckless" cultural attitudes that allow mental survival (12), yet Melville's analysis never makes culture causal because the imposed misery is always contingent—"their vice was like that weed which but grows on barren ground; enrich the soil, and it disappears" (155). Rather than suggesting that ingrained lifestyle values have created material need, Melville understands the culture and psychology of the needy as functional adaptations to harsh environmental conditions. He depicts situational responses to a structural position at the bottom of a stratified society, and reasonable sets of behavioral patterns and ethical values imposed by the social system at large.[67] In this way Melville counters the prevailing opinion of poverty that Israel Potter discovers in Benjamin Franklin's *Poor Richard's Almanac* (1733–58), and that we glimpsed in Thoreau's *Walden:* the opinion that one's financial situation is solely a condition of individual moral responsibility—an idea Potter angrily dismisses as an insulting platitude (53–54).

Melville's ideas may be relativistic in this way but he still recognizes how economic systems can seem rigid absolutes for those involved. If recent critics have tended to theorize class as a category of social movement, then Melville emphasizes class as an imposition of social placement. Hence the images of molding and imprisonment that define the late chapters of *Israel Potter,*[68] and hence the use of a racialized imagery that works not to displace class altogether into race but to understand how aspects of class—those elements of low-class status or social disadvantage we have been calling *poverty*—can behave like race in peculiar ways. Melville employs a composite racial discourse (Potter is figured as black *and* as a "wandering Jew") not like Henry Mayhew to type the poor biologically, but in an effort to understand how poverty too can become legible by marking the bodies of the poor.[69] Injured physically and traumatized emotionally by his poverty, Potter demonstrates what the narrator describes as the mysterious impulses, contradictions, and enigmas that make the poor seem substantially different from mainstream norms (160–62). They seem different not merely in material conditions but in behavior, morality, and psychology—an integral minority group within a nation, something akin to a collective identity that emerges from forms of poverty not conventionally considered constituents of selfhood.[70] In this way, poverty hovers between the contingency of class and the intrinsic nature of race. Poverty is a marginal state connected to the mobility of a class system yet it also limits access to "felicity," removes social agency, and places the individual in an insurmountable position apparently remote from relief (159–60). Resisting the ethical "flip" we glimpsed in the works of Davis and Thoreau, whereby the cultural effects become the causes of poverty, *Israel Potter* describes the poor as blameless, so to speak, within a social condition that is nevertheless extremely difficult, if not impossible, to change. Victimization and exploitation can be experienced as internalized behavioral and mental patterns that act to hinder mobility, but these patterns never cement themselves into the foundations of economic inequality.

Israel Potter ties this concern with the psychosocial lives of the poor to the formal problems of representing poverty in a manuscript that Melville's fictional Editor describes as ragged and materially impoverished itself (v). If at the beginning of the book the rocky landscape of Potter's native Berkshires, exhausted of its potential to support livelihood, yields "ample food for poetic reflection" (3), then by the end this type of mitigating activity is abandoned. The Editor underscores this final refusal of any "artistic recompense of poetical justice" to "mitigate the hard fortunes of my hero" (vi), thus rejecting imaginative devices that might domesticate poverty by appeasing the observer with a compassionate sense of shared suffering. Melville thus self-consciously focuses on a point made by a number of recent anthropologists and sociologists: literature "clearly plays a significant role in orchestrating the language that validates or invalidates certain experiences as suffering," thus prefiguring "what we will, or will not, do to intervene."[71] *Israel Potter* strives to make its readers acknowledge the *experience* of poverty as "extreme suffering" (161). If Potter's little book, the record of his fortunes, long ago "faded out of print—himself out of being—his name out of memory" (169), then Melville's recycling of this source text again brings the ontology and memory of poverty into the textual sphere. The details of labor in particular provide powerful metaphors to understand social alienation and marginalization, whereby workers adapt psychologically and culturally to survive their position. Yet the details of Potter's vagrancy with which the novel ends raise deeper problems of disconnection from the social structure, problems of existential isolation and spiritual exile. There is an asymmetry of access to experiential knowledge implied by the pain that Potter faces,[72] just as the starers who throng to "the craped palace of the king lying in state" rarely "feel enticed to the shanty, where, like a pealed knuckle-bone, grins the unupholstered corpse of the beggar" (161). Melville opens up spaces of incommunicability by removing details from his source text (for example the account of a widow who fed her children on roasted dog)[73] and by drawing our attention to the omission of the really repulsive particulars of Potter's poverty (162). We skim over an entire forty-five-year period of Potter's life because any effort at truly representing it would be emotionally dangerous to the reader. Poverty thus presents a potentially decentering moment in which the appalling scale of human suffering threatens to devastate the observer with intolerable "things of horror" (153). In *Israel Potter,* poverty is not an event within a larger plot, or a power that moves characters up and down the social scale. It is more like a static condition, a location that hinders the movement of individuals within the social structure and equally within the narrative realm. Far from driving characters across the axis of plot, poverty needs to be skipped over altogether.

As in *Redburn,* sympathy collapses and with it the potential for social action that might emerge from the emotional interconnection between rich and poor. If Adam Smith haunts the pages of *Redburn,* then Thomas Malthus emerges at the end of

Israel Potter, in the narrator's recourse to the "well-known Malthusian enigma," whereby Potter's family increases despite his inability to feed them (162). The ideas of Malthus offered a convenient way to rationalize the suffering so clearly attached to poverty, its capacity to destroy life by denying essential goods. But Melville seems unable to accept Malthus's belief that misery and vice are natural forces, necessary to spur men upward, and to bring the level of population down to that of the food supply. There is always a *social* cause of poverty in Melville's world; it is never simply the result of nature or immorality.[74] How adequate, though, is the alternative view: Adam Smith's belief that, relatively speaking, poverty may be inevitable in modern society yet it comes with an economic expansion in which the poor too could share? If Smith's progressive belief hinges on what Himmelfarb describes as his central assumption, that "the poor, as much as the rich, were free, responsible, moral agents," then Melville theorizes poverty as a social state that can pressure individuals so as to deny these degrees of freedom and agency, thus mutating the assumption that "morality" and "responsibility" are universal values.[75] Moments when poverty moves beyond representation always run the risk of being complicit in what Rimstead describes as "a politics of erasure" that keeps the poor outside the field of perception.[76] The silences of *Redburn* and *Israel Potter,* however, should be understood finally not as efforts to exclude marginalized subjectivities but as admissions that the extant languages of political economy were themselves speechless to explain chronic inequality and need.

Despite echoing Redburn's suggestion that Americans, however desperately reduced, never sink to "actual beggary," the ending of *Israel Potter* ironically undermines Potter's reminiscences about his New England youth of "nestling happiness and plenty, in which the lowliest shared" (165–66). When he returns to the "Promised Land" (166), Potter finds a barren and unprosperous place; refused a war pension by the U.S. government, he presumably dies in poverty, after writing his obscure autobiography (169). In the years between *Redburn* (1849) and *Israel Potter* (1855), Melville began to explore how poverty operated more specifically in a U.S. context. These were the years, of course, that saw the publication of *Moby-Dick* (1851), a work that touches on many of the issues that Melville attaches to poverty. *Moby-Dick* explores the movement of world trade, and its relation to social class, particularly in the sense of vocation ("The Specksynder"); the adverse effect of work on the intellectual life ("The Carpenter"); "dependence" as a social category ("The Monkey-Rope"); and the economic metaphysics of the "mutual, joint-stock world" (68) in which man is by definition a "money-making animal" (452). *Moby-Dick* is metapolitically concerned with what antebellum reformers called *sociality,* the ways that communities govern themselves by forming hierarchies in which individuals gain power over others through social forms that command complicity from the disempowered. The novel deals with domination, rather than exploitation and deprivation; it treats the exercises of control, both social and

racial, more than the socioeconomics of need—a subtle distinction that helps explain why *Moby-Dick* fails to tackle the issue of poverty head-on, at least in the
same self-conscious manner that Melville deals with it in other narrative works. The
theme does surface early in *Moby-Dick,* in ways reminiscent of *Redburn.* Ishmael
has "little or no money in [his] purse" (3); he is downwardly mobile, and seeks a
sea voyage to escape poverty and the depressing feelings that accompany it. But
from the moment that Ishmael's despondency melts into the multicultural contemplation of Queequeg, the issue of poverty becomes dispersed and deflected
in the radical rewriting that editorial critics have described as constituting the
novel's vast expansion of thematic scope. If the category of poverty resurfaces
again then it does so as a relatively insignificant part of the novel's encyclopedic
contemplation of racial, metaphysical, political, psychological, ontological, linguistic, sexual, and global questions. We think of Melville's sailors in *Moby-Dick* as
controlled, as totally embroiled in the era's web of global capitalism, but do we ever
think of them specifically as "poor" in the same way that, in *Redburn,* we confront
the sailors as a ragged and deprived class? It does not necessarily follow that a
concern with poverty inevitably coalesces in texts like *Moby-Dick* that deal with issues of marginalization, commerce, and the working man. I suggested in my introduction that poverty resists the metaphysical abstraction of comparable categories because of its material specificity. And thematically, poverty remains a
specific term that gains special attention in a discrete group of Melville's texts, particularly those set largely on land. These are texts in which Melville's interest in the
behavioral and psychological patterns of the poor, and in the external difficulties of
representing them, questioned ideological forces that highlighted the culture of
poverty as a romantic ideal or a sign of inherent degeneracy—"delusive mitiga-
tion[s]" (*Israel Potter,* 161) that were as true for popular entertainment as they were,
at times, for transcendental philosophy.

Melville's Sketches of the Mid-1850s

Critics have debated whether Melville's sketch "Cock-A-Doodle-
Doo!" (1853) should be read as a satire of transcendentalism in general, or of
Thoreau's *Walden* in particular. (Though Melville's sketch was published in the year
before *Walden,* evidence suggests that Melville could have heard about Thoreau's
ideas from elsewhere, ideas to which he would return explicitly in *The Confidence-
Man.*)[77] There are striking parallels between the two works that imply, if nothing
more, a common response to wider considerations of poverty and individualism,
a response that shows how urgent these issues were becoming in the mid-1850s,
when continued economic instability made financial failure seem routine.[78] The
narrator of "Cock-A-Doodle-Doo!" is a depressed bankrupt who comes to hate

the dependence of others on his faltering resources, but who finds a recourse to his pessimistic belief that the poverty of farmers results from the vicious cycle of their own "incipient idiocy" (276). The recourse comes in the form of a poor farmer called Merrymusk, a remarkable character who represents a virtual pornography of poverty in his display of multiple qualities commonly ascribed to an ideal state of worthy want (280–81). His dizzying array of moral virtues revolves around an essential self-reliance, a *manly* independence—manifested in the tale's constant sexual innuendo—that is embodied in Merrymusk's native-born "lusty cock." The cock's tremendous natural beauty glorifies the abject poverty of the family's shanty, a poverty defined not by lack of food ("solid junks of jerked beef" hang from the rafters) but by physical incapacity and sickness that completely remove the family from the productive economy (284). We enter a transcendental world in which the *spiritual* power of the cock's crowing converts Merrymusk from a "poor man" to "a great philanthropist . . . a very rich man, and a very happy one" (286), and makes his dying children seem radiantly heroic, celestial, and noble figures (287–88).

We can think of Merrymusk as Melville's contemplation of the inverse of Thoreau's John Field. He is a figure defined not by Field's virtually biological degeneracy but by a total denial of the body and its needs, which results in the apocalyptic annihilation of Merrymusk's entire family. Melville's tale highlights the unearthly impossibility of self-reliance within need, thus satirizing the belief that a solution to poverty might reside in noble individualism or in an aesthetic appreciation of nature that remains oblivious to irreducible social, economic, and physical limitations. If we read this tale as criticizing Emersonian/Thoreauvian ideas that come to the fore in *Walden,* then it does so not by denying them but by taking such ideas to their absurd extreme. What would happen, Melville seems to ask, if our visits to the poor reveal not John Field but Merrymusk, not someone to build our ideals of voluntary poverty in opposition to, but someone—a poor man—who literally embodies those ideals himself? The result is the quasi-erotic frenzy with which "Cock-A-Doodle-Doo!" culminates. A "wild ecstasy of triumph over ill," crowed over by the cock's "rapture of benevolent delight" (287), removes Merrymusk from the physical world entirely, and terrifies the narrator with an "awful fear" (287). The narrator is converted from his doleful dumps but only by crowing madly like a cock himself (288). There is a conflict here between national ideologies of individualistic independence and the social pressures enforcing need. This conflict requires the poor to be degenerate others whose poverty results from their class-based idiocy (276), or else otherworldly superhumans whose bizarre substitution of the spiritual for the social condemns the observer to a kind of madness.

Supplementing Melville's major novelistic treatments of poverty, his sketches of the mid-1850s represent a remarkably developed and consistent analysis of the literary and social problems of inequality and social suffering in an era of increased economic disparity that was as notable in country as in town, and among whites as well as blacks.[79] The first part of Melville's 1854 diptych, "Poor Man's Pudding and Rich Man's Crumbs," returns to the ideals of poverty tackled in "Cock-A-Doodle-Doo!," in particular the widely held assumption that poverty somehow contains the sources of its own alleviation. This assumption, clearly present in Thoreau's *Walden*,[80] has been traced by a number of critics to Catherine Sedgwick's novel *The Rich Poor Man and the Poor Rich Man* (1837)—an assumption that is implicit too within the broader Christian interpretation of the poor.[81] The sketch returns us to the stark landscape of the Massachusetts Berkshires, where our anonymous narrator is conversing with the poet Blandmour about the apparent physical hardships surrounding them. From the moment that Blandmour personifies nature, as both almoner (official distributor of alms) and philanthropist (unofficial doer of good), Melville's tale becomes an extended contemplation of the poetics of social evasion, the linguistic techniques that can twist a state of poverty from scarcity to abundance—"'Enough is as good as a feast, you know'" (289). Blandmour's power of metaphor inverts the superficiality, whiteness, and coldness of snow, which seem to signal the destitution of Winter, to represent instead a dark, decaying manure, profound in its nourishing effects. Blandmour's figures of speech expand the implicit logic of Boucicault's *The Poor of New York* by presenting poverty as a paradox to be decoded by closely reading the ironic meaning behind the world's superficial signifiers. Not only is snow white as wool but warm, too, as wool, on account of the insulating effect of its entangled fibers, argues Blandmour. He takes the figurative snow-wool equation to a literal level of structural equivalence, which enables Blandmour's crucial belief that "the winter's snow *itself* is beneficent," that "the poor, out of their very poverty, extract comfort" (290–91). Blandmour offers a series of nouns to fill the gaps left by the material things missing from the lives of the poor. Melted snow becomes Poor Man's Eyewater, rainwater becomes Poor Man's Egg, and so on. If language here makes the lack, which defines poverty, a substance, or rather a range of alleviating substances, then the narrator's visit to the home of the impoverished farmer Coulter and his wife shows the materiality of poverty unmaking language itself. The snow and rain *do* penetrate, not to warm and nourish but to dampen firewood and to cripple the physical health of the needy (291–92). When figurative language is employed by the poor farmer's wife, it seeks not to reverse the apparent but to confirm its literal existence, effectively collapsing the tenor and vehicle of metaphor—grief does not drizzle down the soul "like the rain," but rain literally causes grief by helping to kill the Coulters' children (295). The irony of the sketch as a whole is that the narrator finds Poor Man's Pudding quite literally "poor"; the food is ultimately inedible because it contains physically the economic disorder and emotional pains of poverty—moldy, damaged rice, bought cheap, and a bitter, briny taste that embodies its maker's tears (295).

"Poor Man's Pudding" is thus a study of the materiality of poverty, its literal capacity to damage the poor physically and emotionally, its demarcation of class difference at the visceral level of taste. Because of its psychological impact, this materiality has the power to bend and disrupt the linguistic realm—hence Coulter's inability to name the fear and vulnerability of his condition, opting instead to talk indirectly and ambiguously of his psychological insecurity (294). If poverty is defined by material lack, then this lack actively infiltrates the discourse of the sketch, provoking moments of acute communicative crisis that center on the statement that the "native American poor . . . suffer more in mind than the poor of any other people in the world":

> Those peculiar social sensibilities nourished by our own peculiar political principles, while they enhance the true dignity of a prosperous American, do but minister to the added wretchedness of the unfortunate; first, by prohibiting their acceptance of what little random relief charity may offer; and, second, by furnishing them with the keenest appreciation of the smarting distinction between the ideal of universal equality and their grind-stone experience of the practical misery and infamy of poverty—a misery and infamy which is, ever has been, and ever will be, precisely the same in India, England, and America. (296)

The argument that the United States lacks an unstigmatized way for the deserving poor to find relief is made again by Melville in "The Two Temples": the penniless American narrator of this posthumously published tale can only escape psychological stress in a British context that allows him to contravene his national principles by accepting charity. In the passage above, Melville respects the transnational universality of absolute poverty by once more returning to the Malthusian category of *misery,* a category that creates the problem of recognizing suffering without then seeing it as part of a necessary natural force that stabilizes population growth. (Several critics have suggested that the dating of the diptych's fictional events to 1814 may be a specific reference to Malthus, who published *Observations on the Effects of the Corn Laws* in that year.)[82] Malthus paired misery with vice, the latter suggesting how the poor participate in their own extinction. Melville, however, combines misery and *infamy,* a term that not only signifies the notorious vileness of need but also has a specific legal meaning—according to the *Oxford English Dictionary,* a state of being deprived of the full rights of a citizen on account of some serious crime. This implicit discourse of citizenship underscores why nationally specific concerns come to outweigh Melville's comparative, international argument. (Indeed, Malthusian theory, based on overpopulation, always faltered in the open spaces of the United States.)[83] The conflict between poverty, as a form of restricted social agency, and national ideals of universal equality, creates the need to neutralize the human suffering of poverty (the solution of Blandmour), or else to focus structural causes of deprivation inward, toward the moral responsibilities of the individual—the reason for the heightened psychological pain of the Coulters. "Poor Man's Pudding" effectively shuts these escape valves. Rather than removing the poor from the realm of national values, Melville suggests how these values themselves collapse when poverty is recognized as a social crime that compromises the full citizenship of free whites—a point implied by the tale's multiple puns on "enfeebled constitution."[84] The capacity for self-determination and social choice has atrophied for these rural poor, whose communal needs conflict with the assumptions of freedom, universality, and individual agency upon which a dominant national discourse of rights depends.[85]

The point of "Poor Man's Pudding" is that socioeconomic states have cultural and psychological effects that disable communication between the poor and a middle-class narrator who resists recourse to the poetical and figurative tricks that placate public consciousness of material need. The genius of the sketch is that the representational stakes of this cultural difference are implied without constructing an underclass, inferior to bourgeois norms. Behavioral habits, so easily explained as "disgraceful neglect," are not internal subcultural creations but matters of situational expediency (296). And the sketch's constant silences—the narrator's choking on the pudding, his belief that speaking and expostulation will further mar rather than dispel sorrow, and the sketch's final unmentionable word[86]—arise less from the voicelessness of the poor than from profound gaps exposed within mainstream political and social language.[87] The subversive dangers of approaching poverty are as present as they are in *Walden,* but without any corresponding appropriation of the virtues of voluntary poverty, and without the "higher" vision that allows Thoreau to believe he can see through the pretenses and disguises of the poor to find consolation in their alleged shiftlessness.[88] The implication of Melville's sketch is that the persistence of poverty among a white, rural class of hard-working, virtuous, native-born Americans undermines conventional beliefs in equality of opportunity and social mobility to such a radical extent that, without the easy excuse of individual immorality or cultural inheritance, normative discourse is rendered speechless.

"Poor Man's Pudding" is part of a diptych with "Rich Man's Crumbs," the tale of the same narrator's experience, on a subsequent visit to London, of a horrific event in which a mob of paupers is "charitably" fed on the disgusting remnants of an aristocratic banquet. There are certainly parallels between the two sketches, in particular the narrator's repeated feelings of alienation from the poor.[89] Yet what in England is a visceral, physical repulsion (301) becomes in the American sketch a crisis much more intellectual, ideological, and linguistic in nature. A similar contrast appears in another diptych from 1854, "The Paradise of Bachelors and the Tartarus of Maids," although the contrast here is between the English luxury of the Inns of Court and the American poverty of factory life. The bachelors' paradise is a paradise of language: the narrator luxuriates in a homosocial space of storytelling, accounting, erudition, anecdote, translation, and quotation (321–22). Accordingly, the real source of misery for Melville's victimized maids is less the violent physical regime of their work than the intellectual and cultural barrenness of an environment in which human language, whether written or spoken, is either banished or erased.[90] Such analyses of victimization can seem forms of class essentialism, constructions of the victimized as powerless and voiceless others—the implication of Wai Chee Dimock's compelling reading of this sketch.[91] Yet efforts to deconstruct class by unhooking it from the determinism of poverty can leave us without the tools to critique social injustice and suffering at all, just as an emphasis on class as an unstable category of change and movement can work to nebulize the issue and dissolve it into categorical indistinctness and impermanence. Melville's argument in "The Tartarus of Maids" is not that all working women are degenerate victims but that industrialism can, in certain cases, impoverish workers by trapping them in a social position with deleterious consequences for both body and mind. The sketch does not simply erase the poor, but rather it contemplates *the pressures toward erasure,* the social forces that can limit access to the tools of literacy and the means of self-representation by effectively reversing the direction of Locke's metaphor of the tabula rasa (333). Rather than working to isolate the hardships of industrial life, Melville's sketch explores the dangers of poverty for *all* social classes, the capacity of social suffering and unequal cultural distribution to disorient the middle-class observer as well. The key point of the sketch is that cultural desolation fails to remain contained but contaminates the narrator's own intellect and language, obliterating his ability to signify coherently.[92]

Melville's sketches from the mid-1850s suggest that he shared Thoreau's sense that conventional philanthropy was both futile and corrupt. The narrators of "Cock-A-Doodle-Doo!," "Poor Man's Pudding," and the "The Tartarus of Maids" are equally unable to effect social change.[93] There is rarely any potential for reversibility or reform in Melville's view of the poor. His apparent exception, Jimmy Rose, can only rebound from being "a pauper beyond alms-house pauperism" to attain a degree of psychological health and dignity by his miraculous degrees of goodness and kindness, and by his refusal to accept charity in an explicit way ("Jimmy Rose," 342, 345). More typical is Bartleby, the scrivener whose "innate and incurable disorder" is defined as "poverty" ("Bartleby," 27–29), thus returning us to the world of *Redburn,* in which poverty features as a comparative and relational category with relevance beyond the industrialized poor. In many ways, Bartleby represents the end point of Melville's interest in poverty: he is the ultimate vagrant, completely disconnected from conventional social structures. The causes of this disconnection remain murky in Melville's 1853 sketch, which has a problematic focus on poverty as an individual essence, an ontological condition rather than an adaptive response to external social pressures. But the tale is much more about the effects of this poverty on the non poor, its capacity to render the narrator's affections redundant and his charity powerless.[94] Such attacks on charity, or on other forms of public assistance to the needy, can always cut in opposite political directions, toward a conservative vaunting of self-reliance or toward a radical belief that welfare does not alleviate the poor but rather structures and regulates them.[95] In "Bartleby" we get a strange mixture of these motives. Bartleby's total loss of selfhood can be read as an essentializing of need, but it is perhaps more a satire of national ideological pressures that intertwine economic status with individual character to the extent that any loss of status translates into the abyss of language and consciousness that is Bartleby. And this psychological-ideological matrix of poverty is always a danger for those who want to intervene. Bartleby's condition has a deleterious effect on the sanity, morality, and even the vocabulary of the narrator, proving an active menace to the representing agent itself (29). What emerges from Melville's dealing with the poor in an American context is exactly this problem of representation, this ethical, political, and epistemological difficulty, which both drives and complicates narrative interest without simply aestheticizing poverty or else abstracting it as a nonmaterial set of values disconnected from politics and social context. Nowhere is this more apparent and developed than in Melville's landlocked novel, *Pierre* (1852).

Poor Pierre

In this regard, we can think of *Pierre* as a test case in a new way of reading Melville as an author who helps to inaugurate a simultaneously material and discursive interest in poverty—an interest in a national polemics of poverty that would reverberate throughout the literature of subsequent generations. As well as being one of Melville's most "American" novels (in terms of its setting at least), *Pierre* is the text that has most easily offered itself to poststructuralist theory. Its endless ambiguities and enigmas place pressure not on ultimate meaning but on the process of interpretation itself.[96] Attention to *Pierre*'s twisted plot, however, suggests that this novel is less theoretically self-reflexive than socially rooted in Melville's concern with how social rank is far from "unfluctuating" (4), as Pierre's "own voluntary steps" take him "forever from the brilliant chandeliers of the mansion of Saddle Meadows, to join company with the wretched rush-lights of poverty and woe" (111). Thematically at least, *Pierre* can be situated among any number of popular novels from the mid-1850s, such as Ann Stephens's *Fashion and Famine* (1854), which also treats the perils of rural migration to the big city but with special regard to women.[97] *Pierre* shares much with Melville's wider explorations of poverty too: the novel's economic concerns transcend autobiographical sour grapes at the poor sales of his whaling book. *Pierre* presents a thoroughgoing challenge to the strategies by which mainstream society attempted to neutralize the problem of poverty, particularly by viewing it as an inherently aesthetic state— the idea, expounded by Thoreau in *Walden,* that the humble log huts of the poor are pleasing to the imagination.[98] Echoing Orestes Brownson's 1839 criticism of Wordsworth's poetry, Melville's narrator writes:[99]

> If the grown man of taste, possess not only some eye to detect the picturesque in the natural landscape, so also, has he as keen a perception of what may not unfitly be here styled, the *povertiresque* in the social landscape. To such an one, not more picturesquely conspicuous is the dismantled thatch in a painted cottage of Gainsborough, than the time-tangled and want-thinned locks of a beggar, *povertiresquely* diversifying those snug little cabinet-pictures of the world, which, exquisitely varnished and framed, are hung up in the drawing-room minds of humane men of taste, and amiable philosophers of either the "Compensation," or "Optimist" school. They deny that any misery is in the world, except for the purpose of throwing the fine *povertiresque* element into its general picture. (276–77)

Such questions of "optimism" are always part of Melville's engagement with broad philosophical questions of good will and radical evil, his quarrel with whether God had created what Leibniz described as the "best of all possible worlds." Yet Melville's play with the conventions of landscape painting here describes a narrower ideological phenomenon: the tendency for a specific and implicitly sentimental image of the poor to become an autonomous type in the mind's eye of the observer, gaining a permanence and motivating power that can serve as a rigid barrier to social intervention. (The *littleness* of such pictures echoes the social distance that makes this romanticization possible.) Old farmer Millthorpe accordingly draws the *povertiresque* sympathy of Mrs. Glendinning because he represents, quite literally, the "noble poor": claiming descent from an emigrating English knight, he combines a profile of the loftiest aristocracy with the knobbed hands of a beggar (275). The community tolerates poverty within itself by combining *povertiresque* romanticization—Millthorpe remains poor, believes Mrs. Glendinning, because his nobility prevents him from accepting payment for his labor (278)—with moral condemnation: the farmer is accused by the villagers of tipping his elbow too often at the local inn (277). Opposing the "maternal contagion" of optimism, Pierre glimpses the true physical and mental suffering of the Millthorpes' "augmented penury" and thus comes to reject the conventional tendency to root poverty in the "moral derelictions" of the individual (277).[100]

Melville's attack on the conventions for explaining poverty away, however, stops short of deconstructing poverty itself as a material force. Charlie Millthorpe's lack of mental vigor, the result of "having nothing to feed on but his father's meal and potatoes" (276), thus derails his subsequent education in the state-sponsored Saddle Meadows Academy. The latter half of *Pierre* becomes increasingly occupied with the influence of indigence on the mind, particularly in an urban context where the "subtle acid" of democracy corrodes the feudal class system of the countryside (9).[101] *Pierre* outstrips Melville's other works in stressing poverty not as an absence of something needed but as a positive presence, a chronic social state

Fig. 1.3. Frontispiece for Electa Maria Sheldon, *I Wish I Was Poor* (New York, 1864). Courtesy of the Michigan State University Library, Department of Special Collections. In this image from an American Tract Society publication, romanticization of the poor becomes possible when distance reduces the vision of social suffering, and when a window shade lies close at hand to obscure it altogether.

rather than a sudden or temporary condition—one that contains, moreover, a pattern of nonmaterial qualities. The Church of the Apostles, which houses Pierre after he flees home with the "poor castaway" Isabel Banford (66), is Melville's most explicit—and simultaneously his most satirical—recognition of how poverty can power a countercultural community with revolutionary political aims, and with its own aesthetic and philosophical traditions. The Apostles themselves are a collection of impoverished artists, poets, students, politicians, and philosophers for whom "Can't"—the "one great palpable fact in their pervadingly impalpable lives"—becomes "Kant" because their lack of social agency, represented by the absence of material in their stomachs, is converted into a capacity to digest abstract, antimaterialist ideas. Hunger becomes a tangible force that directly motivates philosophy, providing the conditions necessary for idealistic speculation. The Apostles, with their airy philosophy that is abstract to ridiculous degrees of incomprehensibility, may be another part of Melville's occasionally derisive challenge to transcendentalist ideas. Yet there is more than just parody in the narrator's fascination with their "very existence in the midst of such a terrible precariousness of the commonest means of support" (267). Somehow they possess the resources to survive within a social state that, as the novel develops, increasingly disrupts psychological and ethical coherence.

Pierre is labeled a vagabond in New York with remarkable speed; the minute evidence he betrays of dire financial circumstances is immediately detected by the piercing and infallible judgment of the city's "Calvinistical" cabmen (232). Following through on the theme of fallen gentility that begins *Redburn* and *Moby-Dick,*[102] this later novel is concerned again with the power of poverty to pressure individuals from all social classes, just as the down-and-outs Pierre encounters in a New York police house consist of men and women "of all colors" and "of all nations" (240).[103] The Apostles are a lighthearted correlative to Melville's serious study of how poverty represents a special psychological syndrome, a discrete pattern of attitudes and emotions that can easily elude quantification and comparison.[104] Living in a "beggarly room" (270) in the Church of the Apostles, trying to write a great work of literature to support Isabel and his former fiancée Lucy (as well as a destitute servant), Pierre's material "obscurity and indigence" (296) bring into play a complex combination of negative emotions and paranoid thought structures. His abject isolation and underprivilege, verging on hypothermia and starvation, create feelings of public persecution ("All things that think, or move, or lie still, seemed as created to mock and torment him") and self-hatred ("there was nothing he more spurned, than his own aspirations"), which conspire in a vicious cycle to perpetuate his poverty by making the very idea of success seem intolerable (339–40). Pierre's defeatist lack of ambition and self-esteem culminates in a state of absolute mental and physical breakdown. A "dismal lassitude, and deathful faintness and sleeplessness, and whirlingness, and craziness" (339) lead to blindness and vertigo when Pierre enters an existential vortex that attracts him to the mysterious haunts of social castaways, the "night-desolation of the obscurest warehousing lanes" where he collapses finally in the filthy gutter (341).

The word *obscure* features repeatedly in the novel's treatment of Pierre's poverty, operating on a number of different levels. It connects clearly to the psychosocial problems of vision encountered by Pierre, the combined result of his mental "dilapidations" and his "corporeal affliction" (340). Predicting the fates of Bartleby and the Maids of Tartarus, Pierre's impoverished despair becomes one of complete linguistic and literary destitution. His eyes refuse to look on paper, his pupils roll "away from him in their own orbits" and blink shut—a sign of the compromised autonomy and agency that leaves Pierre sitting "without saying one word," suffering from a "nameless torpor," "suspended, motionless, blank" (341–42).[105] If Pierre is to some extent "[s]wayed to universality of thought" by his hunger and his "absolutely penniless" condition among the Apostles (283), then any sense of poverty as a catalyst for creation soon slides into a skeptical analysis of the impact of material conditions on language, literacy, and the writing process itself. Melville uses Isabel's aphasia, her lack of words for basic things (152), to suggest a literal link between the psychological trauma of early destitution (she is exposed to little coherent speech as a poor orphan) and arrested language development (115, 120). In the case of Pierre, this analysis applies not to speech but to literary representation: the young writer discovers how the material pressures of an inadequate living standard cripple creativity in literal ways. The needs of the body come to define a poverty that cannot easily be transcended. The "consumptive dietarian has but produced the merest literary flatulencies to the world" (299) because need operates both emotionally and structurally. Hunger destroys the vigor necessary for protracted enterprise, while the need for rent and bread brings the hurried production of imperfect text (338). "Oh, who shall reveal the horrors of poverty in authorship that is high?" (338), exclaims the narrator. *Pierre* confronts the question of whether individuals *can* be silenced by their socioeconomic context; the novel defines poverty as a potentially insurmountable material state with cultural and psychological dynamics that actively disable its literary and implicitly its political representation in the public sphere.

Obscure describes the politics of vision whereby the impoverished become structurally remote from observation. But *obscure* works in a deeper ethical sense too. It describes the crisis of clear explanation, the sense of an incomprehensible and inherently false world that helps generate the ambiguity and textual instability that have drawn poststructuralist critics to *Pierre*. This metaphysical crisis in Melville's novel, I would suggest, derives in large measure from *socioeconomic* paradoxes provoked by the presence of poverty. We encounter one of these paradoxes in Plotinus Plinlimmon's pamphlet, which Pierre encounters on his journey to New York. The notion of giving "*all* that thou hast to the poor" (213), of living according to heavenly principles on earth, will merely lead to insanity and atheism in a social context defined by selfish acquisition.[106] Poverty thus becomes a subversive not a passive dilemma by exposing how dominant Christian principles—and implicitly democratic, egalitarian principles—are inherently incompatible with the materialism and inequity of Western civilization (207).[107] This recognition of "the world's downright positive falsity" (208), its moral and ideological self-contradictions, gets demonstrated textually. Pierre's inability to comprehend Plinlimmon's pamphlet directly corresponds to the narrator's inability to comprehend Pierre's inner speculation.[108] A similar point is made later by the narrator, at the moment when Pierre turns to writing as his labor, and thus attempts to "live on himself" (261): the world "vows it is a very plain, downright matter-of-fact, plodding, humane sort of world," yet it is governed by a doctrine "so ridiculous and subversive of all practical sense . . . of giving unto him who already hath more than enough, still more of the superfluous article, and taking away from him who hath nothing at all, even that which he hath" (262).[109]

"Liberal society cannot make itself answerable to the poor without threatening its own institutions and disordering itself," argues the cultural critic Ruth Smith. The recognition of individual need clashes with the foundational ideals of the liberal social state, whereby the poor cannot meet the preconditions of autonomous choice within a model of self-interested nature.[110] *Pierre* resonates with this problematic by dwelling on an *increase* of inequality. The widening of distributive injustice cuts against a central tenet of liberal social philosophy, namely that the progressive expansion of an economy necessarily raises the condition of the poor in line with all. By linking the irrational nature of the social order directly to the dilemmas of financial inequality, *Pierre* shows how the psychological and cultural problems of poverty, experienced by Pierre, correspond to contradictions in the ideological and moral realms. They are contradictions that the novel demonstrates formally because poverty presents problems that affect not merely Pierre's production of narrative but the narrator's production of *Pierre*. If the central ambiguity of the novel returns to the abyss of knowledge concerning Isabel's identity, then this mystery stems directly from her condition of being "a poor girl" (273) whose impoverishment has acted to disable the channels of informational access to her past. If Plinlimmon's pamphlet is a "miserable, sleazy paper-rag" (207), then *Pierre* too is an impoverished text, full of holes, riddled with moments of incompletion, ambiguity, contradiction, enigma, and solecism that emerge from the dilemmas of social marginalization it attempts to capture.[111] In addition to the novel's many moments of profound thought and supernatural sensation, which lie beyond verbal rendition and beyond rational comprehension,[112] we find moments of unmentionably and inexpressibly "low" conditions of poverty that remain indescribable because they actively destroy rational comprehension and ethical consistency.[113] Poverty is actually dangerous to, rather than simply lying beyond, language and thought. It harbors social forces that are "unsuspected without, and *undivulgible from within*" (338; my italics), forces that empty Pierre of creative material while simultaneously compromising his ability to structure experience mentally. Pierre's problem is one of method as much as material, just as poverty dominates the style as well as the subject matter of *Pierre* itself. An inverse of the panic texts that Ann Fabian describes as emerging from the economic downturns of the antebellum era, *Pierre* embodies textually the moments of ideological dislocation, intellectual vacuum, and ethical irrationality that the collapse of socioeconomic progress left so many writers with the desire to resolve.[114]

The idea that certain states of suffering and pain tend to strip subjects of language, and hence resist representation, is a major preoccupation of Western literature, with some critics suggesting that the silence of suffering has "turned into something of a modern cliché."[115] Attempts to apply such ideas to social class, or to the act of labor, can fail to account fully for why the working class is any less describable than other social groups or categories.[116] What we find in *Pierre* and in Melville's other writings on poverty is a more nuanced consideration of whether some social states *are* more indescribable than others, whether there might be a degree of representational inequity within specific conditions of socioeconomic inequality. As Melville realizes, the condition of *need* that defines poverty carries over from the material to the ideological, with dominant political discourse lacking the words to explain a social state that unsettles national assumptions of individual agency and mobility. And the capacity of poverty to trouble the linguistic realm is redoubled by the clear connections between poverty and *literacy*—a crucial means by which lower-class status is distinguished, argues John Guillory, because restricted access to the systematic regulation of reading and writing condemns the socially disadvantaged to real historical silence.[117] Melville seeks a definition of poverty in this relationship between materiality and language. By charting the capacity of socioeconomic situations to restrict literary production and linguistic competence, Melville thus predicts a tendency that Cynthia Ward detects in more recent novels about the poor: the way poverty is characterized by a lack of the literary tools necessary to its representation in the first place.[118]

To define poverty in terms of restricted access to literacy always runs the risk of essentializing class status (clearly, one can be lower class *and* literate),[119] or else of identifying poverty too closely with some kind of "intellectual deficit" that returns socioeconomic problems once more to the inadequacy of the individual.[120] Hence the troubling implications of Pierre's intractable "pauperism of the spirit" (*Pierre,* 136) and Bartleby's "excessive and organic ill" ("Bartleby," 29). What emerges most powerfully from Melville's texts, however, is not a simple muting of the poor or a silencing of poverty. Melville's encounters with poverty produce as much discourse as they erase—a point that remains as good for the beggars of Liverpool as for the hyperconscious narrator of *Pierre*. If literature "holds a power to address, or even reverse, the inherent pressure within affliction toward isolation and silence," as David Morris has written,[121] then Melville's works can be read as embodying a struggle *between* representation and erasure. Rather than simply removing poverty from cultural representation, Melville's work subtly registers the pressures that always push toward this removal, pressures that can result in silence but more usually show themselves in the stuttering and the distortions of narrative shock.[122]

Problems of Need in The Confidence-Man

When Melville's writing on the poor is placed alongside his era's more popular literary treatments of poverty, something of a historical disjuncture appears. Joseph Fichtelberg has charted a development of attitudes within antebellum panic fictions, for example, whereby sympathy toward the poor begins to harden, in the 1850s, into negative representations of a degenerate underclass— a result of increased middle-class frustration at its own financial vulnerability in an economy that once more collapsed in the Panic of 1857.[123] There is little sense of this development in the work of Melville. Indeed, his sketches of the mid-1850s contain some of his most subtle explorations of poverty as a social imposition and an ideological contradiction, as well as his sharpest critiques of the larger national values that make poverty both possible and particularly agonizing. Yet there is a definite wearying of the theme of poverty by 1857, with the publication of *The Confidence-Man:* Melville's farewell to extended prose fiction, which is also his farewell to the questions of poverty that had occupied him since *Redburn* (1849). Often seen as an aberration in the Melville canon, *The Confidence-Man* is very much in tune with earlier works. Its succession of poor (or purportedly poor) characters confirms Melville's interest in poverty as a multicultural condition that affects individuals from diverse backgrounds, races, and social classes. Melville returns explicitly to the transcendentalist take on the poor, when the confidence-man meets a Thoreau-like disciple of Emersonian beliefs who argues that any cry for financial help is itself proof of being undeserving because such indigence is a sign of "a defect, a want, in brief, a need, a crying need, somewhere about that man" (206).[124] There are other flashbacks to earlier works, both in terms of specific figures, such as the peddler boy at the end of the book who recalls *Redburn*'s Carlo in his successful trading on ragged identity (245–48), and in terms of broader problems, such as whether the means necessary to alleviate poverty become pure "lunacy" in light of contemporary social realities (5)—a problem that haunts the pages of *Pierre*.[125] But *The Confidence-Man* diverges from earlier works in significant ways, which helps to explain why this novel deals far less with the cultural and psychological lives of the poor, or with the representational difficulties of approaching them. The episode involving Thomas Fry, the "soldier of fortune," is a good example. Fry has been physically crippled by his time in prison after being wrongly convicted by a corrupt justice system; we return to Melville's concern with how society unequally distributes the "freedom" supposed to be at its core (95–98). What matters in this episode, however, is not the situation that has made Fry poor but the ethical question of whether his begging story, of being wounded in the Mexican War, need correspond to the truth of his poverty, irrespective of its success in attracting alms (97–98).

Melville's concern in *The Confidence-Man* is less with how and why certain individuals become poor, and more with whether we can have confidence in their performances of poverty. Melville has swapped the crisis of representation, evident in his previous works, for the crisis of certainty in a world where poverty, as a theme, endlessly generates stories but simultaneously creates doubt over whether a public confession of poverty can ever be sufficiently provable grounds for charitable giving. *The Confidence-Man* becomes difficult to position ethically. It remains problematic to argue that Emersonian ideas on charity and poverty are being satirized, for example, because transcendentalism is criticized by the confidence-man himself, who is begging charity for his own mysterious and potentially iniquitous aims. Simple moral polarity collapses in a situation where we cannot separate the claims of need from the confidence-man's impersonations of the needy. Michael Ignatieff has described Shakespeare's *King Lear* as a play about how pitiless the world becomes when we fail to take the needs of others on trust.[126] *The Confidence-Man* is Melville's approach to a similar theme, one that places the issue of charity in the narrow sense—giving alms to those in need—within a metaphysical crisis of confidence in the knowability of fundamental categories of "good" and "truth."

The Confidence-Man is less a substitution of philosophical for cultural analyses of poverty than a final statement of Melville's methodological diversity in approaching poverty as social state and ethical dilemma. Melville is most concerned throughout his career with the way poverty can limit the social agency of whites, but he resists essentialized arguments for a white "underclass" by exploring poverty as protean and relational, shifting in meaning and content according to time and place. It can affect blacks outside the context of slavery, vagrants as well as factory hands, the working and the middle classes, both rural and urban dwellers, women and men.[127] In other words, Melville isolates poverty as a category of social discourse that operates beyond traditional affiliations of class and race, a condition that may have its origins in social structure, not culture, but one that still requires a qualified, nondeterministic cultural perspective to understand it.[128] This is where Melville finally differs from a writer such as Davis. He remains more rigorous in his focus on nonmaterial patterns as effects rather than causes of material lack. Melville thus keeps more in tune with recent sociological arguments that allegedly ingrained values of the poor are not internal subcultural creations but matters of situational expediency.[129] There is, in this sense, little sign of an "undeserving poor" in Melville's works because he balances an understanding of how external forces push individuals into socioeconomic suffering with a recognition of the ways that behavior can slip into something like identity, as the poor adapt culturally and financially to survive their indigence. Melville may have echoed Emerson and Thoreau in his emphasis on the ineffectual nature of conventional philanthropy, but the unreachability of Melville's poverty, especially in a U.S. context, is always a response to wider social and political values that pressure individuals. Far from a *povertiresque* construction, the narrational efficacy of this material category is a function of its power to upset social conventions and hierarchies—a contagious threat to linguistic competence that is not bound to a particular class or race.

The centrality of Melville in the Americanist canon tests the assumptions of a critic most attuned to the literary significance of poverty, at least in its Canadian context: Rimstead's beliefs that any instituted national literature in a wealthy nation necessarily suppresses stories of need and resistance, as though these subjects were not worthy of cultural reflection; and that any textual, discursive analysis of poverty tends to make it "a pure, abstract, or fixed object of study" and thus becomes complicit in an exclusion of marginalized subjectivities.[130] Neither of these points is true of Melville's writing about poverty. The main purpose of this chapter, though, has been to test my own thesis that the problem of poverty can offer a sophisticated foundation for literary and cultural inquiry. Melville's pioneering definition of poverty, as a state with material, cultural, and literary relevance, resists the essentializing implications that typically accompany efforts to view poverty as more than a socioeconomic condition. The subsequent literature of the Gilded Age would continue to explore the cultural possibilities and dilemmas of contact with the destitute, as Progressive reformers and writers turned their attention to the nation's neediest. Even the literature of naturalism, however, would not always share Melville's resistance to the powerful temptation to turn the effects of poverty into a reassuring explication of their causes.

TWO

Being Poor in the Progressive Era:

Dreiser and Wharton on the

Pauper Problem

"Why, George," she said; "what's the matter with you?"

"I've been sick," he answered. "I've just got out of the hospital. For God's sake, let me have a little money, will you?"

"Of course," said Carrie, her lip trembling in a strong effort to maintain her composure. "But what's the matter with you, anyhow?"

—**Theodore Dreiser,** *Sister Carrie*

"I can see the lines coming in my face—the lines of worry and disappointment and failure! Every sleepless night leaves a new one— and how can I sleep, when I have such dreadful things to think about?"

"Dreadful things—what things?" asked Gerty, gently detaching her wrists from her friend's feverish fingers.

"What things? Well, poverty for one—and I don't know any that's more dreadful."

—**Edith Wharton,** *The House of Mirth*

THEODORE DREISER'S *Sister Carrie* (1900) and Edith Wharton's *The House of Mirth* (1905) have often been intertwined in the minds of literary critics, dating back at least to a 1907 review that noted the novels' parallel concerns with the surrender to sexual pleasure. Recent critics have observed the similar social descents of Dreiser's George Hurstwood and Wharton's Lily Bart,[1] yet over the past two decades criticism has turned its attention from the theme of poverty to the inner workings of capitalist consumerism. For Walter Benn Michaels, Rachel Bowlby, Michael Davitt Bell, and Amy Kaplan (among others), *Sister Carrie* is obsessed with the spiraling desire, spectacular abundance, and consumerist frenzy of unbridled turn-of-the-century capitalism.[2] For Wai Chee Dimock, Ruth Bernard Yeazell, Elizabeth Ammons, and Lillian Robinson, the target of *The House of Mirth* is not the poverty in which Lily Bart dies but the capitalist marketplace, with its inherently sexist values, in which she is totally imprisoned.[3] The most recent pairing of *Sister Carrie* and *The House of Mirth,* by Jennifer Fleissner, further displaces the social dynamics of poverty from the two novels by arguing that Hurstwood's decline is a product of sentimental conventions, while the novel's central concern with Carrie's rise is—like Lily Bart's dilemma in *The House of Mirth*—the result of a feminized quest for successful personal growth.[4]

With one or two notable exceptions, critics have emphasized the questions of wealth, consumerism, and desire in *Sister Carrie* and *The House of Mirth,* making such topics seem the inevitable domain of critical discourse, and relegating issues of material need to the backdrop that gives desire its prominence.[5] When poverty and deprivation *are* tackled in these novels, they frequently become functions of the generic convention of naturalism's "plot of decline"—formalist devices that detract from a more dynamic understanding of the links between the novel's stylistic practices and surrounding social discourses on inequality and want.[6] This tendency to view poverty as a factor of deterministic naturalism helps to explain why the boldest attempts to upset conventional readings of *Sister Carrie* have been so concerned with generic categories. Although Kaplan and Fleissner disagree on whether Carrie's rise represents a consumerist fantasy or the realistic success of female growth, they nevertheless share a desire to place the implicitly feminized conventions of sentimentalism at the center of a genre of naturalism (or realism) that is conventionally considered masculine in its emphasis on work and deprivation.[7] If criticism of *Sister Carrie* has hovered around questions of its purported naturalism, then criticism of *The House of Mirth* has remained remarkably stuck on the social background of its author. Critics may disagree on whether gender, race, or class is the central focus of *The House of Mirth,* but they tend to concur that Wharton was inevitably trapped by the hegemonic, genteel social values she attempted to criticize. Jennie Kassanoff's recent attempt to break new ground by arguing that *The House of Mirth* advocates a racial discourse of whiteness, for example, leaves us with a familiar conclusion: Lily represents Wharton's belief in the albeit vulnerable superiority of an Anglo-Saxon elite.[8] Further underscoring the parallels between Wharton's and Dreiser's novels, Christopher Gair has offered a virtually identical reading of *Sister Carrie.* So great is the critical reluctance to take poverty seriously as a complex category that Gair can only rationalize Hurstwood's "degeneration" by arguing that Dreiser somehow turns him into a dangerous African American presence that must be killed off at the end of the book.[9]

I draw *Sister Carrie* and *The House of Mirth* together once more to establish their remarkably self-conscious theorization of poverty as a social condition partially distinct from the discourses of class and race, and to uncover the dynamic ways that these novels help us to understand competing ways of thinking about poverty and about how knowledge of the poor is constructed and used. These two novels are less concerned with generic conventions (such as the "plot of decline") as patterns established in the past, than with a political process in the making—in Dreiser's case, a rhetoric of poverty with distinct designs on its readers, and in Wharton's case a polemics of poverty that throws into debate many of Dreiser's assumptions. The ethical logic of *Sister Carrie* as a work of fiction is generated primarily by questions of poverty not wealth, even if these two states are always linked in a context of inequality. The narrative pressures that drive Hurstwood's peculiar fate and, in effect, attempt to drive our responses to it as readers, can only be understood in light of the highly publicized and deeply contentious debates over homelessness, dependency, and persistent want that emerged in an era of economic turmoil and widespread efforts to relieve its increasingly visible victims. Although Wharton would return to the urban and rural consequences of poverty in *The Fruit of the Tree* (1907), *Ethan Frome* (1911), "Bunner Sisters" (1916), and *Summer* (1917), it is ironically in the upscale world of *The House of Mirth* that the issue receives her fullest treatment.[10] *Ethan Frome,* for example, may be relentless in its examination of the environmental causes and the crippling mental and physical effects of poverty on a Massachusetts farm family, yet poverty remains an inflexible determinant rather than the dynamic, cross-class, and formally complex category it becomes in *The House of Mirth.*[11] Echoing *Sister Carrie,* virtually all the major preoccupations of *The House of Mirth* relate to the concept of poverty, which functions as a distinct psychosocial force that explains, if not controls, the actions and interactions of Wharton's characters. By comparing and contrasting *Sister Carrie* and *The House of Mirth*—particularly with regard to their interventions in politicized debates about class and gender—we arrive at a nuanced understanding of the possibilities and the limitations of poverty writing in the Progressive period. We are also forced to confront some of the central assumptions that have shaped readings of these novels and the kinds of social realism they represent.

Both *Sister Carrie* and *The House of Mirth* uncannily echo the plotline of Melville's *Pierre* (1852): the desertion of conventional family relationships brings material poverty, psychological degeneration, and physical self-destruction. Dreiser and Wharton share with Melville an identical concern with the experience of poverty as integral to, not an aberration from, life in America; the same sense of poverty as something more than economic or material, something with moral, cultural, even psychological ramifications; a similar confrontation with the sentimental, sensational, and melodramatic modes that drove mainstream representations of the poor in the first half of the nineteenth century. Yet *Sister Carrie* and *The House of Mirth* remain most important for the gateways they offer into their own era's conceptions of the poor. Numerous historians have noted the change in attitude by the end of the nineteenth century, when individualistic and moral theories of poverty were replaced by social and environmental explanations of need, and by a growing awareness of the ways certain groups—women, blacks, and immigrants especially—were particular victims of inequality.[12] We see these developments reflected in the works of Dreiser and Wharton. But we also confront a deeper ambivalence in the discourse of poverty to which Dreiser and Wharton responded— a vacillation between progressive and reductive reactions in the era's social thinking on the poor, and an anxious drawing of class boundaries among those who stressed the heightened impoverization of working women.

Writing Poverty

Although many of the dominant attitudes toward the poor were firmly in place by the Civil War, the period between 1870 and 1910 saw poverty rise from a community problem to a national one, exacerbated by the end of a slavery that had long overshadowed poverty as a national concern.[13] Poverty was recognized as a pervasive crisis that provoked a range of responses, from the private efforts of so-called organized charities and settlement houses to public moves that institutionalized relief and sought to reform the alleged breeding grounds of destitution. The Progressive Era witnessed the development of voluntary social work—inspired by powerful beliefs in the "social gospel" of reform—and of professional sociology, which strove to define and quantify the extent of poverty. Statistical studies uncovered an industrial proletariat for whom work and want were far from opposing states. Highlighted too was the influx of immigrants from southern and eastern Europe whose overcrowded tenements came to epitomize the middle-class view of squalid urban living.[14] Homelessness became a much more widely recognized problem in the 1870s and 1880s, with the emergence of an aggressive and overwhelmingly male class of tramps and vagrants—individuals displaced by the Civil War and by a series of economic downturns.[15] The slumps of the antebellum era were magnified into major cycles of depression, most notably the "great depression" of the 1890s, centered on the crisis winter of 1893–94, which helped create a new public consciousness of unemployment as an inherent problem of industrial capitalism rather than a result of personal handicaps.[16] Although the living standard of some laborers may have risen during this period, nothing could prevent the developing sense that economic exploitation, insecurity, and inequality were all thriving on American soil.[17] Writing in the 1890s, William Dean Howells expressed the widely held belief that poverty had become a chronic condition in the United States. The condition was defined, for Howells, by a preposterous contrast between rich and poor, and was underscored by an ideological belief in the possession of money as a self-justifying fact—a combination that created shame in the poor and an anxiety in all Americans that they might slip into this state of unquestioned inferiority.[18]

Earlier, conservative literary trends continued after the Civil War, when economic anxieties were again assuaged by fictions of class essentialism and stability. At the end of Augustin Daly's popular melodrama, *Under the Gaslight* (1867), for example, we discover that the heroine, Laura—who has been disowned by high society after the revelation that she was originally a ragged pickpocket and merely adopted into wealth—is in fact the natural daughter of the upper class, and was swapped at birth with a poor child, her half sister, Pearl. Laura's high birth explains her inherent superiority and noble temperament, just as her half sister's original low birth explains her dubious moral tendencies. Sentimental "tenement novels" such as Edward W. Townsend's *A Daughter of the Tenements* (1895) again made poverty and wealth reflect individual and seemingly natural moral characteristics of vice and virtue, thus underscoring traditional beliefs in a providential world order. The sensationalism of the antebellum "city mystery" novel was still alive in writers such as J. W. Buel and Thomas DeWitt Talmage. Their righteous indignation at the bestial poor neglected to stress the historical and social factors producing poverty, as Benedict Giamo has argued in his masterful account of the era's various strategies of mystification whereby genteel writers acknowledged the poor but simultaneously avoided confrontation with the social reality of poverty.[19] Supplementing these persistent trends, the late nineteenth century brought a heightened focus to the cultural and psychological ramifications of a poverty that no longer seemed a temporary condition for individuals. (Even the upward class mobility, powerfully demonstrated in the popular novels of Horatio Alger, returned to chance encounters rather than conventional bootstrapping—a point that underscored the arbitrariness of this mobility and reminded readers of the caprices of the market.)[20] This was the era of cross-class representation, whereby members of the middle classes donned the garb of the working classes and the poor in an effort to comprehend the cultural quality of class difference and the subjective experience of want. Alvan Sanborn's collection of sketches, *Moody's Lodging House* (1895), for example, revealed a need common to documentary and creative literature, the need to get *inside* this type of life, to have oneself entirely made over both physically and psychologically so as to understand—in Jacob Riis's classic phrase— how the other half lived.[21] This distinct genre of cross-class memoir developed fully between 1890 and 1910 in protosociological works such as Walter Wyckoff's *The Workers* (1897–99), though many of its implicit assumptions had already been disseminated by Mark Twain's popular children's fantasy, *The Prince and the Pauper* (1881). Predicting Stephen Crane's experiments in misery and luxury from the mid-1890s, Twain's tale concerns a two-way act of class crossing that is fraught with ambivalence. The establishment of common humanity between rich and poor gives way to the wholesale psychological destabilization of both prince and pauper, which necessitates the reestablishment of rightful class boundaries at the end of the tale.[22] If middle-class interest in the poor highlighted the suffering and injustice of poverty, and at times reveled in the vitality of the lower classes, then it also worked to sanction the superiority of genteel values against the threat of "uncivilized" masses — a point that remains especially true of writing by women on female laborers, to which we will return.[23]

Melville's critique of the *povertiresque* was directed at a simultaneous recoil from and aesthetic attraction to the state of poverty discovered in the works of writers like Thoreau. This ambivalence only strengthened in mainstream Gilded Age depictions of poverty. Take, for example, the following scene from Howells's 1890 novel, *A Hazard of New Fortunes*, which describes the search of Mr. and Mrs. Basil March for an apartment in a New York City that seems very different from their native Boston. Driving accidentally down a street that "seemed gayer in the perspective than an L road," they confront the ash barrels, garbage heaps, shouting peddlers, and swarming children of a lower-class, immigrant neighborhood:

> The time had been when the Marches would have taken a purely aesthetic view of the facts as they glimpsed them in this street of tenement houses, when they would have contented themselves with saying that it was as picturesque as a street in Naples or Florence and with wondering why nobody came to paint it; they would have thought they were sufficiently serious about it in blaming the artists for their failure to appreciate it, and going abroad for the picturesque when they had it here under their noses. It was to the nose that the street made one of its strongest appeals, when Mrs. March pulled up her window of the coupé.
>
> "Why does he takes us through such a disgusting street?" she demanded, with an exasperation of which her husband divined the origin. (52)

Giamo has described how genteel local colorists such as Brander Matthews and Julian Ralph "wallowed in the descriptive intoxicants of sights, sounds, smells, tastes, and the general feel of 'the other half.'" Rather than wallowing in the aesthetic, however, Howells is keen to underscore what Keith Gandal identifies as the "schizophrenic" aspect of late-nineteenth-century writing on the slum, whereby fascination with the spectacle of poverty meets deep revulsion from the details of squalid living. Howells implies that the difference between picturesque admiration and disgust is a function of *distance* — a point also true for Thoreau, whose extraction of beauty from poverty depended on his capacity to retreat both physically and imaginatively. What is beautiful in Naples or Florence, and even in a fleeting glimpse of Lower East Side New York can get literally up one's nose when it exists on one's doorstep. (Howells suggests something similar in his sketch "New York Streets": poor neighborhoods can yield the charm of the picturesque and the spectacle of human drama, but to lack distance is to inhale the stenches of neglect.)[24] Howells makes even clearer than Thoreau the true source of disgust: this poverty has come to seem "as hopeless as any in the world, transmitting itself from generation to generation and establishing conditions of permanency to which human life adjusts itself as it does to those of some incurable disease, like leprosy" (53). The distance that makes poverty seem beautiful can easily contract into a belief that social difference is really cultural degeneration.

The late-nineteenth-century fascination with the cultural dynamics of poverty often worked to deflect attention from socioeconomic suffering in need of redress. Either the culture of the poor was degenerate, thus making the poor morally complicit in their degradation, or else this culture bore clear consolations that could negate social problems altogether. According to Julian Ralph's *People We Pass* (1896), tenement dwellers "are not so poor as most of us think! Many are not poor at all; many are poor only as they make themselves so. . . . There is plenty of money for dress, cheap life insurance, father-land societies, for charity to organ-grinders and beggars, for the church, funerals, festivals—and beer" (88–89). Josiah Flynt's *Tramping with Tramps* (1899) reduced much of the era's homeless problem not to economic pressures but to a disease of the youthful imagination, contracted from reading dime novels that romanticize life on the road, or from the pernicious influence of older tramps who bewitch young boys into hoboland with their artfully told tales of adventure.[25] The remarkable public hostility to the new category of the tramp in the 1870s and 1880s—homelessness was considered deeply subversive of the established Protestant ethic, argues Kusmer, while also threatening community control—had clearly abated by the turn of the century. Works such as Jack London's semi-autobiographical *The Road* (1907) again negated the structural problem of poverty by stressing the picturesque qualities of homelessness and by affirming its countercultural resistance to conventional life.[26]

Critics who have uncovered this literary interest in poverty have tended to join historians in arguing for a historical progression toward more sympathetic and to some extent more accurate representations of the poor by the end of the century. At the apex of the era's writing on poverty, for example, Giamo places the work of Crane and Dreiser, which marked a distinct break with the genteel values that went before.[27] These writers stressed the socioeconomic not the individualistic causes of poverty, argues Giamo, and thus offered a more realistic confrontation with the material, subjective, and subcultural qualities of the poor.[28] Critics have debated whether Crane's novel *Maggie* (1896) corroborates Crane's stated intention "to show that environment is a tremendous thing in this world, and often shapes life regardless."[29] Recent attempts to establish Crane's individualistic reasoning have

Fig. 2.1. "I am The New Constitution!" Britton and Rey, Lithographers, 1879. Robert B. Honeyman, Jr., Collection of Early California and Western American Pictorial Material. Courtesy of The Bancroft Library, University of California, Berkeley. The figure of the tramp loomed large in the national imaginary of the 1870s and 1880s. Here the destruction of local community implies a threat to national political institutions as well.

been undercut by Howard Horwitz's convincing argument that *Maggie* resists the era's idealized "sociological paradigm" by refusing to sanction the power of an unconditioned consciousness that might transcend and modify an environmental molding of self.[30] In many other ways, the era's literary interest in poverty showed the impact of Progressive developments in social thought, which stressed environmental origins for patterns of human behavior. The "Social Gospel" novels that burgeoned in the mid-1890s targeted the social and institutional causes of urban poverty, and called for a radical reform of society according to Christian doctrines.[31] In a rural context, Hamlin Garland's *Main-Travelled Roads* (1891) emphasized the emotional and intellectual dimensions of poverty, in which the entrapping drudgery of farm life causes an inarticulate despair that lies beyond the power of money to help.[32] Perhaps the era's best-known and most controversial representation of the impoverishing effects of labor on the self was Edwin Markham's apocalyptic poem, "The Man with the Hoe," which set off a storm of editorials, sermons, and public debates following its publication in 1899.[33] Markham rechanneled a key trope of naturalistic fiction—the power of unstoppable environmental forces to reduce humans to animals—to represent the power of exploitation and deprivation to destroy intelligence, culture, and spirituality.[34] Social suffering amid "the world's blind greed," Markham implies, had created a monstrous proletariat with terrible revolutionary potential.[35] Upton Sinclair would expand on this theme in *The Jungle* (1906), a book that looks back to the "problem of labor" novels of the 1880s, such as John Hay's *The Breadwinners* (1883), and forward to the proletarian novels of the 1930s. Sinclair represents an economic-industrial environment with an almost insurmountable power to trap workers within a poverty defined by physical crippling, psychological anguish, moral degeneration, and spiritual degradation. Even if its social effect was in the realm of food legislation rather than industrial reform, *The Jungle* strives throughout to capture the conditions of destitution that remain beyond polite literature, and to find some sort of political solution to the brutalization of the worker.[36]

No reading of *Sister Carrie* can miss the degree to which Dreiser also shared the realist and reformist urges of the Progressives, the muckraking desire to document and expose the social problems of the era, particularly its extremes of economic inequality. In his nonfictional writing, Dreiser paid careful attention to the physical and emotional suffering of New York's overcrowded masses. He was quick to criticize the sensationalism in journalistic approaches to the poor, and the moralistic sentimentalism of novels such as Townsend's *Daughter of the Tenements,* in which "good" poor people become wealthy and successful without apparent effort, whereas "bad" people are eventually punished financially.[37] *Sister Carrie* directs similar criticism at the conventional ways that details of poverty reached a wider reading public; a steady emphasis is placed instead on poverty as a material condition.[38] In this regard, *Sister Carrie* predicts the findings of

Robert Hunter's *Poverty* (1904), one of its era's most detailed and important studies of inequality (though one that has received relatively little attention, in part because Hunter abandoned the field of social work shortly after its publication).[39] At heart a socialist, Hunter helped spearhead arguments for the environmental causes of want; he worked to establish a material definition of the relative term *poverty,* based on the inability to obtain the necessities for a state of "physical efficiency."[40] Likewise, Carrie's lack of basic resources compromises her health and physical efficiency. The poverty of factory life is defined by basic physical abuses to the human body, which result in substantive states of hunger and sickness.[41] Hunter's focus was tightest on the alleged nonmaterial aspects of being poor. Drawing on the ideas of Tolstoy and Howells, he defined poverty as "not the lack of things" but "the fear and the dread of want" (1). Likewise in Dreiser's novel, Carrie's domestic experience with the Hansons in Chicago is defined as a "way of life" marked by the anxiety of financial insecurity and by entrapment in a dull and narrow round of toil (27–30). Material conditions have psychological consequences that radiate between people to create a broader culture of want and that coalesce into a psychological trauma, the driving force in Carrie's life.[42] The powerful interest in desire ascribed to Dreiser is certainly present in this text, but not as something abstract and in isolation. Desire is a force born from the shame and fear of not having enough, from the trauma of poverty that Howells recognized as emerging when tremendous luxury is struck against the financial insecurity and inequality of American life.[43]

If this is true for Carrie then how do we account for Hurstwood's strange rejection of desire, his failure to strive toward the better thing? "But what's the matter with you, anyhow?" asks Carrie the Broadway star when she meets a shabby, baggy Hurstwood on the street toward the end of the novel (438)—the word *anyhow* highlighting how Hurstwood's decline resists all hope of reversal, a predicament so peculiar that it provokes Carrie to ask the same question many times throughout the second half of the book. Early reviewers of the novel were obsessed by Hurstwood's "evolution" into a beggar, his "slow slackening of will, the subtle growth of indecision and self-abandonment, the loosening of all manly fibre, the crumbling, rotting of character in a kind of narcotic procrastination."[44] Recent critics who share the early opinion that Hurstwood's fall is the book's big achievement—the minority—tend to view it as part of Dreiser's fundamentally sympathetic approach to the poor and the oppressed, or else explain it away as part of the novel's purportedly racial logic.[45] Yet the completeness of Hurstwood's collapse remains a more perplexing phenomenon, as the editors of the Pennsylvania edition note.[46] Dreiser only describes Hurstwood's irritating, supine apathy as "*almost* inexplicable," however (362; my italics): it is far from a mystery without a key. *Sister Carrie* diagnoses Hurstwood with a specific disease, and works rhetorically to prescribe a cure.

The Persistence of Pauperism

In 1877 Robert Dugdale published his influential study, *The Jukes: A Study in Crime, Pauperism, Disease, and Heredity.*[47] Focusing on a single family of rural whites from upstate New York, Dugdale traces a line of persistent poverty and crime, allegedly originating from a single person (Max, born between 1720 and 1740) but now twelve-hundred strong—an extended family that Dugdale claimed had cost the state upward of one-and-a-quarter million dollars in seventy-five years (70). *The Jukes* suggests that environment nearly always has the power to modify heredity: positive moral habits can be inculcated by a discipline imposed from outside, such as enforced industrial training. Yet Dugdale also opens a broad path running in the other direction, with adverse conditions compounding an initial tendency toward debauchery and destitution. Environmental influences effectively enter the blood in a Lamarckian fashion, atrophying the cerebral tissue to produce hereditary habits (66). The result is a breed of hereditary paupers who suffer from a disease of character, a weakness, a lack of will power, a desire to follow the line of least resistance, all described by Dugdale as the sociological aspect of physical degeneration and disease (26, 38). Despite his environmentalist emphasis—or rather, because of his belief in the interaction between environment and individual—Dugdale leaves room for an underclass of the persistently poor akin to incurable sufferers of idiocy and insanity (70), a class whose inborn lack of vitality places them entirely beyond the reach of social and personal reform (47–50).

The idea of pauperism, which marked the difference between the "deserving" and the "undeserving" poor, was nothing new after the Civil War. It is important to realize, however, how extreme this distinction became by the end of the century, and how seriously pauperism was analyzed and defined as a specific disease rather than a vaguely immoral state of financial dependence. "Poverty and pauperism are words which should not be used as equivalents, or even as synonyms," wrote Oscar Craig, former president of the New York State Board of Charities, in 1893: "The terms stand for things or thoughts which in some respects are antithesis."[48] Charles Loring Brace's *The Dangerous Classes of New York* (1872)— an important bridge text drawn from Brace's experiences before the Civil War but written under the influence of postbellum evolutionary thinking—defined *pauperism* not as the consequence or symptom of disease but as the disease itself, a weakness and dependence that was essentially a degradation of character, a loss of manhood and self-respect (389–90). Brace feared that "a community of paupers, transmitting pauperism to children of like character, would soon become one of the most degraded and miserable on the face of the earth."[49] Dugdale later claimed to have discovered just such a community, as did Oscar McCulloch in *The Tribe of Ishmael: A Study in Social Degeneration* (1888), another influential work.

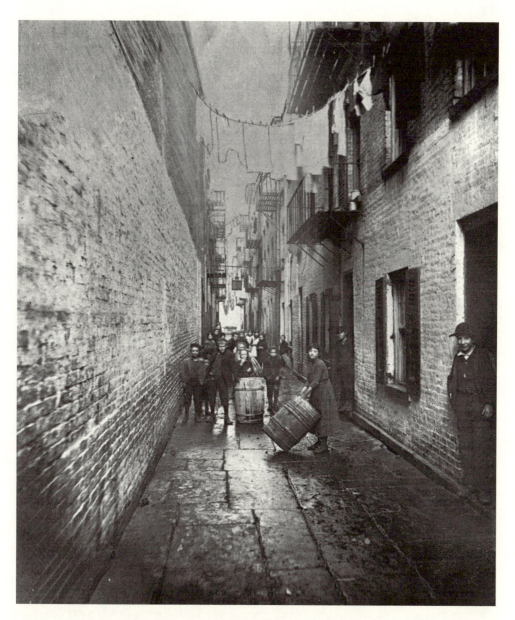

Fig 2.2. Jacob A. Riis, "Gotham Court." Illustration from Riis, *How the Other Half Lives: Studies among the Tenements of New York* (New York, 1890). Museum of the City of New York, Jacob A. Riis Collection, Riis #452. "The true line to be drawn between pauperism and honest poverty is the clothes-line," wrote Riis in *How the Other Half Lives*. This Riis image suggests that such binary thinking fed a visual hierarchy in which cleanliness and whiteness hover as flags of hope above the dirt and darkness of poverty.

McCulloch goes even further than Brace and Dugdale in specifying the difference of paupers and tramps from the poor in general: they are immoral, weak, diseased both physically and mentally, and inherently unfit for hard work (3). Removing any glimmer of environmental reform, McCulloch argues that these pauper families are absolutely determined by heredity, with each generation sinking back to their degraded habits despite perpetual efforts to lift them morally (8).

This discourse of pauperism thus shared in the historical growth of "hard" hereditarian beliefs that culminated in a broad-based eugenics movement that had its greatest influence between 1905 and 1930, when it dominated debates over charity and inspired the American Birth Control League of Margaret Sanger.[50] What Mark Haller calls the myth of the menace of the feebleminded became a major force in American social thought from 1910 to 1920, with poverty being ascribed to the inborn capacity and character of the individual alone, thus making environmental reforms virtually redundant.[51] Within the earlier discourse of pauperism, extreme views would similarly mingle the extremely poor and the homeless with the mentally ill and the criminal, thus making chronic poverty seem both biological and dangerous.[52] The belief of criminal anthropologists, that crime stemmed from the absolute factor of physical atavism, was applied equally to the pauper.[53] Expressing in *The Arena* (1894) an extreme version of views held implicitly by many, Martha Louise Clark described a lowest social stratum that contained sufferers of "moral imbecility."[54] These people with diseased consciences and souls had an incapacity for responsibility or correct judgment, which had become an irresistible biological condition—the direct result of perverse behavior in previous generations.[55] And distinguishing the pauper even more radically from the insane and the criminal were the most disturbing factors of all: a Bartleby-like absence of energy, independence, and substance, a total incapacity to fit into the social structure, an abyss of all those qualities that make for character itself.[56] Such viewpoints were reflected in debates over how best to relieve the nation's growing ranks of the homeless and the extremely poor. The so-called scientific philanthropy movement, epitomized by the Charity Organization Society, held that indiscriminate almsgiving produces the opposite of its intentions, actively pauperizing those it would save.[57] Hardcore Social Darwinians, such as William Graham Sumner, argued for a complete absence of institutional care, allowing the poor to succumb to poverty, intemperance, and disease, and thus ensuring the progress of the race. The incorporation of the pauper into flexible ideas of the "unfit"—a group supposed to be inherently incapable of self-government—allowed for the advocacy and the practice of both institutional segregation and sterilization as solutions to chronic dependency. Laws were established in certain states to prevent marriage between members of the persistently poor.[58] At the furthest extreme were the ideas of W. Duncan McKim, author of *Heredity and Human Progress* (1900): "the surest, the simplest, the kindest, and most humane means for preventing reproduction among those whom we deem unworthy of this high privilege, is a *gentle, painless death.*"[59]

Recent literary critics and social historians have revisited the history and legacy of eugenic thought in the United States, with a particular emphasis on its disciplining of female sexuality as a means to preserve white racial dominance.[60] When class issues are emphasized in this scholarship, as they are in Nicole Rafter's excellent introduction to the genre of eugenic "family studies," the model is one of class domination whereby a vulnerable middle class cements its hegemony by naturalizing social inequality.[61] The discourse of pauperism certainly shared in this class politics by tying poverty to inherent weakness or moral perversity.[62] The pauper as moral delinquent and intellectual imbecile thus helped solve an ideological crisis by explaining the existence of individuals seemingly unable or unwilling to rise up the social scale, and by sanctioning growing socioeconomic inequality by suggesting that the class system inevitably reflected the natural capacities of its members. Within a wide spectrum of opinions on the causes of and solutions to want, the pauper came to seem a real and specific figure in the minds of many social observers, irrespective of whether or not they subscribed to hereditary influence.[63] This persistence of pauperism highlights a wholesale ambivalence within even the most Progressive thinking on poverty at the end of the century. What Horwitz calls the "sociological paradigm," which saw the other half as entirely the mechanistic product of environment, was always in tension with more regressive explanations of need.[64] Amos Warner's influential study of poverty and its relief, *American Charities* (1894), was heavily revised in the early 1900s to reflect the growing understanding that the primary causes of poverty lay beyond moral fault; Warner's study thus looked forward to structural explanations of poverty that would come to dominate sociology in the twentieth century.[65] Yet Warner also sounded the alarm of "race degeneration" that grew from a belief in pauperism as an inborn disease of character, a form of physical decay arising from "scrofulous and neurotic heredity." Johns Hopkins professor Richard Ely identified environmental factors such as unemployment as major causes of poverty, yet he also drifted disturbingly into eugenics when he confronted those who most contravened social norms. Flynt's *Tramping with Tramps,* which celebrated the countercultural tramp, and Riis's *How the Other Half Lives,* which reduced poverty to environment or to a lack of "civilized" traits, also ran up against an implicitly white class of pauper whose peculiar character made him seem harder to deal with than the criminal.[66] In the literary sphere, even Edward Bellamy's utopian novel *Looking Backward* (1888), which projects an ideal world that differs most from the late nineteenth century in its virtual eradication of poverty and the fear of want, still contains an absolute subaltern class that cannot rise, a class essentially deficient in sensibility (61).

Within this particular poverty discourse ran an unresolved conflict between reformist and antireformist positions, between environmental and individualistic explanations of chronic need—a tension that stemmed from the dilemma of confronting the catastrophic breakdown of equality within whiteness itself, as American-born men of working age visibly swelled the ranks of the unemployed after the crisis winter of 1893–94. Because pauperism was most often described as male and white, it does not fit so neatly into the rationalizations, based on female sexuality and racial difference, that have driven recent scholarship on eugenics. The discourse of pauperism was much more messy, with the pioneers of the notion of self-perpetuating pauperism, Brace and Dugdale, never losing faith that the problem could be wiped out entirely by acts of environmental and social engineering.[67] It is not difficult to find calls for the "extermination" or the "elimination" of the tramp, but such extremist language often masked the belief that radical change might come from authoritarian, institutional attempts to impart the unquestioned moral values of work to the offending individual.[68] This was the complexity and the power of Lamarckian beliefs that behavioral traits willfully or necessarily acquired in a specific social environment could be passed on to later generations as a biological inheritance (a view rejected by orthodox eugenicists and by Darwinists, who saw the individual as already molded by environment). It could roll the alleged moral, anatomical, and environmental causes of poverty into one snowballing, degenerate mass, while also allowing some potential for environmental intervention consistent with the Christian reform tradition, some optimism about recovery from this medical condition.[69] Unlike hardcore eugenics, the discourse of pauperism could seem ambivalent and dynamic as well as rigid and absolute. No wonder it intrigued those whose business it was to move characters across narrative space.

What's the Matter with Hurstwood?

Despite some early hints in *Sister Carrie* of Hurstwood's early "lack of power" (202), his social collapse after eloping with Carrie to New York City is notable for its totality and for the degree of detail that Dreiser dedicates to its progression. Trying at first to hide his shame, Hurstwood gradually becomes indifferent and apathetic to his plight, trapped in the present moment of doing anything to satisfy his "craving for comfort" (335). In essence, Hurstwood's problem is a crisis of will, a form of addiction in which agency and self-governance collapse altogether. Following the line of least resistance, he loses his self-respect (326), while his expression of manhood becomes rapidly stultified (343), collapsing into a supine drooping, an ineffectual, irritating, clinging, and complaining manner (362). He is happy to become dependent parasitically on Carrie, making inquiries into how she is getting along with a regularity that "smacked of someone who was waiting to live upon her labour" (353). (He also employs the deceitful tricks that featured prominently in the era's antibegging propaganda.)[70] Hurstwood is devolving biologically too as he adapts to his squalid environment. His physical decay is matched by the onset of a psychological disease manifested in radical lapses of thought, traumatic flashbacks to better times, and unconscious verbal enunciations of remembered conversations that disturb even Hurstwood's fellow lodging-house inhabitants. As the novel progresses, Hurstwood's poverty merges with his insanity. He rambles incoherently in the street, "begging, crying, losing track of his thoughts, one after another, as a mind decayed and disjointed is wont to do" (452).

When Carrie thinks of leaving Hurstwood, in an effort to make him act for himself, she fears "he had developed such peculiar traits" that "he might resist any effort to throw him off" (395). These peculiar traits of dependency challenge Carrie's faith in potential reform, just as they challenge Dreiser's, and—I suggest—are increasingly intended to challenge our own. The forces motivating Hurstwood's drift into absolute dependency and social alienation represent Dreiser's social politics not his response to generic conventions, as the power of the socioeconomic structure confronts the power of individual, behavioral, and psychological disease. The bizarre behavior that leads Hurstwood to desert his family, steal the money, and virtually abduct Carrie seems a true demonstration of what Martha Louise Clark called "moral imbecility," while his nervous failure of resolve after the theft shows how Hurstwood lacks the requisite energy of the criminal mind. Instead, Hurstwood demonstrates the most disturbing qualities of all, the pauper's inherent absence of vitality, willpower, and resistance, his fitness for nothing but the personal comfort of parasitic laziness—an abyss of character itself, represented by Hurstwood's eventual devolution into a featureless entity of psychological blankness.[71]

Dugdale speculated that the emergence of such pauperism in an adult, especially in the meridian of life, indicates a hereditary tendency that may or may not be modified by environmental factors, a tendency that manifests itself in different gradations of waning vitality (*The Jukes,* 38). The possibility of reform within Dugdale's generally hereditarian outlook, however, evaporates entirely where Hurstwood is concerned, though it is not so easy to identify the ultimate source of his waning gradations. We are told nothing about Hurstwood's biological predecessors, even if the novel as a whole ascribes to the existence of instincts and other "inherited traits,"[72] and Hurstwood seems personally weak at significant moments throughout the first half of the novel, as well as pathologically addicted to the comfort of the pleasurable moment.[73] Hurstwood's problems originate in a vague area between potentially inborn and environmental pressures, an area of inherent tendencies whose lack of hereditary specification does nothing to lessen their power. This vagueness surrounding Hurstwood's origins is no oversight, I suggest. It demonstrates how the exploration of pauperism in *Sister Carrie* is driven not by Dreiser's interest in where Hurstwood may have come from but by Dreiser's fascination with Hurstwood as a kind of progenitor himself, a cauldron in which inherent traits of weakness spiral into something sinister. Hurstwood's psychological change in

New York resonates with a crucial element within the theory of pauperism, thus helping us to understand why the nature of this change could be "marked enough to suggest the future very distinctly indeed" (300).

Let us return for a moment to a crucial passage from a seminal text in the late-nineteenth-century discourse of pauperism, Charles Loring Brace's *The Dangerous Classes of New York:*

> It is well-known to those familiar with the criminal classes, that certain appetites and habits, if indulged abnormally and excessively through two or more generations, come to have an almost irresistible force, and, no doubt, modify the brain so as to constitute almost an insane condition. This is true also of the peculiar weakness, dependence, and laziness which make confirmed paupers. I have known a child of nine or ten years, given up, apparently beyond control, to licentious desires and habits, and who in all different circumstances seemed to show the same tendencies; her mother had been of similar character, and quite likely her grandmother. The "gemmules," or latent tendencies, or forces, or cells of her immediate ancestors were in her system, and working in her blood, producing irresistible effects on her brain, nerves, and mental emotions, and finally, not being met early enough by other moral, mental, and physical influences, they have modified her organization, until her will is scarcely able to control them and she gives herself up to them. (43–44)

Brace's use of the unusual term *gemmules* (a zoological term for a bunch of cells that becomes detached from an original body but retains the power to generate a new one) captures the Lamarckian belief that abnormal behaviors can transform an individual's biological organization and get passed on to future generations as the crippled willpower that defines pauperism. For Brace, this is a fairly prolonged process, and the biological determinism is always qualified by tentative doubt ("almost," "apparently," "scarcely"), the result of a hopeful belief—shared by many of Brace's contemporaries—that such forces may indeed be met early enough by other moral, mental, and physical influences. Now compare Brace's language and ideas with this well-known and remarkable description of Hurstwood from *Sister Carrie:*

> Not trained to reason or introspect himself, he could not analyze the change that was taking place in his mind, and hence his body, but he felt the depression of it. Constant comparison between his old state and his new showed a balance for the worse, which produced a constant state of gloom or, at least, depression. Now, it has been shown experimentally that a constantly subdued frame of mind produces certain poisons in the blood, called katastates, just as virtuous feelings of pleasure and delight produce helpful chemicals called anastates. The poisons generated by remorse inveigh against the system, and eventually produce marked physical deterioration. To these Hurstwood was subject. (302)

No early moral or mental influences stand in the way of habits to which Hurstwood may be prone—he lacks training in reason and introspection—but Dreiser's point is not that a hereditary predisposition explains Hurstwood's collapse entirely. Dreiser develops Hurstwood's character to represent the potential effect *and* the analyzable cause of his destitution. In other words, Hurstwood acts as a kind of nexus, a moment in which inherent weakness becomes a condition of full-blown pauperism, precisely because Hurstwood embodies the dynamic biological-social effect that contemporary observers placed at the center of this disease of will and character: the capacity of the environment to enter the blood. Dreiser's *katastates* (a physiological term, in use in the 1890s, for a simpler substance resulting from the destructive effects of metabolism) seem another version of Brace's *gemmules,* with the difference that the changes Brace sees occurring over several generations happen over several years in Hurstwood's case.[74] Hurstwood's decline demonstrates a reciprocal and spiraling interaction of environment, mind, and body. The impact of his new, impoverished environment causes a mental depression that in turn enters the blood, bringing a physical breakdown that can only reduce him to worsening environmental situations.[75] In terms of his overall development throughout the novel, Hurstwood seems a clear demonstration of Brace's belief that the effects of abnormal behavior may become biologically rooted in the blood, determining a degeneration from poverty to the insane disease of pauperism. The key differences in Dreiser's rendition are the acceleration of the effect, the lack of doubtful tone, and the disappearance of any hope in counteractive environmental reform.

Dreiser may have been echoing the ideas of pseudoscientists such as Brace, yet we should not underestimate the significance of historical compression in Dreiser's version of pauperism, the distillation of generations of devolution into a matter of years, for it hints at Dreiser's extremism. It highlights Dreiser's total rejection of hope in personal reform by moral, mental, and environmental influences—a hope that was always part of mainstream accounts of pauperism, such as those of Dugdale and Brace, despite their simultaneous drift into biological determinism. Rather than reenacting a plot of decline, *Sister Carrie* actively participates in a polemics of poverty by seeking a firm position within an ambivalent and complex discourse. Dreiser is not interested in making arguments about historical progression, or in linking Hurstwood to his forebears or progeny. His interest in the poor is synchronic more than diachronic, for it rests finally on the parallels between Hurstwood and the other extremely poor characters in the novel, as narrative attention shifts beyond Hurstwood to pauperism as a general social problem in need of cure. The final scenes of the novel, describing the homeless class at large, as well as Hurstwood's suicide, reveal in greater detail Dreiser's peculiar position regarding the causes of chronic poverty. Disturbingly, this position posits little opposition between an inability to reform the poor and something like a solution to abject want.

The Class That Drifts

If *Sister Carrie* tells the tale of Hurstwood's decline then it also describes how Hurstwood the individual gradually enters the mass, where people take him for "a chronic type of bum and beggar" (449), just as Hurstwood himself comes to recognize the "type of his own kind—the figures whom he saw about the streets and in the lodging-houses, drifting in mind and body like himself" (430).[76] Dreiser claimed to have drawn the character Hurstwood from experiences of his own among New York's homeless class,[77] and *Sister Carrie* bears a close relationship to Dreiser's nonfictional writings on the poor, collected in *The Color of a Great City* (1923)—sketches that Dreiser dates to his experiences in New York City between 1900 and the beginning of World War I, together with a few pieces published before the appearance of *Sister Carrie.*[78] These journalistic sketches dramatically underscore a belief that develops over time in *Sister Carrie:* the causes of chronic want return to the "mental insufficiency" (201) and to the "perverted moral point of view" (234) of the sufferer.[79] Dreiser is particularly drawn in these sketches to the characteristics of "the bum," characteristics that are described consistently and compulsively throughout *Sister Carrie* as well. These literary bums exhibit warped, frayed, and faded clothing; baggy, wobbling, torn trousers, worn almost to shreds; drooping hats and broken-down shoes; faces dry and chalky or blotched and puffed, drained white or brick red; shrunken features, sunken eyes, grizzled beards, and unattended hair; hollow chests, diseased frames, and malnourished bone and muscle; thin, rounded shoulders, wooden legs, flapping clothes, great anaemic ears, swollen noses, sickly red lips, and glinting blood-shot eyes (*Sister Carrie,* 428–29, 446, 455–56). In *The Color of a Great City,* Dreiser describes the chronically poor as a distinct "class" (231), even a "species quite distinct from the body social" (34)—a group whose biological difference makes them immune to the suffering of their poverty (35–38). In *Sister Carrie,* the poor become a group without community or even coherent language (430–31, 456), a group whose physical deformities match profound states of mental illness. There was not "a normal, healthy face in the whole mass; not a straight figure; not a straightforward, steady glance" (456). Even the working poor, as opposed to the complete down-and-outs, combine physical misshapenness with mental derangement (375–76). Echoing the contemporary discourse of pauperism, these men are homeless and poor not because of socioeconomic forces or age (the novel describes plenty of men in their prime who are poor) but because of combined and catastrophic states of physical and psychological abnormality, possessed individually though shared by a mass of people.

Transcending its analysis of Hurstwood's character, *Sister Carrie* highlights the broader persistence of poverty in the United States, with the daily spectacle of need becoming "so common by repetition during a number of years that now nothing was thought of it" (449). The novel seems to be positioning itself alongside contemporary, Progressive efforts to muckrake the era's social problems. But Dreiser's larger point here is not so much that poverty persists, with a certain number of poor people being an inevitable by-product of modern society, but that *the same people will always be poor*—an essential difference of emphasis. The dilapidated specimens who unobtrusively turn in to the mission house of the Sisters of Mercy are either the very same people, who return day after day the winter through, or at least the same *type* of person, a "class which simply floats and drifts, every wave of people washing up one, as breakers do driftwood upon a stormy shore" (446). In a passage borrowed from an earlier sketch, "Curious Shifts of the Poor" (1899), the novel describes how for twenty years Fleischmann the baker has given a loaf of bread every night to a line of men who have changed little in "character or number" over time: "In times of panic and unusual hardships there were seldom more than three hundred. In times of prosperity, when little is heard of the unemployed, there were seldom less. The same number, winter and summer, in storm or calm, in good times and bad, held this melancholy midnight rendezvous at Fleischmann's bread box" (446–47). If Dreiser literally cut and pasted into his manuscript sections from "Curious Shifts of the Poor,"[80] introducing Hurstwood as a character where necessary, then these lines were explicitly added to *Sister Carrie.* The emphasis falls not on how the mental and physical problems of individuals are caused by poverty, but on how poverty—at least this extreme and chronic type— is caused by the mental and physical deficiencies of a consistent number of exactly the same type of individuals.

The Fleischmann bakery scene is taken from the final section of "Curious Shifts of the Poor," the section Dreiser cuts most in *Sister Carrie,* leaving out the final page of explicit commentary that seems to embody the unspoken logic of the novel as a whole. Recalling John Field in Thoreau's *Walden,* the charity cases in "Curious Shifts of the Poor" (and implicitly those in *Sister Carrie*) are intended as the truly poor in body *and* mind (140). They are "driftwood," desensitized to their miserable condition, the "lifeless flotsam and jetsam of society without vitality to ever revive," people who exist beyond the reach of charitable intervention ("Curious Shifts," 140). The complexity of these intertextual relationships between Dreiser's early novel and his journalism is compounded when we realize that Dreiser includes in his later collection, *The Color of a Great City,* sketches that had appeared both in *Sister Carrie* and in "Curious Shifts of the Poor."[81] "The Bread-Line," for example, repeats the Fleischmann bakery scene, though Dreiser adds a passage to the scene as it appears in his novel, stating that he has "quite another purpose than that of description in doing so" (129). He implies that we are being given the moral gloss to a passage that featured merely as description in *Sister Carrie.*[82] "The thing that I protest against is that it [the breadline] endures," writes Dreiser. "It would be easy, as it seems to me, in a world of even moderate organ-

Fig 2.3. "A New York Charity—Distributing Bread at Tenth Street and Broadway after Midnight." Wood engraving based on a sketch by Charles Broughton. *Harper's Weekly,* December 17, 1892. Louis Fleischman's Vienna Bakery began distributing bread to New York's needy in 1877. The brief article that accompanied this image noted that the orderly breadline comprised men of all sizes, ages, nationalities, and "all classes and stations in life." No women were tolerated in the breadline at night.

ization to do something that would end a spectacle of this kind once and for all, if it were no more than a law to destroy the inefficient. I say this not in cruelty but more particularly with the intention of awakening thought" ("The Bread-Line," 131). Dreiser follows this statement with a slight retreat that advocates the merciful arrest of such men, putting them through a compulsory labor system. But the overall tone of the passage has chilling implications that undermine any impetus toward environmental amelioration, effectively closing the door on personal reform. Following the radical fringe of the debate on pauperism, Dreiser's call for the destruction of the inefficient drifts into a eugenic belief that the persistently poor are irreclaimably incapable. The best means of effecting their elimination is thus a legal form of "moderate organization"—compensating for the crisis of biological "organization" in the offending individual—rather than the laissez-faire laws of natural selection. The assumptions of Social Darwinism that punctuate Dreiser's early journalism are in this case insufficient; the impact of environment on individual must be speeded up in the most disturbing fashion. Such explicit commentary may be missing from *Sister Carrie* but I want to suggest that the novel employs the implicit devices of plot, character, narrative voice, and figurative language to awaken thought by other means—a rhetorical push toward an inevitable if disturbing conclusion that the intractable nature of inborn pauperism does not necessarily mean that a social solution to the homeless problem cannot be found.

Where Hurstwood is concerned, the solution to his predicament arises naturally, as "constant want and weakened vitality" inevitably make "the charms of earth rather dull and inconspicuous"; his inability even to beg successfully leads Hurstwood to interiorize opinions of his personal worthlessness (449). Turning toward the Bowery with death in his heart, Hurstwood, otherwise mentally deranged, is allowed one coherent thought: "People had turned on the gas before and died; why shouldn't he? He remembered a lodging-house where there were little, close rooms, with gas-jets in them, almost prearranged, he thought, for what he wanted to do" (449–50). When Hurstwood has begged the necessary fifteen cents, we join him again in a crowd of homeless men, gathered outside the closed door of the lodging house. This scene (again drawn from "Curious Shifts of the Poor") has a close textual resemblance to Stephen Crane's sketch "The Men in the Storm" (1894),[83] though Dreiser's version lacks Crane's description of the "deserving" poor who are pushed into poverty by socioeconomic forces, or the belligerent poor whose "sublime disregard of consequences" gives them genuine social power ("The Men in the Storm," 94–95). In Dreiser's account, we have an undifferentiated mass notable for its physical powerlessness and collective psychological derangement. They are "dumb brutes," gathered in a pack that precludes expression of individual personality and distinctness—the very elements from which sympathy might be generated. The crowd is merely a murmuring "it," fighting without dignity or honor to escape from the harsh elements that inevitably threaten the lives of the weakest. The "melting inward" of the crowd seems largely a passive and indifferent act, less as if they are propelling themselves and more like they are being pushed. But what are they being pushed toward? Why does the appearance of a light inside the lodging house send "a thrill of possibility through the watchers" (457)?

An obvious answer is that this light is a signal that the lodging house is about to open its doors, but these lines take on deeper meaning when we realize that this passage is markedly different from Dreiser's original version in the copy-text of *Sister Carrie,* a version subsequently emended—presumably by Dreiser himself—in the first printing of the novel. The original reads as follows, the italics highlighting the differences removed from the published version: "A light appeared through the transom overhead *where some one was lighting the gas.* It sent a thrill of possibility through the *watcher.*"[84] In this alternate version the emphasis falls on the act of lighting the gas (an implicit reference to Hurstwood's impending suicide), but more significant is the change from "watchers" to "watcher," which shifts the subject of the noun from the crowd outside (the collective watchers) to a solitary watcher, an outside observer of the scene. The watcher becomes the highlighted narrator, and the episode as a whole becomes a moment of narrative realization, I would claim, of a final solution to the intractable dilemma Hurstwood demonstrates. The final scene of Hurstwood's suicide again features this watcher, who observes Hurstwood's final moments of hesitation and preparation for suicide (458). Michael Davitt Bell has commented on the mastery of point of view demonstrated in this scene, its panning outward and away from Hurstwood.[85] But more important is its difference in narrative perspective from anything else in the novel—except, of course, the alternate version of the recognition scene outside the lodging house, when we are first introduced to this solitary watcher, whose eugenic desires become projected onto the homeless sufferers themselves in the published version. We have in the suicide scene a final withdrawal of sympathy, a narrative dissociation from Hurstwood, in which we are refused access to his consciousness, with the strong implication that there is little consciousness left for us to enter. Hurstwood does not think or review his life; there is no emotion or self at stake, no spark of vitality; there appears indeed to be little "use" in keeping such a weak specimen alive (458). Hurstwood's death comes to seem (or at least, Dreiser wants it to seem) the greatest kindness, an act of rest that can happen mercifully out of sight—an easy and gentle solution to a case of incurable and painful disease that lies beyond the reach of charitable intervention.

In *The Color of a Great City,* Dreiser flirts again with the logic of euthanasia—a subject clearly in the air in the early years of the twentieth century, featuring prominently in Wharton's novel *The Fruit of the Tree* (1907), which begins by debating a euthanasic solution to an injured worker but only features the mercy killing of a physically suffering wealthy woman.[86] Dreiser's sketch "A Wayplace of the Fallen" describes a lodging-house institution that may not have the reform of the workless in mind but could bring an end to poverty nonetheless. Poverty "has color and odor and radiation as strong as any gas or ferment" (178), a destructive power that is magnified by the structure of the institution itself. Unlike Hurstwood in his lodging house, these inhabitants live not in enclosed rooms but in cells with mere partitions between them, positioned to give maximum supervision, and allowing the internal circulation of air laden with poverty's destructive fumes (176). Dreiser reinforces these disturbing implications with a further contemplation of a great chemic or psychic force at work in the world at night, "as though these misfits of soul and body were still breathing in unison with something, as though silence and shadow were parts of some shrewd, huge plan to soothe the minds of the weary and to bring final order out of chaos" (179). Writing in *Harper's Monthly Magazine* in 1910, Robert Bruère, former general agent of the New York Association for Improving the Condition of the Poor, suggested that such a "shrewd, huge plan" may already be established. He noted that Bellevue Hospital in New York, which effectively served as the general city poorhouse, was an institution in which unofficial genocide actually took place, as such high mortality rates resulted naturally from the tendency to congregate in one sickening mass the destitute, criminal, diseased, and insane, as well as dependent children.[87] Bellevue Hospital is the place where Hurstwood is sent after his feverish collapse, though it is finally the institutional structure of the lodging house, with its ready supply of gas, that emerges in *Sister Carrie* not as a problem of poverty but potentially its solution, soothing the minds of the weary and bringing order out of chaos with an effectiveness beyond the restructuring of charity or other forms of social welfare reform.

The context of the storm that informs Hurstwood's suicide underscores a point that Dreiser makes in several of his journalism articles, and one that contemporary students of pauperism were also quick to suggest: harsh environmental conditions might naturally destroy the people at the bottom of the social pile.[88] But Dreiser does not trust to nature alone, just as his understanding of the causes of chronic poverty seems more in line with Lamarckian than Darwinian thought. Positioned between laissez-faire and institutional solutions to the pauper problem, *Sister Carrie* implies that a kinder outcome than death from starvation or disease might be found for what Dreiser believed to be a distinct and inevitable segment of people. This is not suggested as a Malthusian check on overpopulation, for Dreiser makes it clear that only a small and fixed number of individuals would be involved—the Hurstwoods of the world, who through a combination of inherent personal weakness and environmental pressure have entered a state of total dependency, social alienation, physical decay, and mental death. Nobody would be turning on the gas in an official capacity; this would not be genocide, technically speaking. More convenient still, in this world of "moderate" organization the conditions of poverty would be allowed to take care of themselves, and the problem of a seemingly unreformable underclass could reach its own solution.

Fear of Falling

Comparison of *Sister Carrie* and Kenneth Kusmer's history of homelessness in the United States suggests that Dreiser made a number of historically pertinent points, especially concerning the proneness of middle-class whites to downward mobility.[89] The novel offers pointed criticism of the harsh working conditions of the Gilded Age, as we saw in the descriptions of Carrie's factory experiences, and as we see again in the account of the Brooklyn trolley strike, which seems largely sympathetic to the demands of the exploited strikers. There is a force in *Sister Carrie* that we can identify as *poverty*. It is a situation of misery and want that affects the working class in general, fixing them in a state of relative suffering, and creating the trauma of uncontrollable desire when placed in the context of spectacular wealth. In this sense, *Sister Carrie* does not simply sanction what critics describe as the era's corporate-capitalist values. But it is not to the world of the working poor that Dreiser's novel finally looks. Dreiser offers *Sister Carrie* as an intervention in a public debate over the causes of a persistently homeless, workless class in a supposedly advanced industrial society, though Dreiser avoids Henry George's conclusion that such extreme poverty was an inevitable product of the very "progress" it opposed. If the novel does contain an aesthetics of consumption for which critics have argued, then it must be seen as inextricably intertwined with, if not actually displaced by, a *rhetoric of pauperism*—just as wealth and poverty are themselves mutually constitutive states—because the book's narrative logic strives to persuade its readers to credit this pseudomedical condition of spiraling degradation, internally generated by the inadequacy of the individual. Rather than stressing the negative psychological and physical results of hunger and deprivation, Dreiser flips the causal relationship to suggest that virtually all extreme cases of poverty, especially when found among white men of working age like Hurstwood, stem from a preexisting and catastrophic breakdown of physical and mental fabric. Though the novel engages occasionally with social class in the traditional sense, the working class is inevitably eclipsed by this new class of pauper, totally beyond the reach of political consciousness. It is a class for whom poverty becomes virtually an ontological condition, an innate factor of identity whose causes threaten to detach entirely from material considerations. The prolonged depression of the 1890s made it increasingly difficult to distinguish the allegedly undeserving among the poor, and thus brought less rigid views of dependence.[90] The image of the homeless became much less vicious and more sympathetic in middle-class literature of the early twentieth century.[91] But these trends in social thought are directly countered by Dreiser. Even in his description of the trolley strike, Dreiser employs skewed economic logic—unemployment and harsh treatment of workers exist despite a scarcity of labor—which shows how his economic ideas were driven not by the laws of the market but by a much more personal sense of individual power that precludes anything like a political solution to problems of poverty.[92]

In its treatment of the causes of pauperism, *Sister Carrie* corroborates the belief that environmental factors can become hereditary, thus rejecting a purely Darwinian or a purely eugenic view. But this Lamarckian position only works in the one-way, negative direction toward degeneration, and it is clearly supplemented by a belief in innate characteristics that preempt cultural influences. In terms of solutions, any Social Darwinian belief in the resolving power of environmental forces also proves inadequate, for such natural processes of extermination must be exacerbated by institutional organization. *Sister Carrie* thus makes a number of complex ideological moves, which add up to a resistance to ambivalence over the causes of and possible solutions to chronic want. The statement that Hurstwood "*must* do it" (335; my italics) not only describes his addiction to ease, the catastrophically diseased will that marks his intransigent degeneracy; it also advertises the degree to which Hurstwood is being compelled, by the narrator, to enact so absolutely his inactivity. The complete or partial absence from *Sister Carrie* of contemporary issues such as temperance, the settlement-house movement, even Christianity itself in any prominent sense,[93] further suggests how Dreiser is actively closing off avenues of medical, educational, and spiritual reform in his exploration of Hurstwood's peculiar predicament.

Possible motivations for Dreiser's feelings about poverty can be found in his autobiography and in sketches such as "On Being Poor," where Dreiser dwells on the traumatic experience of his own hardscrabble upbringing and his early experiences as a down-and-out. Poverty made Dreiser "nervous, really very sick mentally, and very depressed," and thus "all but destroyed [his] power to write."[94] The solution to this crisis of creativity emerges from his encounter with the poverty of others, particularly the "spectacular" figure of the homeless bum, which has "always had a peculiar interest for me, even a kind of fascination, such as an arrestingly different animal might have for others."[95] Extracting literary material from these social victims, Dreiser strives to save himself from poverty in another sense, by constructing difference and creating distance between himself and the poor characters he describes. Mark Pittenger has suggested that the alarmist view of the poor at century's end, the insistence that the neediest were a degraded, constantly devolving, subhuman race, was a means to cement class boundaries at a time of pronounced middle-class insecurity—an intensification of patterns established by panic fictions in the 1850s, and traceable again to the eugenic "family studies" of the early twentieth century.[96] An antidote to the fear of falling that Barbara Ehrenreich has identified as plaguing the inner life of a vulnerable middle class, Hurstwood offers the counteracting and potentially reassuring sense that such precipitation derives from specific forms of personal disease, and cannot simply be thrust upon people by external economic pressures.[97]

When we recognize the rhetoric of pauperism at work in *Sister Carrie,* it becomes difficult to accept traditional arguments for Dreiser the naturalist, or revisionist alternatives such as Fleissner's thesis that Hurstwood's plight is a recourse to sentimentalism. If anything, Dreiser erases sentimental sympathy by underscoring Hurstwood's moral bankruptcy, though this erasure is no prelude to systemic analysis because it lacks a revision of the moral essentialism upon which such condescending attitudes were founded. *Sister Carrie* may resist the sentimental but only by leaving the assumptions of melodrama firmly in place. Dreiser's novel is thus more in accord than is usually thought with the themes and ideas of Augustin Daly's play *Under the Gaslight* (1867), large sections of which appear word-for-word in *Sister Carrie.* Dreiser echoes Daly's central moral that biology will inevitably win out over environment, that hereditary wealth is a prerequisite of blood not an arbitrary convention. Hurstwood may be offered primarily as an example of how environmental and behavioral forces conspire to *become* determining biological traits—the crucial dynamic that differentiates the discourse of pauperism from eugenics proper—yet his decline is still related to the key convention of traditional melodrama, the tendency for inherent moral character (or in the pauper's case, a profound lack thereof) to prevail over social and environmental pressures.[98] What distinguishes *Sister Carrie* from the works of writers like Daly is finally a matter of structure, not ethics—the whole technical drama whereby ideological tensions are muted, hopeful alternatives are shut down, and an antireformist position on both cause and cure is enacted quite literally under the gaslight.

It is tempting finally to see the decision to end the 1900 edition of *Sister Carrie* with Carrie, not Hurstwood, as a retreat from the issues of poverty emphasized by the ending of the Pennsylvania edition. Yet the culmination with Carrie only highlights a series of parallels between Carrie and Hurstwood, undermining any effort to create difference, and suggesting that Carrie may be heading toward a state of pauperism herself.[99] We are told at various points that Carrie prefers comfort to activity, that "[u]nconsciously her idle hands were beginning to weary" (419), that an addiction to the easy life may seal her doom. Throughout the novel Carrie predicts Hurstwood's end by quickly abandoning the struggle of looking for work, choosing instead a dependency on unearned income, from Drouet and then from Hurstwood, to relieve her distressing thoughts. An analysis of gender difference shimmers behind these events. Is Dreiser suggesting that social expectations make it possible for a woman to exist in a state of dependence that would be shameful and soul destroying for a man? *Sister Carrie* touches upon this question but only hints at what would become a pressing issue by the end of the nineteenth century: the special links between poverty and American womanhood.

The Feminization of Poverty

Robert Hunter confessed in the preface to *Poverty* that "the working woman and the mother are left almost entirely out of consideration" (vii), largely because he was not personally familiar with their conditions. His interest lay instead in questions of "manhood" (127, 131); pauperism itself was assumed to be specifically a disease in men. That the most extensive account to date of American poverty neglected to emphasize the situation of women is remarkable.[100] Reflecting a homeless world that had become overwhelmingly masculine by the turn of the century, this omission also implied the development of pronounced gender lines in social investigations, which rendered poor and homeless women largely invisible.[101] Historians such as Mimi Abramovitz and Christine Stansell have shown how the identification of the moral problem of work with masculine duty during the Victorian Era made it difficult to criticize unemployed homeless women, while patriarchal beliefs in the family ethic forced, and condoned, women's dependence on men. A powerful reaction to this sexist dependency emerged in the works of writers such as Thorstein Veblen and Charlotte Perkins Gilman, who targeted a sexism in economic relations that seemed most pronounced and damaging in the wealthy classes. Gilman's *Women and Economics* (1898), like Veblen's *The Theory of the Leisure Class* (1899), described marriage as "economic beggary," and women as "starved" individuals who had fallen behind in evolutionary growth (89, 75). Yet Gilman's social vision failed to stretch to the working women who eked out some degree of financial independence in an economy of sexist inequality. (In this regard, Gilman's work matches a broader cultural movement that Richard Brodhead detects in postbellum novels such as Louisa May Alcott's *Little Women* [1868]: an emerging middle-class concern to define itself against the affluent leisure class rather than against the poor.)[102] For other observers at the turn of the century, it became increasingly difficult not to notice that women did indeed swell the ranks of the working poor, as those "undeserving" individuals who strayed outside the bounds of domesticity were punished with low-paid labor.[103] The Progressive Era saw the rise of the settlement-house movement, of the Social Gospel reform movement, and of voluntary social work, particularly among women. This era also witnessed the emergence of a brand of literature that stressed the special links between poverty, work, and womanhood—a literature that suggested how working-class women have always been particularly prone to poverty in the United States, even as it revealed class divides widening within female identity itself.

Helen Campbell's *Prisoners of Poverty: Women Wage-Workers, Their Trades and Their Lives* (1887), Mrs. John [Bessie] and Marie Van Vorsts' *The Woman Who Toils: Being the Experiences of Two Gentlewomen as Factory Girls* (1903), Dorothy Richardson's *The Long Day: The Story of a New York Working Girl as Told by Herself* (1905): these major studies of working women in the Progressive Era reflected different motivations, though they all shared a middle-class desire for contact with the poor, a need for sympathy and for bonds of sisterhood between different social classes.[104] These works represent a gender-specific manifestation of the cross-class representation that was so prominent at the turn of the century, when earlier trends became fully established.[105] By 1860, writes Stansell, bourgeois women had gained moral power and some freedom of movement in their communities, manifested in a reformist zeal to understand and to help poor women. Yet any gender consciousness, any sympathy between women, came at the expense of a rigid cultural division between classes.[106] Such trends can be seen in Elizabeth Stuart Phelps's novel *The Silent Partner* (1871), which strives to establish close parallels between rich and poor. Perley Kelso's voicelessness as a woman who must remain a powerless silent partner in a Massachusetts cotton mill echoes the political voicelessness of the laboring poor, represented by Catty Garth, who is literally deaf and dumb. (Phelps's short story, "The Tenth of January," repeats an imagery of scarred mouths and marred lips that captures the ways harsh factory labor damages women physically and psychologically, rendering their suffering speechless.)[107] In *The Silent Partner,* women do finally gain voices, but in ways that reinforce class hierarchies and that give genteel women a nonthreatening power within their male-dominated communities. Catty's sister Sip becomes a preacher, teaching meekness to the poor, while Perley gains her own power to preach cultivated values to the lowly. Sympathy is reached between Perley and Sip, but—as Amy Lang has argued—it is largely a prerogative of Perley's middle-class status.[108]

Echoing this class consciousness and an ambivalence within Progressive class-crossing narratives as a whole, the literature of female philanthropy reveals revulsion from the impoverished lives that attract it. Campbell's *Prisoners of Poverty* positioned the saintliness of the charity worker and the virtuous refinement of the wealthy against the female factory hand who was unemotional (45), barbaric (130), and unreflective (222), "hardly higher in intelligence than . . . the limpet on the rock" (112). At root, Campbell cannot accept the different culture of poor women, their alternative ways of living and thinking (232), their desire for some degree of economic independence that might resist the subservience of a domestic environment (16–17).[109] She blames the poor for their poverty, failing to understand those who choose what seems a degraded lifestyle over her own cultivated ideals (184). Richardson and the Van Vorsts run into similar problems. The great trouble in alleviating the condition of the working woman, writes Richardson, is that she is "too contented, too happy" with her lot despite failing to read the right books or to think the right thoughts (*The Long Day,* 89, 299–303). Bessie Van Vorst notes the amazing cheerfulness and stimulating companionship of her fatigued workmates, which makes her fear the sociability and discipline of factory work—a dangerously attractive alternative to the family unit (*The Woman Who Toils,* 33, 28). The Van Vorsts express the most hope in real empathy between the classes; they believe that the difference between rich and poor is less natural than "merely a thing of culture" (69). But their desire for cultural reform presupposes a realm of intellectual, aesthetic, and moral ideals into which the poor girl will be lifted (20), a realm that stresses above all the values of domesticity over any desire for independence.

These women writers tended to regularize female labor as a monolithically devastated entity. The Van Vorsts describe women as particularly vulnerable to exploitation and poverty because of their inferior womanly sentiment and because they lack the same class solidarity as men (both Campbell and the Van Vorsts stress how women allegedly tyrannize other women in the workplace).[110] The overwhelming conclusion is that working girls are deficient in the fundamentals of language, morality, emotion, aesthetics, and thought itself.[111] According to Richardson, women lack the same intellectual and moral capacities as men. They are

1. SCENE IN A "SWEATER'S" FACTORY.   2. THE END.   3. SCENE AT THE GRAND STREET FERRY.
THE FEMALE SLAVES OF NEW YORK.—"SWEATERS" AND THEIR VICTIMS.
FROM SKETCHES BY A STAFF ARTIST.—SEE PAGE 191.

Fig. 2.4. "The Female Slaves of New York—'Sweaters' and Their Victims." *Frank Leslie's Illustrated Newspaper,* November 3, 1888. Clara Goldberg Schiffer Collection, The Schlesinger Library, Radcliffe Institute, Harvard University. The suffering of women in the workplace is both physical and deadly in this image of male power and exploitation. According to the accompanying article, these female victims of "absolute slavery" are inevitably "ground down to starvation, insanity or lingering disease."

innately unequipped for the ignorance and hardship of a laboring environment, and thus fall rapidly into states of degradation, delinquency, and even insanity.[112] Possible reasons for these disparaging attitudes toward working-class women's culture and intelligence are suggested by Jane Addams in *Twenty Years at Hull-House* (1910), the classic text of the settlement-house movement. The independence of the working girl only highlighted fears that, as Gilman had argued in *Women and Economics,* an even deeper kind of poverty might afflict the non-working woman too. Addams emphasizes from the outset how her concern with the poor comes directly from what she perceives as her own relative indigence as a woman. This indigence is revealed in the nervous depression following her failure to break through sexist limits and pursue a professional career (48–49), and in her feelings of hopeless futility emerging from the emotional malnourishment of an overcultivated upbringing (51–53).[113] For Addams, the solution to her gender-based sense of impotence is to advocate philanthropy as a kind of purposeful labor in which middle-class women can become empowered and balanced individuals by conferring their cultivation on those beneath them (59).[114] In an era when analysts of the upper classes highlighted gender imbalance by arguing that marriage, for women, was a form of servitude at best, genteel women countered attributions — and fears — of pervasive female "lack" by producing a social literature that spiritualized the female domestic role by demonstrating the impoverished alternative of the working woman.[115] The needs of gender were answered by the virtues of class. In effect, the works of Addams, Campbell, Richardson, and the Van Vorsts painted a picture of working poverty that sanctioned a version of sheltered femininity, thus strengthening the hegemony of their own cultivated class values and salvaging some moral authority from what Henry James called the "abyss of inequality" between the sexes.[116]

Poor Lily

The House of Mirth bears a close relationship to its contemporary genre of philanthropic writing by women. Like Jane Addams, Lily Bart's closest friend, Gerty Farish, responds to her subordinate status by taking up charity work as her "trade" (163), thus using a relationship with the poor to elevate her own sense of professional significance and moral authority. Gerty runs a Girls' Club, a social institution that, like its big sister the settlement house, sought to elevate the minds of working women by encouraging contact with their social "betters." When Lily Bart encounters the girls in Gerty's club, however, she resists succumbing fully to "one of those sudden shocks of pity that sometimes decentralize a life" (150–51), the shock that Addams would describe when she sees for the first time the need and suffering of the hideously poor (*Twenty Years at Hull-House,*

49–50). There are, I suggest in the following pages, significant reasons for Lily's divergence from this genteel convention of conversional sympathy for the worthy poor. *The House of Mirth* was written against these philanthropic assumptions, which echoed closely an earlier sentimental literary tradition of representing "low" characters—a tradition, found in Maria Cummins's *The Lamplighter* and still alive in Phelps's *The Silent Partner,* that tended to neutralize poverty with a naturalized ideology of domestic femininity.[117] Wharton complained to the head of Scribner's book-publishing department about "the assumption that the people I write about are not 'real' because they are not navvies & char-women."[118] She overcame such assumptions, however, not by displacing the poor altogether but by revealing poverty in a radically different environment.

Critics have dismissed the role of poverty in *The House of Mirth* as sentimental at best, simplistic at worst, their readings bounded by the safe parameters of Wharton's own perceived identity as an "upper-class" writer.[119] Rather than an unreflective victim of her era's social ideologies, Wharton employs *The House of Mirth* to rewrite a discourse of poverty clearly on display in *Sister Carrie*—a discourse that depicted the neediest class as naturally male, and that cast problems of homelessness and unemployment in a predominantly masculine light. Wharton thus follows her philanthropic sisters in identifying special links between womanhood and want. But she does so by introducing another element into her thought, one that sought to liberate the concept of poverty from the hierarchical confines of caste even as it paid little attention to the female poor. Wharton's power as a social theorist is established by the way she both intuits and refigures emergent sociological theories, such as the understanding of poverty as a psychological force, described by Hunter in *Poverty.* (Hunter's work was well known in its time, just as Hunter himself was fairly prominent in New York's elite social circles, though the relevance of *Poverty* to *The House of Mirth* has been eclipsed by a critical obsession with the themes of wealth and consumption described in Veblen's *The Theory of the Leisure Class.*)[120] Wharton plays with sociological ideas, placing the psychology of poverty, ironically, at the heart of high society—an elision of class boundaries that makes *The House of Mirth* a radical critique of gender relations.[121] Reassessing the psychological and cultural reasoning that underpinned both scientific and popular interpretations of inequality, Wharton executes a series of brilliant maneuvers that break down elite assumptions about natural class difference while simultaneously isolating new and radical ways to conceive of female consciousness.

Like his contemporary Dreiser, and echoing earlier social thinkers such as Dugdale and Warner, Hunter dwelt on the perennial distinction between poverty and pauperism, though he was most concerned not to separate them but to explore their dialectical interaction—an interaction essential to an understanding of Wharton's novel. Workers will often accept the agony of poverty in preference to the horrors of charity, argued Hunter, but here he observed a curious fact, "which psy-chology alone explains." The men who will suffer almost anything rather than be-come paupers

> are often the very ones who never care to be anything else when once they have become dependent upon alms. When a family once become dependent, the mental agony which they formerly had disappears. Paupers are not, as a rule, unhappy. They are not ashamed; they are not keen to become independent; they are not bitter or discontented. They have passed over the line which separates poverty from pauperism. (3)

Such a passage hints at the recognition of a degree of adaptive rationality in a state supposedly antithetical to reason itself. An understandable desire for release emerges from the extreme psychological pressure placed on the relatively poor by wealth ideologies and by beliefs in the normalcy of upward mobility. Yet for Hunter, the cycles of this situation were always vicious because—ironically—the inde-pendence of poverty signaled pain whereas the dependence of pauperism offered perversities of pleasure that inevitably caused the catastrophic and irreversible transformation not just of cultural patterns but of an individual's entire mental fab-ric. According to Hunter, lack of work among able-bodied men led to wholesale physical degeneration (128) and to a peculiar mindset clearly evident in the vagrant pauper—a menacing figure that focused the era's special concern with home-lessness and tramping, the most visible aspects of the poverty problem. Recalling the ideas on display in *Sister Carrie,* Hunter defined this mindset as an absence of systematic memory and stable associations, which forced the individual to live in a perpetual present (129); a radical weakness in concentration, discrimination, and critical capacity, which disabled the grasping of abstract ideas or generalizations (129–31); a lack of coherent philosophy concerning one's own life, which com-promised even a basic degree of self-consciousness and self-control (129). Pau-perism signaled a collapsed selfhood, thought Hunter, which he attempted to cap-ture with an image used increasingly to describe the most profound depths of penury that seemed beyond the bounds of charitable intervention: an "abyss," an absolute void of consciousness.[122] (Both Richardson and the Van Vorsts also de-scribed extreme poverty as a vortex, a whirlpool sucking fragments of humanity into its mysterious depths.) Hunter believed that the working poor were uncon-sciously producing a traumatized generation of the culturally deprived because these workers were trapped in a psychological double bind whereby the only re-lief from unbearable misery was an even deeper degree of degeneration.

In a conversation with Gerty Farish toward the end of *The House of Mirth,* Lily Bart expresses her dread of the dingy world into which she is heading (266). Significantly, though, Lily's past life of apparent luxury is described as another form of poverty—a relative poverty, defined by the nerve-racking battle to keep up, on diminishing resources, with the living standards of the wealthy (266). This is the governing irony of *The House of Mirth.* While suggesting that Lily is not made "for mean and shabby surroundings, for the squalid compromises of poverty," the narrator reveals the perpetual undercurrent of Lily's need, the stressful consciousness of struggling "to pay her way" (26), the "daily friction of unpaid bills, the daily nibble of small temptations to expenditure" (77). Of all the complex emotions to which Lily is prone, an "old incurable dread of discomfort and poverty" is perhaps the dominant force in her life (295).[123] It is tempting to dismiss this employment of poverty as merely a figurative equivalent to the limitations of Lily's self, or as an inappropriate metaphor that describes relative differences among the very wealthy, and thus ignores the real sufferers of want. But poverty is treated much more seriously in the novel as an actual psychological condition of "real stress," with Wharton taking special care to distinguish Lily's "practical strain of poverty" from less accurate applications of the term (77).[124] Poverty is a state of mind, a dread of worse horrors figured in images of "mounting tides" and "dark seas"—images of a self being submerged in abysmal depths of destitution (77). A real psychosocial presence, poverty shapes a complex network of emotions and fears that dominates Lily's behavior and shapes the plot of the novel, a network with roots deep in the early formation of Lily's consciousness.

Lily is clearly victimized by her early training, but the real impact of Lily's upbringing rests not on the point to which critics have drawn most attention—that she is raised as a luxurious ornament with no practical purpose (297).[125] The deepest psychological scar Lily bears is made by the pressure of growing up relatively poor. When Lily first contemplates why she seems to be failing in life, her thoughts return immediately to her childhood, the memory of which is dominated—as it was for Melville's Redburn—by the horror of her father's financial ruin, followed by "the underflow of a perpetual need—the need of more money" (30). Lily is clearly exposed as a child to the psychology of striving poverty, to the stress of keeping one's head above a flood of want (39), represented most vividly by her father's mental and physical enervation, which comes from the anxious struggle to meet the material needs of his family. But the reactionary view held by Mrs. Bart, her belief that the dingy condition of living "like a pig" (30) arises from the moral failure of the individual, is only sustained by her parasitic dependence on the earning power of men—the kind of gender subjection that Gilman exposed as beggary. Alongside the anxiety of relative poverty, Lily becomes increasingly aware of being a "mere pensioner" on "the luxury of others" (26), of living thoughtlessly off unearned income—the very situation defined as pauperism by Hunter. Lily's life is the story of her vacillation between these relative and absolute states of destitution.

Close and sustained attention to the plot of *The House of Mirth* reveals Wharton's remarkably developed psychological language of poverty, which accounts for the "zig-zag broken course" (29) that critics have noted in the novel.[126] The contemplated prospect of marrying Percy Gryce is the first of several crucial moments when Lily zigzags between the psychologies of striving poverty and pauperism. Marriage to Gryce would lift "a heavy load from her mind" by freeing her "from the shifts, the expedients, the humiliations of the relatively poor" (49), and from a stressful overexpenditure of emotion. The word *shift* in this instance works on multiple levels to signify Lily's poverty, which registers as a lack of choice (*shift* as a verb, "to take whatever course is available"), a material inability to afford glamorous clothes (*shift* as a noun, "women's dress of oblong form"), and, implicitly, a state of being *shiftless,* an adjective that was most often associated with the "undeserving" poor.[127] Ironically, though, this shiftlessness is exactly what Lily is heading toward: her marriage to Gryce would turn her from an active (albeit overstressed) spender into the passive thing spent upon. By marrying Gryce she would indeed be freed from the shifts of the relatively poor—*shift* in the sense this time of movement, as she would come to lack the social agency to move freely in her environment. Lily's "sense of relief" is not "happiness," we are told (49), because Lily's dependence on Gryce would necessitate an erasure of personality, a total identification with the desires of another (49). Marriage signifies entrance into an abyss of self, a radical loss of independence and self-respect that connects with Wharton's wider inquiry into the problems of female consciousness, as we shall see later. The point to note here is that the temptations of marriage are, with varying degrees of self-awareness, resisted by Lily. Earlier in the novel Lily realizes that the reason for her failure in life lies in her inability to accept the rewards of marriage, which "would be a rest from worry, no more" (28). She later rejects Simon Rosedale's proposal in a similar manner, considering the desire to be free from the anxieties that arise "when one is poor and lives among rich people" as insufficient reason to marry (178). And of course, whether intentionally or not, Lily's chance of solving her troubles by marrying Gryce is destroyed when she temporarily absconds at the crucial moment for a walk and talk with Lawrence Selden. We begin to suspect that there is a state of being that Lily holds more horrifying than the worry and anxiety of relative indigence.

By resisting marriage to Gryce, Lily maintains her independence at the expense of suffering the stress of being relatively poor. Her subsequent business arrangement with Gus Trenor, in which Lily believes that Trenor is merely making her own small investments work for her on the stock exchange, again releases her from "the need of economy and self-denial" (85). She loses her sense of risk (85), which had fed her anxiety, entering instead a state of complacency and "disinterestedness" (86) that lasts for five chapters, during which Lily enjoys the cessation of pain and the freedom from minor obligations that her new income provides. Yet Lily's release is always about to spin into less desirable behavior, verging on a loss of self-respect marked by her tolerance of Trenor's inappropriate advances (85), which culminates in the pseudorape scene that makes Lily's sexual victimization obvious. The reality and power of sexual victimization should not be underestimated at this moment, though Lily's thoughts turn quickly from her physical vulnerability to the nature of her debt to Trenor: she has been unconsciously subjected to Trenor's charity, and has thus been living off unearned income all along. Lily's sense of humiliation brings "wave crashing on wave so close that the moral shame was one with the physical dread" (146)—a moment of gender subjection that merges with a discourse of pauperism that was itself conceived as both moral and physical in kind. If Hunter saw pauperism marked by a loss of self-respect and weakness of cognitive power, then Lily too loses her self-esteem and her ability to think coherently, as her consciousness drowns (146). If the pauper lacked self-consciousness, according to Hunter, then Lily comes to seem "a stranger to herself" (148). Pauperism for Hunter was a state of social dislocation whereby the subject lives, childlike, in a perpetual present. Lily also feels "alone in a place of darkness and pollution" in which time seems to cease (148). Sexual victimization is thus always linked with socioeconomic context, to the extent that the economic tends to outweigh the sexual as a way to describe the *complexity* of Lily's material and emotional situation. Following this realization of the nature of her debt to Trenor, Lily contemplates horrific depths of dependence. "I've sunk lower than the lowest, for I've taken what they take and not paid as they pay" (166), confesses Lily to Gerty—a sinking described in the kind of abyss imagery that Hunter used to capture the pauper's voided consciousness, and that Upton Sinclair would use again in *The Jungle* to describe the relentless pressures toward debt and destitution.[128] This imagery of sloughs, chasms, and spatial voids, which captures Lily's radical social dislocation, is accompanied by further signs of impending pauper psychology. Lily loses her self-confidence (130) and self-respect (169); she suffers the mental prostration of disconnected thought (168); she experiences a "paralyzing sense of insignificance" (169). When Selden sees Lily on the brink of a chasm, it is her "unconsciousness" of failing ground, her lack of thought, that strikes him most (192).

If the total loss of care and self-respect were considered key signs of pauperism, then Lily maintains enough of these qualities to reemerge, quite remarkably, from this moral abyss—a point that distinguishes Wharton's ideas from those of Hunter, who suggested that dependence would tend to annihilate individual agency irredeemably. By repaying her debt to Trenor, Lily moves from shame and misery into the worry and striving of relative poverty (229), a "nervous tension" that again brings a slip into the "moral lassitude" of dependence on the Gormers (234). As the plot of *The House of Mirth* unfolds, it becomes increasingly difficult to understand the forces pressuring Lily's movements *without* reference to this poverty-pauperism dialectic, wherein Lily detests her ethically "insidious" dependence yet feels that "to be excluded from it would, after all, be harder still" (234). If poverty features in Dreiser's *Sister Carrie* as a device of consistent descent where Hurstwood is concerned, and of consistent ascent where Carrie is concerned (in the sense that the fear of poverty drives Carrie upward), then *The House of Mirth* is remarkable for its compounding of these forces into a single character. And if Dreiser's novel engages in a rhetorical strategy that attempts to push its readers toward certain conclusions about the causes of chronic need, then Wharton is keen to uncover, through narrative movement, a polemics of poverty—a dynamic controversy, an engagement within debate that is enacted by Lily's constant zigzagging between opposing yet interconnected states of being (even if this zigzagging has a downward pitch overall). Lily rises into self-sufficiency by leaving the Gormers and refusing to marry George Dorset (238), yet she is pushed by her "urgent and immediate need of money" (267) into the service of Mrs. Norma Hatch (a wealthy divorcée desperately attempting to enter high society), a relationship that eases her discomfort but again destroys her ethical powers of "[a]nalysis and introspection" (273).

At this point in the novel Lily is forced actually to enter the working class, in an effort to avoid further welfare from her friends (282), though this crossing of class lines brings little difference to the issues confronting Lily. As a worker in a fashionable millinery establishment, Lily continues to strive to maintain her independence against a "mounting tide of dinginess" (295), and against the haunting fear that her self-respect will disappear into the sink of shameless dependence if she accommodates herself to remaining indefinitely in Trenor's debt, or if she relies again on unearned income by accepting Rosedale's offer to lend her money (295–96). Following her meeting with Nettie Struther, a member of Gerty's Girls' Club who has been earlier rescued from lung disease by Lily's spasmodic benevolence (316), Lily comes to the full realization that material hardship is by no means her greatest dread:

> She had a sense of deeper impoverishment—of an inner destitution compared to which outward conditions dwindled into insignificance. It was indeed miserable to be poor—to look forward to a shabby, anxious middle age, leading by dreary degrees of economy and self-denial to gradual absorption in the dingy communal existence of the boarding-house. But there was something more miserable still—it was the clutch of solitude at her heart, the sense of being swept like a stray uprooted growth down the heedless current of the years. That was the feeling which possessed her now—the feeling of being something rootless and ephemeral, mere spindrift of the whirling surface of existence, without anything to which the poor little tentacles of self could cling before the awful flood submerged them. (319)

Here lies exposed the narrative dynamic of the novel as a whole, a dynamic powered by the fact that even compared with the misery and dreariness of poverty there is *something more miserable still*. The materiality and psychological stress of poverty are opposed to the ontology of pauperism, defined by social disconnection, by vagrancy, by a failure to control time (Lily feels disconnected from "a slowly accumulated past" as well as powerless to control her future), and by a curious annihilation of selfhood captured once again in an abyss imagery that represents the dissolution of character in the novel. Placing this passage in the context of the discourse of pauperism makes us realize how language that can seem merely metaphorical, merely an expression of Lily's spiritual "homelessness" and "vagrancy," is in fact tied to a quite literal understanding of a purported psychosocial disease, just as Lily's condition is linked at the end of the novel to the materiality of working-class want. Lily's "inner destitution" can be read as generally existential or specifically female, yet it returns fundamentally to a social discourse that sought to explain the *economic* situation of individuals. Lily realizes here that this confrontation with vagrancy has always shaped her life, even from her childhood experiences, and we as readers accordingly come to see that the power of poverty and pauperism lies in their capacity to transcend conventional class boundaries, which is why they have been so active in the novel all along.

The persistence of Lily's economic vulnerability is implied by a subtle use of imagery in which Lily is shown either attempting to form edges, surfaces, and lines against an inner void, or trying to float above vacuous states that threaten to overwhelm her.[129] Though present throughout the novel in this way, the danger of pauperism takes on special significance in the final chapters because here Lily suffers her most radical psychological change, connected to her use of the drug chloral as a cure for sleeplessness. The question of addiction was central to theories of pauperism, largely because the pauper's alleged lack of willpower and self-control left him open to a multitude of "sins." Consistent with Lamarckian thinking, writers such as Dugdale and Warner suggested that pauperism arose *from* bad habits, like alcoholism, which could become biologically rooted. The more extreme position held that pauperism constituted an addictiveness in the abstract, the cause of alcoholism and substance abuse rather than their effect. This is clearly the case with Dreiser's character George Hurstwood, who seems addicted to nothing but dependency itself, one of several points that close off avenues to reform in *Sister Carrie.* Wharton subtly revises such assumptions by describing an addiction that results from rather than creates Lily's poverty, as Lily seeks understandable relief from nervousness and fear. Yet there is still a sense here of crossing a line after which there is no turning back, a point at which the vortex of dependence resists the reforming counterweight of environmental intervention. Lily's zigzag course effectively comes to an end. The drug allows Lily to enter a timeless state of dreamless annihilation in which she is totally mastered by the moment.[130] She becomes stranded in a "great waste of disoccupation," her willpower collapses totally, and she forms a strong armor of indifference to outside opinion (302–303, 311–12). Although she has flickerings of independence in her insistence on repaying the debt to Trenor (299–300), Lily's final slip into the "dim abysses of unconsciousness" bears all the characteristics of the transition that Hunter feared the most about pauperism, particularly the "soft approach of passiveness . . . the sense of complete subjugation" (322–23)—the languid relief from the fear and dread upon which poverty was seen to depend.

Lily resists the escape route that would be taken by Charity Royall, the heroine of Wharton's novel *Summer* (1917) who acquiesces to the subjection and dependency of marriage to avoid a return to the miserable poverty in which she was born.[131] Poverty is instead a dialectical trap in *The House of Mirth*. On the one hand it describes a stasis: the location—or dislocation—of pauperism that resists representation by shutting down narrative progression and access to linguistic production, just as Lily finally loses the ability to represent herself. The word that would make all clear between herself and Selden lingers "on the far edge of thought" and eventually fades away altogether (323).[132] This aspect of want destroys Lily's individual autonomy and social agency. But on the other hand, poverty represents a force of mobility, a category of transition that is constantly pulling Lily toward and pushing her away from dependency—not the eraser of language but the enabler of narrative itself. An awareness of poverty as a complex psychosocial condition is thus essential to understanding character and narrative movement in *The House of Mirth*. Formally we can understand Wharton's novel not as literary realism or naturalism but as an instance of the self-conscious kind of poverty writing I argue for throughout this study, because it responds discursively to the social and political debates surrounding it. It seems ultimately reductive to follow the wave of recent critics who have explained the narrative of *The House of Mirth* as a function of Wharton's unconscious racism.[133] The point about the polemics of poverty in the novel is the dynamic interaction it establishes between materiality and identity, between the contextual and the essentialist. The end point of Wharton's narrative—the triumph of dislocation over mobility—seems at first to sanction beliefs in the power of poverty to destroy subjectivity, just as Lily's character dissolves from the medium of language. But there are limits to the parallels between the fates of Lily Bart and George Hurstwood, limits that arise from Wharton's effort to reach broader conclusions about the relationship between gender and social class. Wharton's conclusions differ sharply from those of the philanthropic tradition in which this relationship was most commonly regarded, and they counter the leisure-class ethos of which Wharton is typically considered an exponent.

Class and Gender

Critics have tended to downplay the significance of the working classes in *The House of Mirth* by stressing Lily's essential difference from the poor, or by arguing that Lily's entire encounter with Nettie Struther—the poor girl whom Lily meets at the lowest point of her career—is sentimental and romanticized, even regressive and facile.[134] Nettie is, in fact, far from the sentimental image of the poor seamstress, popular among charitable ladies. She is a woman who has fallen, albeit to an unclear extent, from the moral standards of her society.[135] In this respect, she offers a parallel (if more extreme) case to Lily's effort to maintain her standard of living against the threat of social censure. But here is the significant difference: Nettie is able to bounce back from possible pauperism into a state of striving poverty that, while full of worry—Nettie remarks that she "can't afford to be sick again, that's a fact"—maintains an independence and self-respect above the "social refuse-heap" (313–14). Wharton conceives of Nettie's situation in the sociological imagery that we have seen at work throughout the novel:

> The poor little working-girl who had found strength to gather up the fragments of her life, and build herself a shelter with them, seemed to Lily to have reached the central truth of existence. It was a meager enough life, on the grim edge of poverty, with scant margin for possibilities of sickness or mischance, but it had the frail, audacious permanence of a bird's nest built on the edge of a cliff—a mere wisp of leaves and straw, yet so put together that the lives entrusted to it may hang safely over the abyss.
>
> Yes—but it had taken two to build the nest; the man's faith as well as the woman's courage. Lily remembered Nettie's words: *I knew he knew about me.* Her husband's faith in her had made her renewal possible. (319–20)

Wai Chee Dimock has argued that, because Wharton is unconvinced by the virtues of the working class, she can only represent Nettie as an ideal by romanticizing her, by imbuing the "bird's nest" of Nettie's household with the permanence of an organic, natural force. But the very point of Wharton's nest image is its vulnerability not its permanence, its precarious position above an "abyss" of dependence. Nettie might not quite represent the transcendent strength and triumphant rebirth of the will for which Donald Pizer argues, but neither is she the naïve (or eugenic) fantasy that most critics would have her be.[136] Nettie is not an ideal but a survivor, a qualified recognition of what can be salvaged from social injustice. Rather than "curiously unexamined," as Dimock suggests, Nettie is the final piece in Wharton's extensive examination of the psychology and culture of poverty, a piece that gives ultimate clarity to the conjunction of class and gender in *The House of Mirth.*[137]

Wharton's novel challenges in several ways Lily's belief that class differences are "in the natural order of things" (150). The very fact that Lily enters the same abyss of pauperism that Nettie hangs above suggests how Wharton's psychological understanding of poverty allows her to break down the absolute class ideology found in writers such as Richardson, Campbell, and the Van Vorsts—the "strong barrier between money and labor" that would reappear in Wharton's next novel, *The Fruit of the Tree* (97). But Lily's encounter with Nettie Struther also differs in a fundamental respect from the sociological perspectives with which Wharton seems to play. Hunter believed that poverty was a dangerously negative cultural force, defined by an inescapable misery that pushed poor workers toward the downdraft of greater destitution. If Lily represents the destructive irony of this dilemma, then the appearance of Nettie Struther delineates a noncausal culture of poverty, a pattern of behavior and a common mindset that allow Nettie and her husband to create a way of living on the edge of socioeconomic suffering. (Nettie's working-class community thus differs fundamentally from the degenerate counterculture of poverty that Wharton describes on the Mountain in *Summer,* and hints at in *The Fruit of the Tree.*)[138] We can also understand Lily's encounter with Nettie as part of Wharton's attempt to develop what Michael Ignatieff describes as a "language of need," distinct from the language of desire with its assumptions of rights, freedom, and individuality. "To define human nature in terms of needs is to define what we *are* in terms of what we *lack,* to insist on the distinctive emptiness and incompleteness of humans as a species," writes Ignatieff in an effort to establish need as a category of the essential and urgent qualities that unite individuals—a category beyond the invidious distinctions of competitive emulation.[139] Lily's belief that Nettie had reached "the central truth of existence" (319) is not intended ironically but is rather a statement of the philosophical dimensions of Wharton's inquiry.

Wharton's double take on poverty results from an effort to prioritize the special considerations of gender in her analysis of human relations. Hunter described particular social groups as especially prone to the cycle of poverty and pauperism; some economic classes were free from its extremities. *The House of Mirth* suggests the proclivity of *all* women toward this condition, a point that makes the novel particularly prescient from a historical perspective. As historians such as Kathy Peiss and Mimi Abramovitz have argued, nineteenth-century ideologies of domesticity forced women into dependency on men (through marriage or other forms of assistance) or else into the poverty of work that remained low paid as punishment for independence, or because of occupational segregation whereby employers "justified women's low wages and their exclusion from higher-paying skilled trades by claiming that women were temporary wage-earners who worked only until marriage."[140] This gendered dynamic of poverty, employed by Wharton, helps to explain the psychological parity between Lily and the charwoman Mrs. Haffen: both are marginalized women who must resort to similarly shifty measures to survive.[141] Hence too the novel's networked imagery of "lack," seen most powerfully in Lily's inner indigence, which allows her to be just what the occasion requires (89), an indigence intertwined with transcendent syndromes of need that are specifically feminized.[142] Wharton's cycle of poverty is thus more absolute than Hunter's, yet despite—or rather because of—this pervasiveness, it also incorporates some room for cultural consolation, some respectable means of individual survival. If women are inevitably perched above dependency, then the striving of poverty becomes, relatively speaking, a valuable escape into a type of independence—in Wharton's vision, the only hope for a lifestyle not necessarily awash with misery, or submerged in a flood of subservience.

Lily's encounter with Nettie Struther supports the conservative ideology of the family ethic only to the extent that it offers partnership, some degree of equality and mutual support, as an alternative to poverty that threatened women in special ways. And Lily's final human encounter upholds a class bias only insofar as it criticizes the increased restrictions that upper-class life places on women, restrictions which mean that Lily Bart can never enjoy even the tenuous independence of the working poor. There is one character in *The House of Mirth* who recognizes how Lily's apparent social privilege is really dependence, who can offer Lily the type of belief that might sanction a communal shift toward nonmaterialistic values, thus offering a nonpauperistic alternative to poverty. This character, moreover, has grown up in a culture of relative indigence at least structurally similar to that which supports Nettie Struther.[143] But Lawrence Selden fails to recognize that his republic of the spirit, which he defines as the middle ground between poverty and dependence (68), is closed to Lily because she lacks access to the type of professional career, the breadwinning opportunities, that could make it possible. Selden accuses Lily of sanctioning values to which she has no alternative. Lily is a victim of her relative poverty in a way Selden is not, and Selden's inability to realize this point lies at the heart of Wharton's critique of masculine ideals that refuse to acknowledge their gendered exclusivity.

To some extent, Lily's downward course toward "bare unmitigated poverty" (329) can be read as a conscious choice, a virtuous self-privation amid conscienceless affluence, as Lawrence Buell has argued. Or Lily's oscillation can be read as a form of seeking that lacks the historically older alternative of feminine domestic fulfillment, as Jennifer Fleissner suggests.[144] Yet such readings do not quite account for the novel's specific and detailed account of poverty as a materially based psychological syndrome with a determining strength that cannot be fully contained or explained by the literary discourses of sentimentalism, realism, or voluntary simplicity. Awareness of how the trauma of want dictates Lily's behavior in *The House of Mirth* helps to explain several problems that critics have had with the novel, for example Percy Lubbock's difficulty understanding the rapidity of Lily's disappearance into obscurity, or Gloria Erlich's questioning of why Lily feels such extreme shame and self-degradation when she realizes her debt to Trenor.[145] Knowledge of the role of poverty in the novel also leads us to reevaluate the reigning view that Wharton is largely trapped in a genteel ethos. Wharton echoed writers such as Veblen and Gilman in her stinging criticism of the sexist leisure class. Gilman's emphasis on the greater dependence of women on men among the wealthy, for example, is paralleled by Wharton's identification of a type of pauperism within "that little atrophied organ," as she described the "idle & dull people" of New York high society.[146]

But Wharton's critique of the leisure class has only been part of my argument. Gilman's demand for female access to recognized work failed to acknowledge that there *were* working women in her world—a narrow approach to gender that Wharton counteracts with a vision of working women that is neither sentimental nor denigrating.[147] True, Wharton follows Dreiser and philanthropic writers such as Campbell and the Van Vorsts by suggesting that factory life can compromise the intellectual and cultural lives of its workers. But there is little effort on Wharton's part to construct absolute differences between the classes in an attempt to assuage middle-class fears of falling down the social scale. When Lily descends into the millinery business she discovers no awkward sense of distinction between herself and the working girls (285–86). Different social classes share an ideology of success, with class itself coming to seem a wholly contingent product of material achievement rather than a natural quality.[148] Lily remains on the outside of a working-class culture that has become a normative state with clear consolations for workers. Because she views women as sharing a complex psychology of poverty, Wharton is able to sympathize with the relatively rich and poor alike, thus criticizing her own social class while seeing clearly beyond it. Although Lily cannot ultimately achieve class transit by accepting a working-class life, I hope to have convinced the reader that this is, in part, a function of Lily's similarity to, not her difference from, the poor women in the novel. She has by the end of the story slipped too far from poverty to pauperism to effect a recovery.

In *The Long Day,* Richardson describes her descent into the extremes of need, which matches Lily's final experience closely, and confirms a consistency within the literary tropes by which poverty was getting written at the turn of the century.[149] Richardson can emerge from this trancelike abyss and regain self-consciousness, however, through the profession of authorship that enables her to heal some of the suffering, horror, and loathing of being poor (273). Amy Kaplan has outlined the similar importance of professional authorship to Wharton, whom she describes as coming into being through the development of a professional self producing written work in the context of the literary market—an argument that once more implicates Wharton's identity in the growing consumer society she depicts.[150] It may thus seem ironic that Wharton removes from Lily the possibility of a middle-class escape from trauma, placing her instead in opposite class extremes of intolerable pauperism or impossible poverty. But Lily's only difference from other women in the novel lies in the degree and not the kind of her dilemma. Rather than constructing middle-class identity or sanctioning the values of consumer capitalism, Wharton's point is that the middle-class brand of genteel work—as a writer, or a social worker, or, as was often the case, a writer about social work—is really no solution to the gender injustice that cripples women in the workplace, and in social life more broadly. Wharton recognizes the unwholesomeness within even the brand of "aesthetic" labor, such as hat making, that female philanthropists saw as an ideal solution to factory work.[151] *The House of Mirth* may not be a revolutionary feminist text celebrating a rebellious and independent heroine; criticism that suggests so is rarely convincing.[152] But Wharton's novel *is* revolutionary in recognizing a form of female victimization that breaks through the class prejudice of its era to expose how the idealization of domestic femininity masked deeper degrees of indigence. The pattern of Lily's life highlights the very point that female philanthropists sought to disguise. Owing to the deep-rooted sexist ideology of contemporary society, the anxiety of relative poverty and the pauperism of absolute dependence were complementary, if critically dissimilar, psychological states thrust upon womanhood itself.

Critics seem to want Wharton to imagine some way out of the problems she depicts, some alternative vision to Lily's socioeconomic environment, or else they force the novel into the mold of racial reasoning.[153] *The House of Mirth* fails to offer its readers a comforting ideal of class, race, or gender, just as it refuses to push toward the final solution that structures *Sister Carrie.* Lily's death demonstrates rather than resolves the ethical problems in the novel, but something positive also emerges from this situation. Far from judgmentally constructing "the poor" as an inferior underclass, Wharton conceives of poverty as a broad and complex state of marginalization, a dynamic dialectic of transition and location that allows for an alignment of gender and class much more radical than most critics would allow, at least at this stage of Wharton's career.[154] This alignment works directly against the tendency within the era's sentimental domestic literature to solve class problems by simultaneously universalizing bourgeois values and naturalizing gender differences—a tendency discovered in Phelps's *The Silent Partner.* If Nettie Struther's working-class culture relates directly to a specific social context, then Wharton suggests how the differences between the consciousness and cultural situation of men and women are not preestablished but rather emerge alongside their relative economic positions and political struggles over the distribution of social resources.[155] The critical neglect of poverty in *The House of Mirth* not only furthers the class essentialism by which Wharton is typically judged.[156] It leaves us powerless to perceive how this social problem provides the nexus of cultural, psychological, and socioeconomic forces that merge into perhaps the most complex exploration of female consciousness yet to appear in American literature.

The Depression in Black and White:

Agee, Wright, and the Aesthetics

of Damage

*[T]his is a book about "sharecroppers," and is written for all those who
have a soft place in their hearts for the laughter and tears inherent in
poverty viewed at a distance, and especially for those who can afford
the retail price.* —James Agee, *Let Us Now Praise Famous Men*

*I had written a book which even bankers' daughters could read and
weep over and feel good about. I swore to myself that if I ever wrote
another book, no one would weep over it; that it would be so hard
and deep that they would have to face it without the consolation of
tears.* —Richard Wright, "How 'Bigger' Was Born"

H ISTORIANS of 1930s America have sought to distinguish the Great Depression from earlier economic crises by highlighting the effects of the era's endemic want on observations of the psychological and cultural health of the nation. According to Richard Pells, the Depression brought a new sense of decomposition at every level of public and private life; there was no longer a belief, as there was in the Progressive Era, that economic development would solve social problems. The Depression was seen by many as a cosmic catastrophe beyond explanation. Society seemed to be literally falling apart, the world grown suddenly irra-tional and absurd.[1] Commentators were quick to suggest reasons for this alleged bewilderment in the face of economic crisis, this turning inward to the psychiatric, marked by the dominance of the term *depression* to describe the downturn.[2] Ac-cording to Sherwood Anderson's *Puzzled America* (1935), the position of Ameri-cans was different from that of any other people in the world because the perverse indoctrination of the success ethic in early youth made the experience of poverty seem a personal failure and disgrace, which led to shame and guilt, and to a col-lapse of self-respect and moral fiber—a blaming of the individual rather than of so-ciety as a whole.[3] Though some historians have questioned the pervasiveness of such views among the public at large, there is little doubt that the economic crisis brought many observers to a wholesale reevaluation of national values.[4] The United States came to seem a sick civilization where individualism tortured people with fear of failure.[5] Once again a clash between chronic want and deeply held so-cial doctrines was believed to have special ramifications on American soil. Re-sponding to the quality of stasis in the Depression photography of Walker Evans, the art critic A. D. Coleman wrote that the termination of "all American dreams, all futures, save a few apocalyptic ones" meant this was "a time when the country did not, in a certain sense, even exist." "The land no longer knew what it was," wrote Nelson Algren in 1935, "so the men and women moving across it no longer knew who they were."[6]

The focus of the final part of this study is on two nonfictional genres in which the psychological dynamics of the Depression received their fullest expression—the genres of documentary and autobiography that both responded in special ways to the era's economic catastrophe. Documentary expression has been variously described as the characteristic genre of the 1930s, as writers sought to realize subtle economic forces that remained "so nearly invisible to the casual eye."[7] The era's desire to seek truth in personal impression led to what William Stott has called a "cult of experience," an outpouring of explicitly or ostensibly autobio-graphical works and documentary records that sought to understand the peculiar personal and cultural crises of the Depression years.[8] The two texts that concern us most are ones that contemplate, in an unusually explicit and sustained manner, the material, cultural, and—following the direction of social thought in the 1930s—psychological significance of poverty as a social state. James Agee's textual col-laboration with the photographer Walker Evans, *Let Us Now Praise Famous Men* (1941), is typically considered the apotheosis of 1930s documentary writing. Rich-ard Wright's *Black Boy* (1945)—a book that deals with the Depression but is more concerned with the ways poverty affects African Americans beyond this narrow historical context—has been read as a classic account of black self-making that expands the concerns of the ex-slave narrative, with its movement from dehu-manizing captivity to the fulfillment of freedom. What ties these texts together,

I suggest, is an identical concern with the power of poverty to bewilder both the subject and the observer of socioeconomic suffering, its power to destroy coherent thought and to limit access to the stuff of consciousness. Both Agee and Wright confront once again the literary conventions for representing poverty, particularly the kind of perspectival distance that Agee mentions with savage irony in *Let Us Now Praise Famous Men* (14), and that Wright saw as a cause of the consoling sentimentalism he later regretted representing in his story collection, *Uncle Tom's Children* (1938).[9] (As Lionel Trilling put it in his review of *Black Boy,* Wright does not allow the reader to "vicariously suffer in slippers," or be "morally entertained by poverty, seeing it as a new and painful kind of primitivism which tenderly fosters virtue.")[10] Both of these writers seek to break down, with strikingly different results, the conventional boundary that separated the observer from the alleged damage, degeneration, and delinquency of poverty. The 1930s may have been the decade in which the "luxurious" and "aesthetic" functions of literature came to seem most inappropriate in the face of widespread suffering, as the prominence of literary nonfiction suggests. Ironically, though, Agee's and Wright's encounter with the injuries of class leads them *toward* the aesthetic significance of poverty — its power as a category to structure literary technique and to provide the foundation for theories of representation.

To recognize the centrality of the category *poverty* in both of these texts is to reevaluate critical assessments of Agee and Wright in radical ways. *Let Us Now Praise Famous Men* (hereafter abbreviated to *Praise*) has been described repeatedly as the greatest literary achievement of the 1930s, a "supremely fine book," the culmination of modernism.[11] Indeed, Agee seems to have shaped the very historiography of the era, for so many historians and literary critics have been deeply influenced by Agee's methods and beliefs, and have ended their studies with a discussion of his book.[12] This overwhelming admiration for *Praise* has centered on Agee's ethical stance toward the poor tenant farmers he encountered in Alabama in the summer of 1936. Richard Pells believes that *Praise* contains the most sensitive and compassionate writing of which the 1930s was capable; abhorring the tendency to treat people as abstract categories, as mere victims of deprivation, Agee saw his poor farmers as distinct individuals whose inner feelings were crucial — creative and adaptable people with spontaneous intuition. Similar testaments to Agee's commitment, respect, and sensitivity can be found in the criticism of Warren Susman, Laura Browder, David Peeler, Victor Kramer, William Stott, Michael Staub, Sylvia Jenkins Cook, and T. V. Reed.[13] Critics have been especially attracted to Agee's methodological iconoclasm and formal self-consciousness, his deconstruction of the conventions of documentary and the assumptions of ethnocentrism. Hence *Praise* is an example of "avant-garde modernism" for some critics, or "postmodern realism" for others.[14] Even Paula Rabinowitz, who in less enthusiastic fashion highlights Agee's narcissistic and colonizing middle-class gaze, is still drawn to the way Agee supposedly undermines the guilt-appeasing conventions of "proletarian" and "objective" writing by including anxious moments in which the objects of political desire actively resist bourgeois inscription.[15] The textual difficulties of *Praise,* the book's linguistic complexity and methodological self-consciousness, seem to affect the way critics evaluate Agee's ethical position, with the assumption being that he shares "our" postmodern, relativistic, skeptical, deconstructive values.

The critical history of Wright's *Black Boy* has been dominated by the volume's editorial problems (Harper and Brothers urged Wright to remove the second part of the autobiography just prior to its publication in 1945), and by interpretive difficulties emerging from a passage early in the autobiography, where Wright seems to lambaste the "essential bleakness," "cultural barrenness," and emotional pathology of black life in America (37).[16] Although the 1991 Library of America edition of Wright's autobiography finally unites its two parts, the choice of *Black Boy* as the primary title of the restored text (Wright's title on the page proofs was *American Hunger,* which became the title of the second half of the autobiography when published posthumously in 1977) reflects the critical obsession with race (blackness) rather than poverty (hunger) in the autobiography.[17] In a valuable essay, for example, Abdul JanMohamed follows Robert Stepto and others by placing *Black Boy* within a transhistorical racial tradition, emerging from the structures of slavery and racism.[18] JanMohamed describes *Black Boy* as the successful story of how literature allows Wright to overturn racist hegemony by bringing his independent subjectivity into being, a story founded on a paradox: "It is a remarkable document of Wright's total absorption of the racist attempt to negate him and his own total negation of that attempt." Yet JanMohamed hovers around a point that troubled early reviewers who found it "hard to believe that the dismal, maltreated colored lad who is the central character of 'Black Boy' could grow up to become the author of this powerful, disquieting volume." In JanMohamed's view, *Black Boy* yields no adequate explanation of how Wright was able to survive his experience of environmental forces so overwhelmingly negative.[19] Racially based interpretations of *Black Boy* have thus run up against a problem never far from literary approaches to poverty: the apparent power of poverty to restrict the accrual of cultural capital and the attainment of tools that might enable its literary representation. As Wright puts it in the conclusion added to the 1945 edition of *Black Boy:* "How dare I consider my feelings superior to the gross environment that sought to claim me?"[20]

The problematic at work in both *Black Boy* and *Praise* is at heart a problematic of poverty, as Wright and Agee grapple with the ethical, cultural, and linguistic difficulties of recognizing and representing material need. To confront the full workings of poverty in *Praise* is to overturn the conventional wisdom regarding Agee's radical class politics with a view that verges, at times, on a regressively cultural and a disturbingly biological view of the causes of inequality. And to analyze poverty fully in both parts of *Black Boy* is to supplement racial readings of Wright's auto-biography with an awareness of a socioeconomic syndrome that governs Wright's behavior and his forming consciousness. But this is not simply to say that race surprisingly trumps class in *Praise,* or that class outstrips race in *Black Boy.* Rather, both of these ostensibly nonfictional studies (there has been some debate over the "truthfulness" of Wright's autobiography) attempt to acknowledge poverty as a category with some degree of autonomy that both connects it to and sepa-rates it from the discourses of identity and socioeconomic location.[21]

Understanding the Depression

If the persistence of widespread poverty in the Depression pro-voked such profound ideological crises, then it also brought a radical release of aesthetic energy. A. D. Coleman recognized this in the photographs of Walker Evans, which supposedly found "[i]n the clarity of this full stop" a country that had turned into a series of works of art.[22] Mainstream literature of the period may have turned, at times, away from an explicit contemplation of the era's economic prob-lems, yet the fiction of the 1930s still offers a dizzying array of responses to pov-erty.[23] A dominant focus was the power of poverty to damage the poor not only physically—through hunger, exploitative labor, or environmental decay—but also emotionally, intellectually, culturally, and even morally, as material need seemed to rip apart conventional human relationships and to degrade behavioral norms. This was especially true of the literary concern with the poor southern white, which de-veloped in the nineteenth century, began to escalate in the 1920s (see, for example, Sherwood Anderson's *Poor White* in 1920 and Ellen Glasgow's *Barren Ground* in 1925), and peaked in the Depression years in novels such as William Faulkner's *As I Lay Dying* (1930) and Erskine Caldwell's *Tobacco Road* (1932). Faulkner's novel, written immediately after the 1929 stock-market crash, illustrates the complexities of representing characters who are both poor and white. At times, poverty is the-orized as primarily a socioeconomic condition. Hence Cora Tull's early monologue, which describes the weak social agency and the small margin of error that defines the poor, who lack the freedom to change their minds, and who are forced to eat their own mistakes (6–9). Yet the spectacle of poverty presented by the Bundren family, who become a traveling circus of incompetence and want in their quest to bury Addie's corpse, is never far from the comic vulgarity, grotesque violence, and obsessive illogicality that Sylvia Jenkins Cook describes as driving literary interest in the poor white character. This ambivalence over poverty centers on Anse Bund-ren's body. Anse's splayed feet and warped toes represent the ways that poverty marks the body and traumatizes humanity, just as the Bundrens are to some de-gree victimized by their environment and by a middle class that looks on them with pity and horror. Yet Anse's body also suggests nonsocial origins for his degradation—a cunning laziness (Anse claims to suffer from a sickness that will kill him if he ever sweats) or perhaps even an abnormal genetic background implied by his humpback. The Bundrens are associated repeatedly with an essentialized whiteness (just as Vardaman is named after the white-supremacist governor of Mississippi, James Kimble Vardaman), though this racial status confers not social entitlement but a virtually biologized poverty and ignorance, with the body coming to seem more the cause than the effect of poverty.[24] Anse's desire for a new set of teeth, which helps shape the quest narrative, is on one level a resilient attempt to replace the manhood and self-respect destroyed by his destitution. But it is also a bathetic and absurd quest that dissolves class consciousness into the kind of grotesque humor common to the poor white stereotype.[25]

The major concerns of Faulkner's novel can be viewed in light of the theme of poverty: the characters seem to be falling apart because of their need.[26] But Faulkner's socioeconomic interest is always expanding into a universal philosophical inquiry into human identity and integrity, consciousness and being.[27] In the work of Caldwell, the ambiguity of the poor white character remains much more focused. The Lester family in *Tobacco Road* are desperately poor to the point of frantic hunger and actual starvation, which threaten their sanity toward the end of the novel (175). Caldwell offers some clear economic explanations of this poverty: wealthy capitalists and credit organizations fail to educate poor sharecroppers in modern methods of agriculture, trapping them in cycles of debt.[28] Yet the Lesters' total dislocation from the economy has roots in individual, cultural, and perhaps genetic problems, which add up to a combination of perverse desires, moral hypocrisy, physical deformity, sexual promiscuity, ignorance, and laziness. Like the useless firewood that Jeeter Lester insists on trying to sell throughout the book, these characters are stunted and diseased spiritually, morally, and intellectually— the source of a freakish humor when they engage in acts of almost unspeakable moral depravity, physical brutality, and financial irresponsibility.[29] Jeeter and his wife, Ada, are finally consumed by fire themselves, destroyed by Jeeter's ignorant desire—really an absurd instinct—to burn over land he has no chance of farming. Caldwell's representation of southern poor whites thus differs markedly from Sherwood Anderson's earlier exploration in his 1920 novel, *Poor White*. Anderson's hero, Hugh McVey, is born amid "a race of long gaunt men who seemed as exhausted and no-account as the land on which they lived" (3). His early poverty becomes a physical and intellectual "handicap" (8), a blood disease of laziness and shiftlessness, as well as a psychological syndrome of inferiority and isolation. Yet— as is no longer the case in Caldwell's world—McVey is still able, more or less, to root the stupidity out of his mind through a process of self-education. He becomes upwardly mobile economically, as a successful inventor of labor-saving devices, and culturally, whereby he manages to "whiten" and purify his "trash" background through marriage.[30]

Opposing Caldwell's literature of moral degeneration, the Depression years of-fered ways to rationalize and to escape the destructive poverty of the era. John Steinbeck's classic *The Grapes of Wrath* (1939), for example, sought solutions to the social suffering of the Depression in the heroic self-sufficiency of the folk and in the agrarian promise of a return to a healthy relationship with the soil—just as the poverty of Steinbeck's Okies originates less in a dysfunctional economic sys-tem than in the ecological catastrophe of the dust bowl.[31] Hunger is a sin in Stein-beck's novel, but hunger is also a positive, passionate force, an emotional power that drives the dispossessed toward a collectivist repossession of the land. "Need is the stimulus to concept, concept to action," as men are driven toward populist revolution by "a hunger in a stomach, multiplied a million times; a hunger in a single soul, hunger for joy and some security, multiplied a million times" (207, 204). Even if the exodus to California ends in the same poverty and natural disaster that pro-voked the journey in the first place, the novel still offers a powerful image of a col-lectivist solution to hunger when Rose of Sharon offers her full breast to meet the needs of strangers—a moment that Michael Szalay places in the context of broadly welfarist, New Deal concerns about the operation of the national domestic econ-omy. What Michael Denning calls the Popular Front laborism of Steinbeck's novel displaces class struggle into natural history and conservative vitalism.[32] In a simi-lar fashion, Betty Smith's popular novel, *A Tree Grows in Brooklyn* (1943), turns again to the squalor of grinding poverty, yet represents the hopeful rise of the poor into middle-class national belonging through individual strength and self-help, as the critic Judith Smith has argued.[33]

From the opposite side of the political spectrum, the proletarian novels that ap-peared throughout the first half of the 1930s found alternative routes to an ideal-ization of the poor and the working classes. As Barbara Foley argues in her recent study, this interest in the working class was defined by a political instrumentalism: the majority of literary leftists sought not merely a heightened awareness of ex-ploitation and suffering but the revolutionary establishment of a socialist system.[34] Jack Conroy's *The Disinherited* (1933) concentrates on the impact of an abusive environment of labor on the body and mind of the worker, both through physical injury and through the escapes of sex and alcohol. When the novel turns more generally from the practice of work to the problems of hypothermia, hunger, and exhaustion during the Depression, this suffering is presented as an inevitable stage in the developing class consciousness of the disinherited. The "slow worm of mo-notonous poverty" (279) finally turns. Yet this leftist desire to write "a truthful book of Poverty," as Michael Gold put it in his proletarian classic, *Jews Without Money* (1930),[35] could also compromise any easy political conversion—as could the per-sistence of individualist ideologies in radical novels such as Robert Cantwell's *The Land of Plenty* (1934).[36] The twelve lines of socialist conversion at the end of Gold's novel do little to counterbalance the overwhelming sense that the material misery of poverty indelibly scars and wounds individuals both physically and psychologically. Marxist critics from the 1930s, such as Joseph Freeman and Granville Hicks, may have criticized literature that stressed "the parasitic experience of personal sensation, emotion, and conduct" over the material and the socioeconomic, yet many radical writers of the period emphasized exactly these internal dynamics.[37] While poverty physically removes eyes, shatters limbs, and sickens bodies in *Jews Without Money*, its peculiar humiliations in an American context break the will and torture the individual into fits of miserliness or hopelessness. "Poverty makes some people insane," writes Gold (76). There is virtually no escape from a world of "vast anemia and hunger; a world of feebleness and of stomachs, livers, and lungs rotting away. Babies groaning and dying in thousands: insomnia—worry . . . screaming, hysteria, nervous disease" (225).

The tradition of African American social realist writing that Stacy Morgan traces in writers such as Willard Motley, William Attaway, and Ann Petry also portrayed the power of poverty to destroy class consciousness, with the poor even becoming complicit in their own social degradation.[38] The classic example here is Ann Petry's *The Street* (1946), another work that takes the question of black poverty beyond the immediate context of the Depression. *The Street* is the story of Lutie Johnson's ultimately futile determination to resist the power of an impoverished environment to suck humanity out of people. The racism of whites is clearly responsible for the entrapment of blacks, though Petry focuses most closely on the internal patterns of black poverty, whereby women are sexually victimized by frustrated men, children are traumatized by unstable families in which mothers are forced to work, and people have adopted the low educational expectations that help keep them poor. For Petry, poverty is more than a material condition. It is an entire mindset, a psychology of unhappiness, resignation, and bewilderment that—as in Gold's *Jews Without Money*—can easily degenerate into outright insanity.[39] By the end of *The Street*, the poverty and oppression of Lutie's environment has turned her into a violent criminal who accepts the inevitability of black ignorance, and is largely unable to understand the twists and turns of her own fate (436).[40]

The literature of the Depression and its aftermath found it difficult to retreat too far from the brink of outright disillusionment. Paula Rabinowitz has described a tradition of radical writing, by women such as Meridel Le Sueur and Tillie Olsen, that cataloged social lack but, according to Rabinowitz, was more concerned with the mobilized desires and bodily "plentitude" of female intellectuals.[41] Yet the feminist collectivity that ends Le Sueur's *The Girl* (a novel that originally appeared as sketches in radical magazines between 1935 and 1945) is haunted by the power of poverty to cripple human relationships, and by the power of public institutions to further degrade and punish the poor. "It seems like my family was crippled and hurt just as much as if their flesh had been riddled by bullets and their limbs torn apart," writes Le Sueur's anonymous narrator about her impoverished youth and about her father's fury and insanity in face of his hungry children (36, 39). James T. Farrell may have turned away from what he called the "immediate economic roots" of slum neighborhoods in his *Studs Lonigan* trilogy (1932–35), but he still emphasized a destructive and pervasive "spiritual poverty" within the lower middle class, a kind of poverty caused by a collapse of cultural and educational institutions, and manifested in Studs's profound failures of articulation.[42] If the 1920s saw works such as Nels Anderson's *The Hobo* (1923), which romanticized the countercultures of hoboes and tramps, then the 1930s brought the literature of the "marginal man," which stressed meaningless violence, alienation, and antisocial play.[43] In the preface to his 1935 novel *Somebody in Boots,* Nelson Algren accordingly describes his antihero, Cass McKay, as "a youth alienated from family and faith, illiterate and utterly displaced . . . belonging to nothing and nobody . . . exiled from himself and expatriated even within his own frontiers. A man who felt no responsibility even toward himself" (8–9). Poverty—represented through hunger, thirst, cold, and fatigue—is at some level responsible for the physical wounding and the psychological bewilderment of Algren's hoboes, whose hopeless lives are torn apart by relentless pain, shame, and fear. Yet material forces do not quite account for the apocalyptic moral decay and spiritual degeneration of characters such as Cass who form an unreachable Lumpenproletariat motivated by a meaningless evil that grows inexplicably in their blank minds.[44] In a similar but less extreme fashion, Vag, the dislocated young hitchhiker who ends John Dos Passos's *U.S.A.* trilogy (1930–33), suffers from the physical pain and the psychological disorientation of a poverty that cannot be explained but merely repeated in cyclical phrasing: "Head swims, hunger has twisted the belly tight. . . . Head swims, belly tightens, wants crawl over his skin like ants . . . waits with swimming head, needs knot the belly" (1238–40).[45]

Nowhere was this "psychologizing" of poverty more apparent than in the era's outpouring of documentary expression. As critics and historians have noted, documentary could easily slide into Steinbeckian affirmations of a spiritually unsubdued people, or into sentimentalized calls for social action.[46] But often these solutions could barely disguise the profound bewilderment, discord, uncertainty, and personal ambiguity that seemed to emerge from the confrontation with economic hardship. Writers and documenters of the 1930s, such as Sherwood Anderson, Nathan Asch, and Louis Adamic, observed the effects of the psychological trauma of the Depression on themselves—an inability to perceive reality as a coherent whole, a verging on the edge of personal breakdown—and on the lowliest victims of the crisis who seemed totally baffled and overcome with feelings of incompetence and worthlessness.[47] Observing a pervasive dreariness and apathy among the American people in *Where Life Is Better* (1936), James Rorty commented that the victims of the Depression "did not know the name of the disease from which they were suffering; did not know its causes, let alone its treatment and cure. The word 'despair' did not describe their condition. Despair implies consciousness and

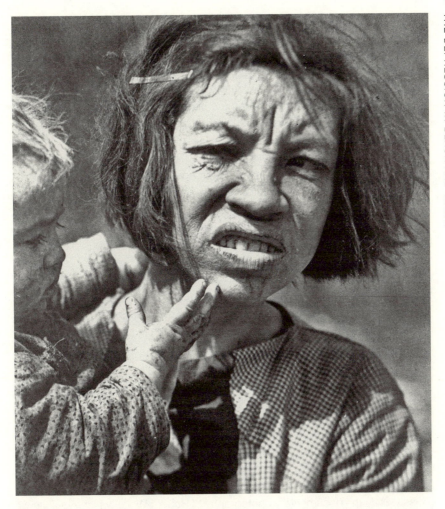

Fig. 3.1. Margaret Bourke-White, "McDaniel, Georgia. 'Snuff is an almighty help when your teeth ache.'" Illustration for Erskine Caldwell and Bourke-White, *You Have Seen Their Faces* (New York, 1937). Margaret Bourke-White Photograph Collection, Special Collections Research Center, Syracuse University Library. Courtesy of the Estate of Margaret Bourke-White. Bourke-White's close-up photographs force viewers to read the signs of poverty in the face, though she framed her subjects in such a way that the causal relation between poverty and the body can seem reversed. The whiteness of this subject becomes a horrifying hue.

they were far too gone for that" (117). Touring America in *The Road* (1937), Nathan Asch discovered a country in confusion and mad darkness, its citizens unable to make sense of the world around them.[48] Caldwell's collaboration with the photographer Margaret Bourke-White, *You Have Seen Their Faces* (1937), is particularly extreme in its depiction of tenant farmers as "degraded" and "defeated," "beaten" and "subjected," "depleted" and "sterile" (75, 168). Caldwell's white tenants are hopeless victims of plantation- and tenant-farm owners, who have degraded them into "an inferior race specifically bred to demonstrate such characteristics as indolence and thriftlessness, cruelty and bestiality" (76). The shame and degradation of whites is particularly intense. When they speak, supposedly in their own words, these tenants are pitiful, bewildered, and desperately depressed — "*All I feel like doing most of the time is finding me a nice place to lay myself down in and die. . . .* I've done the best I knew how all my life, but it didn't amount to much in the end" (114, 183).

Caldwell's animalistic and pathetic view of the poor, which has received harsh criticism from scholars, is precisely the view that Agee's text in *Praise* is conventionally thought to oppose.[49] Agee is the writer who allegedly undoes the sentimentalism of Steinbeck, the political idealism of the proletarian novel, and the belittling view of the mental capacities of the poor — particularly poor rural whites — found in fiction and documentary both. While other documentaries "contributed to the tenants' poverty through impoverished representations that could see them only as victims," argues T. V. Reed in a recent essay, Agee respects their ambiguity as complex human beings, and forges a genuine democratic discourse from the recognition of radical difference.[50] The critical framing of *Praise* is fairly clear. Unfortunately, though, the ethical direction of Agee's approach to poverty is not.

Agee's Uncertainty

There is plenty of material in *Praise* to justify the view of Agee as an iconoclast, a radical disrupter of established conventions for approaching and representing the poor. Undermining its foundations in a *Fortune* magazine commission to write a story on sharecroppers in the deep South, Agee's text explicitly attacks the motives of "honest journalism" and moral crusading "science" (7), as well as the documentary photography of Bourke-White, which Agee views as a callous and hypocritical theft of artistic material from the disadvantaged.[51] At times, Agee situates this criticism within a broad exposure of the attitudes within public consciousness that neutralize poverty as a pressing social problem, either by blaming it on the behavior of the poor, or else by viewing it as an inherently desirable if not beatific state.[52] The epistemological dilemmas and formal self-consciousness of *Praise,* which have encouraged critics to place Agee on the borders of modernism and postmodernism, derive directly from Agee's confrontation with conditions that coalesce to define the tenants' poverty specifically — their burdens, isolation, sorrow, and tremendous vulnerability (53). There is an intractability within the original material that makes the subject of poverty "unfathomably mysterious," makes Agee's insights almost intangible, and makes any sense of truth inevitably "undiscernible" (8–9). When Agee is deep in his stalling description of the house occupied by the Gudgers (one of the three tenant families featured in the book), he highlights the differences between the qualities of houses in general and qualities that are "the privilege only of the houses such as this one I am talking of" (183)—that is (the word *privilege* ringing ironically), the houses of the poor. The poverty of a single room means that "all materials of structure are bare before one," every inch of structure is open to the eye, all things, relations, substances are "*at once*, driven upon your consciousness" (184). Yet Agee can "tell very little about it" (185) because of the substantive and qualitative *difference* of an impoverished environment—a laying bare, an exposing of essential structure that annihilates consciousness when perceived, and thus actively resists literary description.

This awareness of inadequate, collapsed representation is accompanied in *Praise* by an opposing attempt to define poverty as a substantial condition with material, psychological, and cultural values, even if—ironically—these values are often of the type that make such definition problematic in the first place.[53] Agee examines the *environment* of poverty: its composite and constantly noticeable odors, which saturate the very materials of the Gudgers' house (154–55); its dirtiness, determined in part by lack of water (196–97); its tastes, which derive directly from the cheap metal cutlery the tenants are forced to buy (181). Echoing the conclusion of Melville's "Poor Man's Pudding," food plays a vital role in establishing the all-suffusing atmosphere of want (an odor of pork and sweat becomes infused throughout the house and its contents) and in its capacity to establish the substance of class difference, marked by the "quiet little fight [that] takes place on your palate and in the pit of your stomach" when you bring this food to your mouth (416). Agee reveals a powerful sense of how the lives of the tenants are determined in literal ways by their economic situations. The structural deficiencies of these houses, for example, actively prevent privacy and cleanliness (210). Agee goes even further to suggest that the tenant condition itself—living in unowned property—physically determines the quality of the property as well as the overall emotional and mental health of the family in it.[54]

Numerous passages in *Praise* correspond to currents within recent sociological thought on the structural causes of poverty. Agee shows sympathetic understanding of the socioeconomic and material forces that reduce people to, and keep them in, a state of want: the debt cycles and wagelessness inherent in the sharecropping system (115–20); the general inapplicability of welfare to the sharecropper, who is officially "employed" (326); and the nature of the cotton itself, which demands much work but yields little reward, and remains enormously vulnerable to elements of chance (334–36). Agee suggests that the physical nature of cotton labor affects the spirit of the laborer, destroying the appetite for living, creating a "knotted iron of sub-nausea" that literally weakens body and being (327). Poverty creates a distinct mindset, an ethical viewpoint that plays out materially in the labor process, as the underpaid house builders in *Praise* take vengeance on the world in a cynical, part willful apathy (142–43). Agee thus strives to understand the complex behaviors and habits that have grown from socioeconomic conditions—what Agee describes as the "less sociological" things about the tenants, which are difficult to define or understand, and are "merely tiresome to those whose intelligence is set entirely on Improving the Sharecropper" (215). Whether concerning the naming practices of the tenants, their violent cruelty to animals, or the rituals surrounding the wearing and decoration of hats, Agee attempts to understand, from a relativistic viewpoint, how these psychological, emotional, and cultural patterns have distinct social meanings, and have emerged from dynamics of deprivation and oppression.[55]

These aspects of Agee's text have naturally encouraged claims for Agee's progressive politics, as indeed has the antireform agenda of *Praise,* which critics tend to view (and praise) as part of Agee's fundamental iconoclasm.[56] Agee harkens back to earlier thinkers such as Emerson and Thoreau when he positions the artist as the enemy of conventional society, deplores middle-class tastes and practices (he despises flush toilets), and rejects, often angrily, the traditional modes of social reform.[57] When Agee criticizes, for example, the inadequate and inappropriate schooling that cripples the tenant child's understanding, it seems that Agee's frustration follows a belief that universal human potentiality is getting institutionally wasted (289). But his criticism of Alabama schools develops into a much more fundamental criticism of the whole idea of learning and intelligence, the implication being that more education would place the tenants at just as great a disadvantage (305, 290). This move away from specific causes captures the rhythm of Agee's thought, which tends to retreat from a belief that the tenant system alone is responsible for the disadvantage in the tenants' physical and mental living—a dangerous assertion with "little effect save to delude the saviors into the comfortable idea that nothing more needed doing" (207). This might seem an admirable radicalism when Agee targets not only the "tenant system" but "the whole world-system" (207) as the ultimate cause of the poverty he witnesses. Yet Agee follows his radical statement with an immediate retraction that demands the closest attention: "there are in the people themselves, and in the land and climate, other forces quite as powerful but less easy to define, far less to go about curing: and they are, to suggest them too bluntly, psychological, semantic, traditional, perhaps glandular" (208).

Agee is concerned with the effects of what he considers bad education on child psychology because this is the level at which poverty supposedly gets passed along behaviorally and emotionally, with "exquisitely sensitive" children adopting a series of values—cowardice, brutality, deception, crime—to survive a harsh environment (311).[58] Rather than maintaining that the poor are victims of their environment, however, Agee suggests that the tenants' situation remains unreformable because their poverty rests squarely on causes in past generations (305). At several points, *Praise* seems to blame poverty on the shiftlessness and the *taste* of the tenants—the determining inheritance of their internal values. The Gudgers

Fig. 3.2. Walker Evans, "Sharecropper Bud Fields and his family at home. Hale County, Alabama." Illustration for James Agee and Evans, *Let Us Now Praise Famous Men: Three Tenant Families* (New York, 1941). Library of Congress Prints and Photographs Division, FSA/OWI Collection, LC-USF342D008147-A. The word *shiftless* moved historically from a term of sympathy for the poor (to be without a shift or shirt) to a pejorative synonym for "lazy" and "inefficient." Both attitudes toward the poor seem alive simultaneously in Agee and Evans's photo-text. (Agee changed the Fields family name to "Woods.")

avoid pleasantly scented soap not because of cost but cultural preference (151); the Ricketts' seemingly "insane" level of dirtiness arises as much from relative cultural standards as from infrastructural limitations (196–97); the pulley device at the Woods' spring is in such bad shape because of an inability, unwillingness, or lack of intelligence to keep it in good working order (192); the poor upkeep of many tenant homes may be part of what Agee calls *tradition* (207). We return to a distinction that had shaped perceptions of the poor for at least a century, a distinction between those who have self-respect and strive to maintain a way of life, and those who have lapsed into moral and emotional apathy. When Agee turns to the tenants' clothing, we realize that the differences in quality between the families are mostly to do with Mrs. Gudger's "good taste" and respectability (275–76, 281). Once more, the signs of being poor arise directly from the ethical and cultural traits of individuals, not primarily from their socioeconomic situations.[59]

We should not lose sight of the moments in *Praise* when Agee reveals a sensitive, compassionate, and implicitly democratic respect for the tenants' complex subjectivities. Hence his patient descriptions of the tenants' daily rituals (89–90), his discovery of a technique to describe the mundane with dignity (90), and his detection of beauty and cosmic significance in the tenants' trials.[60] Yet there is throughout *Praise* a constant pressure on Agee's environmentalist and circumstantial explanations of the spiritual and mental ruin he sees before him.[61] There is thus a tension in *Praise* between relativistic explanations of cultural and psychological poverty and an absolutist understanding of the inner damage of tenant life—with the latter making Agee seem much closer to the trends within 1930s writing that he is conventionally thought to oppose.

Damage and Disadvantage

It is worth spending time on this aspect of *Praise,* if only to realize the dizzying extent of Agee's fascination with the degeneration of his tenants within their socioeconomic situation. The "Colon" section of Book Two contains much of this material, where Agee reverts to a religious discourse by emphasizing the outrageous vulnerability of the *soul* to damage, the ease with which it can become measurelessly discredited, harmed, insulted, poisoned, and cheated beyond "power of rectification" (100). Human consciousness is so easily wounded by the input of the senses that a radical kind of transformation takes place in the tenant's mental-spiritual makeup: "a benumbing, freezing, a paralysis, a turning to stone, merciful in the middle of all that storm of torture, relatively resistant of much further keenness of harm, but always in measure of that petrification obtuséd ten times over against hope, possibility, cure" (106). The very formation of consciousness becomes tantamount to a kind of mental cauterization, with each impression cutting its mark, each time "a little deeper, a little more of a scar" (106). Agee's use of the archaic *obtuséd* captures the tenant's inability to feel and perceive, and alludes to the stupidity that allegedly results.[62] And the tautological density of Agee's "word piles" establishes stylistically the kind of intellectual density that emerges from the repetitive impacts of the tenants' poverty. This tautological effect is repeated across pages as well as between words, as Agee repeats his points again and again. In the section "Work," for example, Agee writes that physical labor absorbs the tenants so absolutely that "life exists for them scarcely more clearly or in more variance and seizure and appetite than it does for the more simply organized among the animals, and for the plants" (319). Any consciousness beyond that of the simplest child becomes a painful encumbrance (320). (*Praise* is full of suggestions that any more intelligence, knowledge, and consciousness would not only be irrelevant to the tenant's life but an active danger if not "thus reduced or killed at birth" [295].) In the section "Education," Agee considers the adult tenant capable only of the manifest meanings of the simplest few hundred words, and totally incapable of critically examining any ideas, or even physical facts beyond the simplest and most visible (306). The tenants are blinded to what Agee calls consciousness and knowledge in human relationships, and to "those unlimited worlds of the senses, the remembrance, the mind and the heart" (306). They cannot comprehend their own existence (306), or the beauty, ambiguity, and darkness that swarm every instant of a healthy consciousness (307). Essentially childlike, the tenant is left with "[n]o equipment to handle an abstract idea or to receive it: nor to receive or handle at all complex facts: nor to put facts and ideas together and strike any fire or meaning from them" (313).

In essence, Agee suggests that socioeconomic contexts allow for different quantities and qualities of mind and spirit. The tenants are unable to reach something like "genius" or "consciousness," which would allow full perception of the world's emotional range, argues Agee in "Colon" (108). Full levels of consciousness are all "gifts or thefts of economic privileges," only available to the leanest classes "by the rare and irrelevant miracle of born and surviving 'talent,'" he writes in "Education" (307). Agee thus seems not to have abandoned relativistic and environmentally contextual reasoning entirely.[63] The great majority of tenants may be born with as healthful intelligences as any on earth, he suggests at one point, yet "by their living, and by their education, they are made into hopeless and helpless cripples, capable exactly and no more of doing what will keep them alive" (305–306). If there does seem to be hope in social change then we have underestimated the absolute power of the environment to leave the tenants less equipped than animals, and "incurably" so (306). We come uncannily close here to the situation depicted by Nelson Algren in his novel *Somebody in Boots* — one of the most pessimistic works to emerge from a disoriented decade. Algren also represents a rural class of whites who remain utterly beyond the realm of social reform or class consciousness because consciousness itself has been crippled by poverty. In Algren's world, hunger destroys thought (69, 120), and the poor are reduced to a "helpless bewilderment" (112) in which they cannot understand any of the social forces that have "cheated" them.[64]

Agee's cultural explanations of mental and spiritual impoverishment drift, disturbingly, into the realm of the biological — a natural consequence of a powerful interplay in Agee's text between physical and psychological states.[65] Describing all of the forces that turn the young child, during his most defenseless and malleable years, into "a cripple of whose curability one must at least have most serious doubt," Agee suggests ominously that the *blood* becomes stained, bearing the weight and impingements of past generations (108–109). When Agee describes in detail how the tenant soul gets damaged, he makes clear that this soul is brought forth of a chain that goes back centuries to ancestors with heads scarcely above "the blind bottom of the human sea," woven up on this continent from their own "disadvantagings" (John Field, we recall, is imagined by Thoreau as emerging from a primordial "bog" of poverty). Generations have been dwelling

> in bestial freedom or in servitude, shaken with fevers, grieved and made sick with foods, wrung out in work to lassitude in the strong sun and to lack of hope or caring, in ignorance of all cause, all being, all conduct, hope of help or cure, saturated in harm and habit, unteachable beliefs, the germens they carry at their groins strained, cracked, split, tainted, vitiate to begin with, a wallet of cheated coinage. (102)

Recalling the passage from *The Dangerous Classes of New York* (1872), in which Charles Loring Brace describes the power of pauperism to enter a girl's blood in the form of inherited "gemmules" that produce "irresistible effects on her brain, nerves, and mental emotions" (43–44), Agee posits an identically Lamarckian process. The deleterious physical effects of environment (sickness, sunstroke) morph into moral and cultural patterns (lassitude, habit), into intellectual traits (unteachable beliefs), and finally into biological inheritance, with Agee's "germens" (a term for the rudiment of an organism) embodying physiologically the damage of poverty.

Agee's targeting of the causes of poverty thus moves from the environmental to the behavioral to the genetic, with this generational determinism becoming absolute, finally outstripping altogether the influence of family or school. Every act of procreation is thus "a crucifixion of cell and whiplashed sperm" (103)—a phrase that merges religious and medical discourses in a close echo of late-nineteenth-century thinking about pauperism. This ancestral damage is subsequently compounded by socioeconomic, cultural, and psychological forces, leading to children who are "nursed and emboweled among the discouragements of this beating of beaten blood" (103).[66] Even at the points where Agee seems to be admitting some degree of intelligence in the tenants, as in the case of Mrs. Gudger and her father, Bud Woods, such concession is immediately (and with not a little self-contradiction) retracted for a prenatal determinism: "But these intellects died before they were born; they hang behind their eyes like fetuses in alcohol" (305). The "globular damagements" of the tenants are physical, mental, emotional, and economic, but also *glandular* (106)—a key word of Agee's that reinforces the genetic causes of impoverishment.[67] It is finally the language of eugenics that emerges in *Praise,* with references to feeblemindedness giving way to suggestions of racial degeneration, and to a disturbing series of tropes in which the poor are compared directly with animals.[68]

Rather than a radical departure from traditional ways of describing the poor, this progression in *Praise* from environmental to individualistic explanations of poverty echoes the broader shift from nineteenth-century Lamarckian thinking to the hereditary explanations of poverty on display in Henry Goddard's influential *The Kallikak Family* (1912), which sought rhetorically to blame the degraded environment of a single family on its allegedly inherited feeblemindedness.[69] Such paral-

Fig. 3.3. Detail from "Great-Grandchildren of 'Old Sal.'" Illustration for Henry Herbert Goddard, *The Kallikak Family: A Study in the Heredity of Feeble-Mindedness* (New York, 1912). In his classic eugenic family study, Goddard literally wrote on the bodies of the poor to create the appearance of their "feeble-minded" defectiveness. Despite the poor quality of Goddard's original photography, his pen marks are clearly visible in this detail.

lels become more remarkable still when we realize the changes in dominant hereditarian attitudes that had occurred by the time Agee came to write *Praise* in the late 1930s. A number of recent scholars have challenged the conventional historical view that eugenics declined in the 1930s, pointing instead to the ways that "positive" eugenic ideas penetrated the culture at large, especially in assumptions about the fitness of individual mothers.[70] Eugenic ideas would remain alive and well at an institutional level, as Meridel Le Sueur records in her harrowing collection of stories, *Women on the Breadlines* (1932–39), and in her novel, *The Girl*, which tell of the abortion, incarceration, and sterilization forced upon poor women who stray from familial norms.[71] But as an explicitly advocated movement, with widespread intellectual respect, eugenics had undoubtedly faded by the 1930s. Its impetus was partly neutralized by harsh immigration restrictions, and its assumptions were undermined by awareness of unscientific eugenics in Nazi Germany and by the broadcast poverty of the Depression itself, which made genetic explanations of social failure seem, to some at least, particularly inappropriate.[72] Whereas the Progressive motivations of Theodore Dreiser finally drown in a burgeoning doctrine of pauperism, Agee appears to be swimming against an intellectual tide—or at least he keeps explicit what had become deeply implicit at an institutional level— by maintaining the essentialized view of a bestial poor often criticized in the work of Caldwell, who described the poor as "an inferior race" with "perverted" instincts in *You Have Seen Their Faces* (75–76). Yet even Caldwell, so often the straw man in arguments about Agee, resists the kind of *causal* thinking on display in *Praise,* whereby the biology of the poor determines their poverty.[73] What remains most at stake here, though, is not the question of whether *Praise* is in tune with the think- ing of its era, but the way in which a book that has had such an impact on radical thinking since the 1960s contains a vision of the poor as virtually another species in their cultural-psychological-biological damage. Such contradictions are always possible when poverty is the text.

The Beauty and Erotics of Poverty

If Agee dwells on the degeneration of his impoverished tenant farmers, then he is equally and ironically attuned to their alleged blessedness and beauty. Agee thus establishes simultaneously the reassuring binary that Fredric Jameson has detected more broadly in nineteenth-century European fiction, the tendency to denigrate the poor as bestial or to celebrate them as divine—a binary captured succinctly when Agee describes the eyes of one of the tenants as those "of a trapped wild animal, or of a furious angel nailed to the ground by his wings" (99).[74] *Praise* centers on Agee's vision of the grandeur, holiness, and intense beauty within the humble dwellings and structures of "simple people" (134)—a vision re- peated in the still-life emphasis of Evans's photographs. In the case of the Gudgers' palings, this beauty derives directly from the poorness of the original material, from an exposure to the weather (the wood is not treated or painted), and from a deficiency in construction and a lack of maintenance. The "tensions sprung against centers" (144) upon which Agee repeatedly dwells, derive from unintentional "fail- ures" to execute design, which themselves come from a weakness of timber and time (144), neither of which can be afforded.[75] As Agee says of the houses in gen- eral: "this beauty is made between hurt but invincible nature and the plainest cru- elties and needs of human existence in this uncured time, and is inextricable among these" (134). The poverty *makes* the beauty, rather than threatening it. In sum, the "esthetic success" of these houses is inextricably shaped by "economic and human abomination" (202–203). It is the product of people whom Agee con- siders deficient in consciousness, and of a degenerate "local-primitive tradition" (203). And here lies the essence of Agee's moral dilemma: this beauty is irrelevant to those who own and create it, but remains "discernible to those who by eco- nomic advantages of training have only a shameful and thief's right to it" (203).

"Aesthetics of poverty" may seem an inherently problematic term, for all the reasons Melville outlined in his critique of the extraction of beauty from situations of suffering, and for all the difficulties that the critic Peter Hitchcock identifies in attempts to maintain the aesthetic as a viable category in readings of working-class culture.[76] Yet it seems perfectly appropriate to talk of such an aesthetic at work in *Praise*. There are definite ways in which poverty is understood to generate the conditions of description even more than it brings ethical problems of perception to the fore. As becomes most clear from Agee's descriptions of the tenants' cheap and patched overalls (268), it is less the concept of *use* that Agee values aesthetically than the physical and psychological dynamics of damage.[77] This point goes beyond Agee's encounter with the surface beauty of damaged mirrors and garments to include his entire emotional response to the poor. Take for example the early episode, "At the Forks," where Agee encounters a young couple—clients of Rehabilitation (state welfare)—and a mentally retarded man who is presumably their relative. This may be the passage Lionel Trilling had in mind when he criticized the lack of "human unregenerateness" in Agee's poor, being "of a kind not safely to be described in an account claiming to be unimaginative or trustworthy, for they had too much and too outlandish beauty not to be legendary."[78] Agee is not distancing himself here from a dangerous overinvolvement with the horrifying reality of need by retreating into the mythological mode that Thomas Woodson finds at work in Thoreau.[79] Rather, he finds the beauty and the blessedness of this couple to stem directly from the damages they have sustained. The exquisite fineness of the young man's face and body emerge directly from his sickness, from the closeness to death of his hardscrabble life (33). The couple's eyes contain "so quiet and ultimate a quality of hatred, and contempt . . . toward the damages they sustained, as shone scarcely short of a state of beatitude" (33). They are blessed and beautiful *because* of the emotional harm that emerges from their disadvantaged situation.[80]

Agee's detection of blessedness within poverty clearly relates to the Christian urge to love the poor and the despised—the merger between poverty and piety that becomes established in the New Testament and can be glimpsed occasionally in the Old.[81] Agee's immediate love on witnessing the pitiful and unanswerable need of the Ricketts (363–64) can be read as an exaggeration of the New Testament urge to love the poor unconditionally, irrespective of the innocence or the guilt underpinning their suffering. Agee's poor are blessed and beautiful not despite but because of their brutalization, with the distance between spiritual value and worldly degeneration collapsing utterly. If such attitudes can be found in the Epistle of James, in Matthew, and in the Gospel of John, for example, then they are founded on the belief that good works toward the deprived and the marginalized are at the heart of spiritual redemption, with agape love for the poor providing the conditions for final salvation.[82] In Agee, however, the desire for social amelioration inevitably evaporates; there is no emphasis on Christian ministry, or on any sort of ministry, as a solution to the suffering of the poor.

Instead, a different form of personal salvation emerges from Agee's encounter with extreme poverty—a salvation that further highlights why socioeconomic difference seems so insurmountable and need so unanswerable in Agee's world. In Part Three, "Inductions," Agee describes the uncleanliness of the tenants' food, which sickens Agee and thus establishes class difference at a physiological level of taste. Yet "much as my reflexes are twitching in refusal of each mouthful a true homesick and simple fondness for it has so strong hold of me that in fact there is no fight to speak of and no faking of enjoyment at all" (416). Agee's revulsion from the food is thus *simultaneous* with his enjoyment of it. He similarly describes the milk he drinks as "somehow dirty and at the same time vital, a little as if one were drinking blood" (416)—an image that hints at the vampirism in Agee's relationship with the poor, compounded by the irony that the tenants' blood, their genetic heredity, is partly what makes them poor in the first place. Later in this same chapter, Agee turns his attention to the dirty and insect-ridden bedding in which he has to sleep at the Gudger house. Whereas the presence of bedbugs epitomizes the disgust at poverty in Michael Gold's novel, *Jews Without Money* (71), Agee's initial revulsion at the lice and bedbugs that pierce and munch at his body gradually turns into something else:

> I don't know why anyone should be "happy" under these circumstances, but there's no use laboring the point: I was: outside the vermin, my senses were taking in nothing but a deep-night, unmeditatable consciousness of a world which was newly touched and beautiful to me, and I must admit that even in the vermin there was a certain amount of pleasure. (427–28)

This passage focuses a pervasive pattern within Agee's experiences of aesthetic and sensual pleasure.[83] His transcendent state of getting "outside the vermin" is interlinked with his *getting off on* the vermin. The squalor is not just fascinating but inherently beautiful—the aesthetic correlative of a situation in which the poor are blessed not because they conform to social and moral ideals beneath their poverty, but because there is *nothing beneath* their poverty at all, they are so blank and bewildered.

It remains difficult not to view Agee's aesthetic pleasure in overtly sexual terms: he describes the bedbugs as "pricking" and "tooling at me" (427, 425), while his contact with the hard and smelly bedding leads to a state of sexual arousal that culminates in a lustful desire to be naked (425–26). Agee's masochistic extraction of pleasure from his own pain gets outweighed by a virtually sadistic response to the pain of others. Undercutting the occasional, vague hope that the damage of the tenants will be cured one day in the future, Agee finds sexual healing in the exhaustion and discomfort of others, particularly in the physical scarring and the mental crippling of an impoverished environment.[84] When he turns to the special case of Louise Gudger, the "intense sleaziness" and "meagerness" of her clothes provoke erotic desire, as his eyes are drawn to the "animal litheness" of her country body (367). A similar situation results from Agee's earlier attraction to the mentally retarded man who, with his distinctive utterance of *awnk, awnk,* symbolizes the extremes of psychological injury. The encounter has a homoerotic quality throughout. The man is spoken to "as if he were a dog masturbating on a caller" (35), and there is a thick roll of saliva that hangs "like semen" in his beard (35). The troubling possibility emerges that the semen is, metaphorically at least, Agee's own—a powerful symbol of the spontaneous degree to which he is aroused by this example of mental wounding.[85] There is nothing new, of course, in such an erotics of poverty. Amy Lang has shown how the gaze of the wealthy patron on the poor orphan, in the works of Horatio Alger, is rich with a homoerotic tension that emerges in part from disparities in social power. And Michael Trask has argued that the dislocation and groundlessness present in modernist writers such as Henry James and Hart Crane emerges from an anxiously erotic attraction to the risky transience of working-class pleasures.[86] It is not difference to which Agee is attracted, however, but degeneration; not risky otherness but restriction and harm.

Rather than simply responding to damage already present, Agee himself seems—at times self-consciously (370)—the active inflicter of wounds, his very art a form of damaging. A range of critics, such as Stott, Reed, and Williams, tend to read this textual tendency ironically, as part of Agee's recognition that discourses attempting to document or reform the poor are inadequate, inappropriate, or even disingenuous in their effort to understand or help. Yet there are too many ways in which Agee's text literally participates in rather than ironically works against such tendencies. Agee cannot approach admitting that the tenants have any sense of taste or beauty: their preference for enamelware is only referred to as "'good taste'" (in quotation marks), an example of choice and will "in a sort of semi-esthetic awareness" (151). This reluctance to allow any conscious sense of beauty in the tenants leads Agee into some obvious self-contradictions.[87] The tenants clearly *do* have an aesthetic sense "in their terms," as Agee puts it (210). Yet Mrs. Gudger's aesthetic desire to make her house pretty is qualified immediately by Agee's belief that these people "are also, of course, profoundly anesthetized" by the shame and insult of their poverty (210). The ritual of decorating the headstones of dead children with an image or engraved poem is deemed far beyond the reach of Agee's "beloved" poor (439). The habit of cutting patterned ventilation holes in shoes, whereby the desire for "a kind of beauty" greatly reduces their durability, is generally speaking the work of African Americans (263), with Agee again shying away from an acceptance of such aesthetic capacity in his white sharecroppers. The position of blacks in the text, as barely present yet tremendously sophisticated aestheticians, makes a certain sense.[88] Rather than being of "no use" to Agee (26), these African American characters act as a textual magnet that attracts the elements of aesthetic consciousness, if not consciousness itself, that Agee wants to avoid seeing in the poor white tenants. There are even moments when we can catch Agee actively removing, or ignoring, the signs of literacy evident in Evans's photographs.[89] Poor whites come to seem an underclass, beneath even the African American race, isolated in a barren intellectual and cultural sphere.

These issues climax at the end of the "Education" section of the book in Agee's contemplation of whether a sense of beauty is an instinct or a product of training. Agee notes, yet again, that the tenants are beautiful beyond almost anything else he knows in their "intense and final commonness and purity" (314). Yet they are less aware of beauty, or of themselves as beautiful, than many animals (315); the sense of beauty in the white tenant class is "limited and inarticulate . . . almost beyond hope of description" (314). The answer to this paradox—of being extremely beautiful but having absolutely no awareness of it—goes far beyond Agee's lame suggestion that "the 'sense of beauty,' like nearly everything else, is a class privilege" (314). The answer lies in the very essence of Agee's own aesthetic sensibility, his belief that "there is a purity in this existence *in* and *as* 'beauty,' which can so scarcely be conscious of itself and its world as such" (315). Agee believes that the beauty he sees is no projection or abstraction but inheres within the world he perceives; in effect, he denies its constructedness, its relative status. And if beauty inheres in this world, rather than being merely a matter of perspective, then the tenants' failure to see it makes them in essence deficient—the very deficiency, of course, that Agee finds so attractive. The crucial point here is not just that Agee ascribes this lack of aesthetic sense specifically to the *poverty* of the tenants, to the fact that they live in such a state of subsistence that they can only view nature in terms of "need and use," or else fear nature as the agent that can increase their poverty by destroying their crops (314). Even the aspects of the natural world that fall outside this economic explanation—"the profoundest and plainest 'beauties,' those of the order of the stars and of solitude in darkened and empty land"—still fail to be appreciated *as* beauty because the tenants cannot escape the feeling of awe that "in a simple being is, simply, unformulable fear" (314). Any gaps in Agee's argument for the situational influence of poverty on the tenants' viewpoints are filled by the implication that the simplemindedness of the tenants precedes the material need in which they live. Here, once again, a eugenic predeterminism seems to outweigh environmental context.

Agee's responses to poverty had historical precedents. The genre of "dark reform" literature of the 1850s dwelt compulsively on the behavioral sins and social iniquities it wished to eradicate, just as the urban "local color" movement of the Gilded Age contemplated both the alleged beauty and the social horror of poverty. Sylvia Jenkins Cook has shown how the stereotype of the southern poor white in literature of the 1930s was driven by the imputed and equally questionable qualities of extreme degeneracy (the laziness, grotesque behavior, and lack of rationality visible in Caldwell) or extreme virtue (the rugged masculinity, courage, and self-sufficiency that define the heroic individuals found in Steinbeck). Reformist writers of the 1930s were particularly ambivalent, being intrigued by the grotesque and violent associations of the poor white tradition despite their ethical protest at economic inequality.[90] In Agee's *Praise,* the distance—the *contradiction*—between the degeneration and the beauty of poverty collapses entirely. This collapse undermines the dominant critical view that Agee finds beauty in poverty despite recognizing how mentally crippling it is, or that he is creating a truly "anti-aesthetic" text.[91] The objects Agee perceives in the tenant world are not beautiful unintentionally, but the incapacity for intention itself becomes beautiful. We can finally understand why Agee's suggestions that the tenants are no more "incapable of learning" than those in economically luckier classes (305) are overwhelmed by implications that they suffer from an absolute degree of imbecility more genetic than cultural—why the "whole world-system" contracts into the "glandular" (207–208). Any lingering hope in human equality cannot withstand an overpowering desire for the tenants to be incurably crippled, for it is within this transcendental degree of psychological and cultural damage that Agee finds aesthetic value. In effect, *Praise* realizes a nagging idea inherent in the literary discourse of poverty—that the poverty *itself* is attractive and valuable from a literary standpoint. Agee demonstrates how ethically problematic poverty writing can be by allowing us to glimpse one of the most troubling implications of the documentary motive: that the documenter actually enjoys viewing the damaged humanity before him.

Race, Class, and Poor Richard

Agee's challenge to progressive social values echoes Dreiser's *Sister Carrie,* though there, at least, possible motives were more easily apprehended. Put simply, perhaps Dreiser was attempting to create psychological space between himself and the poor—part of a desire to distance the thought of returning to the hardships of his youth. Agee, however, is not running away from the poor but running toward them, pen in hand. We could reduce this again to the class origins of the writer by arguing that Agee merely exaggerates a condescending superiority inherent in a comfortable middle-class affection for the least fortunate—the result of class complacency, not the class insecurity manifested by Dreiser. There are scenes in *Praise* where Agee seems to follow the direction charted by Jane Addams in *Twenty Years at Hull-House* (1910): a profound middle-class boredom, emptiness, and sickness, a desperate desire for something to *do,* can be answered only by contact with and knowledge of the poor, which give Agee personal significance and spiritual replenishment.[92] But such an explanation, based on class position, only belies the complex layering of social, religious, psychological, sexual, class, and literary motivations in Agee, a layering that matches the composite and shifting qualities of poverty as a category and a problem.

Whatever the differences between Agee and Dreiser, one point remains clear. The most challenging texts we have encountered are those in which writers seem to focus on a socioeconomic class but then deny class its contingent qualities. In these texts, characters—often white and male—fail to be upwardly mobile within a situation of alleged potential for such movement. Cook has argued that many of the "negative" qualities within literary depictions of poor whites arose from the status of the poor white as a kind of oxymoron.[93] The unhappy coincidence of poverty and whiteness creates an ideological crisis, a gap that gets filled by absurd laughter or by blaming poverty not on a broken class structure but on the cultural complicity or the genetic deficiency of the poor themselves. In this light, the curious position of African Americans in *Praise* is worth revisiting. They seem culturally and materially better off than whites, as Agee puts pressure again on the special dilemmas of white poverty amid dominant national and racial ideologies.[94] In *Praise,* class proves finally inadequate as an interpretive tool because it gets overwhelmed by poverty as a category with the potential to become an absolute essence not a description of relative and ultimately changeable social position. This is not to say that racialized thinking simply outstrips explanations based on social class. It is not the "whiteness" of Agee's sharecroppers that explains their economic situation. An explanation based on race oversimplifies the issue by substituting one conventional category for another, when it is precisely the capacity of poverty, as a category, to hold in balance the biological and the cultural, the essentialistic and the contextual. The drama of *Praise* (and, indeed, of Davis's "Life in the Iron Mills," Thoreau's *Walden,* and Dreiser's *Sister Carrie*) is the way that social status *moves* from environment to biology—a dynamic process more complex than a rigid establishment of racial distinction.

Race and class were often linked in analyses of poverty in the Depression. Caldwell and Bourke-White's *You Have Seen Their Faces,* for example, juxtaposes black and white poverty throughout, and argues that the extreme poverty of rural whites (and accordingly their cruel racism) emerges from an economic process in which landowners prefer black tenants who are easier to control through racial terror—the legacy of southern slavery. From a black perspective, William Attaway makes a similar point in his novel of African American migration, *Blood on the Forge* (1941).[95] The vacillation between race and class was always inherent within eugenic thinking, and it was common in sociological approaches that tied the heightened poverty of African Americans to the nation's ongoing race problems. The black sociologist E. Franklin Frazier's influential *The Negro Family in the United States* (1939), for example, focused less on racial heritage than on social class— a focus that has earned Frazier harsh criticism for abandoning race as cultural adaptation along with his rejection of racial absolutism.[96] Frazier sought to under-mine the racism within turn-of-century social thought by arguing that the pur-ported problems of the black community, in particular the so-called disorganiza-tion of its family life, were not the results of racial inferiority but responses to the structural aftereffects of slavery and the social pressures of urbanization.[97] Pre-dicting the recent sociology of William Julius Wilson, Frazier understood class in opposing ways. On the one hand, he emphasized class variability among African Americans, and thus recognized some capacity for transition or "uplift."[98] But class is more usually a location for Frazier, something that cannot easily be tran-scended because it becomes determined by the forces of cultural "deficiency" and "disorganization." These ideas are clearly reflected in the following excerpt from Gunnar Myrdal's *An American Dilemma* (1944), one of the era's most important and influential analyses of the "Negro Problem":

> *In practically all its divergences, American Negro culture is not something independent of general American culture. It is a distorted development, or a pathological condition, of the general American culture.* The instability of the Negro family, the inadequacy of educa-tional facilities for Negroes, the emotionalism in the Negro church, the insufficiency and unwholesomeness of Negro recreational activity, the plethora of Negro sociable organiza-tions, the narrowness of interests of the average Negro, the provincialism of his political speculation, the high Negro crime rate, the cultivation of the arts to the neglect of other fields, superstition, personality difficulties, and other characteristic traits are mainly forms of social pathology which, for the most part, are created by caste pressures. (2: 928–29)

Such ideas were in line with the era's anthropological and psychological insistence that—in the words of Richard Pells—"the emotions and attitudes of individuals were irrevocably conditioned by the norms and institutions of their society."[99] But Myrdal's emphasis on the influence of social structure was by no means a form of class analysis that denied racism as a factor altogether. The problem was that the racial pressures (what Myrdal calls the caste pressures, rejecting the term *race* be-cause of its biological associations) were all one way. Black culture becomes a re-action to white racism at the same time as white models of the middle-class fam-ily become the norms against which blacks are judged "pathological." The pressure to blame poverty on the internal cultural values of the poor, found in the era's representation of rural whites, was especially intense where African Ameri-cans were concerned because it punctuated even the sociological thought that sought to save blacks from racist accusations.

This sociological context helps us to understand the controversial passage early in Richard Wright's autobiography, *Black Boy,* in which he mulls over "the strange absence of real kindness in Negroes": "how unstable was our tenderness, how lacking in genuine passion we were, how void of great hope, how timid our joy, how bare our traditions, how hollow our memories, how lacking we were in those intan-

Fig. 3.4. Edwin Rosskam, "Negro family and their home in one of the alley dwelling sections. Washington, D.C.," 1941. Library of Congress Prints and Photographs Division, FSA/OWI Collection, LC-USF34D012828-D. The African American family became a major focus of mid-twentieth-century sociology, with black urban children appearing trapped by the allegedly pathological cultural forces surrounding them. Richard Wright selected this photograph for inclusion in *12 Million Black Voices* (1941).

gible sentiments that bind man to man, and how shallow was even our despair" (37). Alienating him from his critics, both at the time of *Black Boy*'s initial publication and since, Wright seems to deny any sense of a transhistorical racial tradition—of cultural resistance to the effects of racism—valuing instead the hierarchical notion of an implicitly white "Western civilization" from which he suggests blacks have been largely excluded.[100] Rather than simply signaling his rejection of black culture, Wright's depiction of the "bleakness" of black life reveals the depth and detail of Wright's engagement with the complex issues underpinning the association of race, class, and poverty in sociological and anthropological literature of the period (Wright was intimately familiar with both Frazier's and Myrdal's studies).[101] Relativistic notions of black culture as creative adaptation to social structures were certainly available, in the anthropology of Melville Herskovits, for example. But the dominant strain of sociological thought, represented by the work of Frazier and Myrdal, tended to emphasize a *lower-class* culture over race, even as it implied a racialized perspective by conflating this supposedly pathological culture with the black urban community in a special sense. Wright signifies on this sociological discourse throughout his autobiography, as we shall see, and thus he revisits and redirects Agee's fascination with the way poverty seems to damage the cultural, emotional, and intellectual life of the poor—a common theme in literature of the 1930s. Only by placing *Black Boy* in the context of its surrounding poverty discourse, moreover, can we begin to answer the question that has stumped critics such as Abdul JanMohamed: the question of how Wright transcends a dominant environment that seems so absolute in its power to destroy consciousness and social agency.

In his last major work before *Black Boy,* the partly sociological, partly prose-poetic text of *12 Million Black Voices* (1941), Wright describes how the traumatic dislocation of slavery combined with the racist economics of sharecropping to produce the pervasive poverty of black America in the Great Depression.[102] Wright reduces this poverty, this "tied knot of pain and hope," to its fundamental essence: a "feverish hunger for life" (11, 128). This same hunger, I suggest, is the motive force of *Black Boy,* dominating and at times displacing the dynamics of "social death" and racist hegemony that JanMohamed detects in Wright's text.[103] By structuring his autobiography around the thematics of hunger, Wright thus revisits proletarian novels such as Conroy's *The Disinherited,* and Popular Front novels such as Steinbeck's *The Grapes of Wrath,* in which hunger features prominently both as social problem and as a progressive force that pushes the poor toward class action in the case of Conroy, and toward agrarian collectivism in the case of Steinbeck. Wright also comes close, as we shall see, to more pessimistic fictions such as Algren's *Somebody in Boots,* in which hunger becomes the central trope to describe not desire but an entirely negative state of shame, pain, and sickness that crushes the poor into bewildered defeat.[104] Yet Wright's dealing with hunger does not necessarily place *Black Boy* outside an African American tradition of writing. Attaway's *Blood on the Forge*—a novel admired by Wright—also begins with a contemplation of the "hungry blues" (2) of black life in the sharecropping South, which is only replaced by exploitation in the industrial North. Back further in black literary history, Harriet E. Wilson's partly autobiographical novel, *Our Nig* (1859), also centralizes poverty in the story of a free black servant in the North. ("You can philosophize . . . on the evils of amalgamation," writes Wilson's narrator, but "[w]ant is a more powerful philosopher and preacher.")[105] Frederick Douglass's 1845 *Narrative,* to offer another example, reveals how the suffering of hunger was deeply rooted in slave consciousness as well. For Douglass, hunger represents the ultimate cruelty of slavery because it emphasizes the slave's total subjection, his inability to control his own food supply; bondage signifies a natural condition of hunger for the slave, while freedom means to feed rather than to be fed upon.[106] This racial trope of opposition gets reversed by Wright in *Black Boy,* where he formulates an idea of hunger that stretches beyond the realms of race and racism to include a wider sense of suffering and oppression—what Wright describes in his introduction to the sociological study of Chicago *Black Metropolis* (1945) as the "hunger of millions of exploited workers and dissatisfied minorities" (xxiii), the idea of exploitation here carrying a potential for historical consciousness that domination does not.[107] The "social death" that JanMohamed sees in *Black Boy*—a social state that JanMohamed's authority, Orlando Patterson, only ascribes to the total powerlessness of slavery specifically—is replaced by poverty as a complex category that describes a vacillation of power within a condition of deeply compromised freedom, whereby blacks live between dependence and independence, between domination and autonomy.[108]

When Wright's father deserts his family in the first chapter of *Black Boy,* he leaves hunger in his place, a "grim, hostile stranger" that becomes virtually a character in its own right (14–15). From this moment, long before Wright gains his first sense of racial identity, hunger begins to infiltrate his mind, becoming his most abiding feeling (29), "a vital part of [his] consciousness" (161) that remains a "daily companion" throughout both parts of the autobiography (261). Hunger emerges as a substantive material force that affects Wright's behavior in detectable ways, from his strange custom of warding off potential hunger by stealing and hoarding biscuits in secret corners about the house (50–51), to his aberrant eating habits and odd cravings for unusual foods (103). Biting hunger affects Wright psychologically, making him restless, nervous, and hateful (103); it also impacts him physically, with his malnutrition lasting well into adulthood, initially preventing him from meeting the weight requirement for a permanent job in the U.S. Postal Service (277–78). The major obsessions of Wright's life—with language, literature, religion, sex, and politics—are all figured in relation to the central fact of his hunger, whether it be physical, spiritual, cultural, or aesthetic in nature. Even racial tension, described by Wright as the habitual passion of his life (149), is intertwined at key moments with an imagery of hunger and starvation.[109] Poverty, defined by this hunger, becomes a distinct category of social being because it marks the body in lasting and noticeable ways, while effecting psychobehavioral patterns that remain powerful and consistent over time.

Wright echoes Agee when he recognizes the power of poverty to threaten healthy living and to compromise coherent consciousness. Wright's early description of his experience in an orphan home, for example, is marked by a hostile, vindictive atmosphere of nervousness and intrigue that comes from the orphans' deprived environment of constant hunger. Wright feels "suspended over a void" most of the time (30), teetering on the brink of a psychological abyss: "I would grow dizzy and my mind would become blank and I would find myself, after a period of unconsciousness, upon my hands and knees, my head whirling, my eyes staring in bleak astonishment" (29). Such passages resonate with dominant tropes that stretch back through the history of poverty writing. In Algren's *Somebody in Boots,* for example, hunger dulls the vision (230), turns the mind into an empty "cavern"

(30), and spins the head "like a top" (104). The impoverished collapse of Melville's character Pierre is also described as a "whirling" vertigo that blanks the mind and disables the eyes.[110] Echoing the fate of Wharton's Lily Bart, Wright's fear of *dependence,* represented by the governess of the orphan home who threatens to dominate young Richard by adopting him, places him above an abyss that represents an ontological crisis of dislocation. Yet Wright's hunger also merges in much more positive ways with his imagination and individuality (30). Wright's memory is sharpened, his senses made more impressionable, and he becomes aware of himself "as a distinct personality striving against others" (29–30) in reaction to the purportedly dysfunctional, delinquent emotions of dread and disgust that stem directly from the material lack within his institutional environment. The conditions of Wright's poverty thus contain an element of independent striving toward self-consciousness and imaginative fulfillment, a "hunger to be and live" (122)—a craving for being that propels self-formation.

Wright's sense of the connection between his hunger and his individuality develops quickly in the autobiography, even if the reasons for his reliance on a state of inadequacy and disadvantage take longer to emerge. Reflecting on a hungry moment watching his school friends split open loaves of bread and line them with juicy sardines, Wright vows "that someday I would end this hunger of mine," yet his hunger is gaining value by becoming so intertwined with his "apartness" and "eternal difference" (126). Poverty is far from equivalent to blackness, but instead creates an internal racial disconnect. The poverty of Richard's home life, in which he lives "just on the borders of actual starvation," gains importance because it keeps him *out* of the world of his friends, making him "acutely self-conscious" (126), and forcing him down his "own strange and separate road" (126). In a later moment, racial identity seems less important to Wright than the belief that he is *poorer* than his peers, that his "mush-and-lard-gravy poverty" has cut him off from "the normal processes of the lives of black boys my own age" (173). When forced by his family to attend a religious school, Wright's impoverished condition—his experience of saloons, street gangs, and an orphan home—differentiates him from children "claimed wholly by their environment" (104). His hunger again leads to a heightened awareness of society and self.[111]

Throughout the middle and late chapters of "Southern Night" (the first part of *Black Boy*), Wright develops the idea of an inverse relation between the acquisition of food and the acquisition of knowledge, thus reversing the equation of bread and knowledge central to Douglass's *Narrative* and to the Western intellectual tradition more generally.[112] That Wright has to "starve in order to learn about [his] environment," however, is not as irrational as he first thinks (127). Attempting to solve his plaguing hunger by selling newspapers in his neighborhood, Wright for the first time has money for food *and* material to read (the magazine supplement serializes popular stories such as Zane Grey's *Riders of the Purple Sage*), yet the newspaper turns out to be a Klan publication that propagates racist ideology (130–31). To be in possession of both words and food means accepting the racist values of a Jim Crow society that dictates the conditions by which black hunger can be satisfied, an irony reinforced in a later conversation between Richard and his friend Griggs, who accuses Wright of failing to show sufficient respect for whites.[113] "Oh, Christ, I can't be a slave," exclaims Richard. "But you've got to eat," replies Griggs (184)— an exchange that defines the hunger of poverty as an inevitable condition of relative black freedom. These issues reach their climax toward the end of "Southern Night," during Wright's encounter with a northern white man who asks Wright directly if he is hungry, and thus "touched the very soul of me" (231). To accept money from this white man and satisfy his hunger would be to admit the parasitic dependence of black on white, the shameful lack of racial agency, and the terrible reduction of black desires to the tiny items of survival.[114]

If hunger sets Wright apart as an individual, then the effects of race, or at least of racism, are altogether different. The news of a lynching induces "a temporary paralysis of will and impulse," compelling Wright "to give my entire imagination over to it, an act which blocked the springs of thought and feeling in me" (172). In this respect, Wright's experience of racism does bear qualities that Patterson ascribes to the slave state: a fear of total violation, a threat to the integrity of the whole personality, a voicelessness and invisibility.[115] The world of black relative freedom thus contains the consciousness-destroying domination that always threatens to overwhelm the self-awareness and agency that Wright describes as the autonomous act of "starving myself" (231). Racism provides such a "corroding and devastating attack upon the personalities of men" because it offers no cultural "way of life" or "function in society" (265), argues Wright in parenthetical comments that mark the return of explicitly sociological concerns. The potential effects of this social death become clearest at the end of chapter one of *Black Boy* (just before his comments on "the cultural barrenness of black life"), where Wright records a 1940 visit to his father, by then a ragged sharecropper on a Mississippi plantation. Wright describes his father as a black "peasant," a term he uses again to describe the Moss family with whom Richard stays in Memphis—a term that suggests an absence of anything like class consciousness, and even approaches implying an absence of consciousness itself.[116] Wright seems to follow Frazier's argument that urbanization disastrously tears blacks loose from a simple folk culture (*The Negro Family,* 363–64), by describing his father as having hopelessly failed in the city. Predicting the anthropological ideas of Oscar Lewis, Wright describes his father as embodying the most negative and irredeemable aspect of the "culture of poverty" thesis, namely *a poverty of culture:* he is portrayed as an animalistic, intellectual delinquent who is utterly ignorant of the meaning of loyalty, sentiment, tradition, and joy (34).

To some extent, we return here to Agee's world in which poverty brings cultural and intellectual damage. Echoing the works of Myrdal and Frazier, any sense of sit-

uational adaptation collapses into a hierarchical understanding of behavioral de-
viance as negative illness.[117] Yet following Myrdal and Frazier in another sense too,
race loses its causal power in episodes such as this. Ironically, Agee's ostensible
study of class relations returns to a hereditarian essentialism, whereas Wright's explicit study of blackness seems at first to reject "race" as a unified category of identity or as a binding force, even between family members. The situation of Wright's
father is primarily the result of external pressures, with racial culture being overrid-
den and destroyed by socioeconomic forces (34).[118] A difference within blackness
emerges because the category of poverty fails to behave as an absolute term for
social inadequacy or degeneration. Indeed, it is Wright's father's *lack* of hunger, not
his poverty, that dictates his emotionless dependence: there are ways in which he
endures "hearty, whole, seemingly indestructible, with no regrets and no hopes"
(34). The experience of racism is tantamount to an oversatiated social death,
which threatens Wright on numerous occasions (194), but which he can escape
through a rejection of his father—an acceptance of hunger that resists an absolute
equation of poverty and powerlessness (33).

Thus far, then, it seems that poverty, in *Black Boy,* is a complex, composite term
for competing social forces. On the one hand, it describes a stasis, a social location within dependency that is something like race in its stability of being, just as
racial experiences get associated with lines, boundaries, and immobility (83, 198).
This is one way to understand the role of Wright's controversial description of black
"cultural barrenness": an attempt to capture the collapse of autonomy and social
agency. On the other hand, poverty, as a category of social being, also embodies
the force of mobility in its connection to hunger—a negative yet dynamic condition
associated throughout with running, tramping, and escaping. His mother's socioeconomic suffering, for example, keeps Wright in the blueslike condition of being
forever "on the move" (100).[119] In this sense, poverty is not a location but a temporal condition of transition marked by a yearning "for a kind of consciousness, a
mode of being that the way of life about me had said could not be" (169), a tortu-
ous process of striving that becomes a technique of self-formation. The answer to
the question that has preoccupied critics, the question of how Wright overcomes
his environment, lies in the extent to which Wright resists the "pauperizing" force
of racism by maintaining a self-consciousness *beyond* race—a poverty, founded
on hunger, that sets him apart from his fellow southern blacks, actively preventing
him from acculturating to black subservience within a racist society, and offering
some degree of shared cultural values with whites.[120]

We could describe this as Wright's engagement with *want,* a term that unites a
sense of material deficiency with a powerful desire for the things held necessary for
completion. *Black Boy* thus resonates with the state of "hankering" that Le Sueur
theorizes in *The Girl*—a positive desire on the one hand, yet always related to the
stress and malnutrition of poverty, as women nurse their hungers "like cancer"

(78). If the idea of poverty as a spur toward self-improvement has tended historically to sanction free-market ideology, as Jonathan Glickstein points out, then this
idea can maintain an oppositional energy in relation to certain social groups, such
as women and blacks, who were not fully included in that ideology in the first
place.[121] Yet as a bridge between poverty and desire, Wright's hunger is not wholly
a resistant or oppositional state. This becomes clear in a passage toward the end
of *Black Boy,* which seems to celebrate the individualistic Protestant ethic of "self-
achieved literacy" and "self-generating energy" (370). If Wright learns the values of
bootstrapping from a mainstream tradition of rags-to-riches writing, represented
by the works of Horatio Alger and by George Randolph Chester's Get-Rich-Quick
Wallingford series (168–69), then his association of poverty and mobility becomes
relevant to his extraction of *literary* values from the material lack, social exclusion,
and alleged cultural disorder that would seem to destroy literacy altogether.[122] Unlike Agee's *Praise,* in which poverty eliminates the intellectual and aesthetic sensibility of the impoverished, *Black Boy* entertains the possibility of overcoming the
delinquency that Wright attaches to his father. Even in its depths, poverty contains
an inherent potential for heightened language consciousness.[123] "Because my environment was bare and bleak, I endowed it with unlimited potentialities, redeemed
it for the sake of my own hungry and cloudy yearning"—the point being not that
imagination allows Wright to transcend the poverty of his environment but that this
impoverished environment itself *creates* an imaginative sensibility (72–73).[124] When
Wright applies the idea of poverty to his emotional life, to describe his denied
knowledge of the lives and feelings of others that should hinder his ability to write,
instead it creates a "new hunger" for books that open "new avenues of feeling and
seeing" (250, 252). Signifying on Myrdal's belief that "[p]overty itself breeds the
conditions which perpetuate poverty" through the degenerating interplay of environment and behavior (*An American Dilemma,* 1: 208), Wright describes environmental deprivation leading to a social powerlessness that breeds not illiteracy but,
ironically, the need for imaginative development.

Wright's early aesthetic theories, when he falls under the influence of Gertrude
Stein's *Three Lives* (1909), revolve around his attempt to transcend cultural impoverishment by making language into an alternative material in itself, completely
self-sufficient in a virtuous cycle whereby words mutually feed one another
(280).[125] This is a language of want that posits an end point of substantive completion—a final escape from "poverty"—by providing a linguistic food that will both
satisfy his spiritual appetite and bring passionate communion with others. Wright
aims to surmount the absent things in black life by turning words into physical, intellectual, and emotional sensations that establish presence against an ontological void. Through the discourse of food, Wright links the material and the bodily to
the power of cultural taste and to the intellectual bread of knowledge. As he moves
from the first to the second part of his autobiography, from South to North, it

seems that literature will continue to provide him with the intellectual material to feed his hunger for knowledge of social and environmental structures. Wright describes how his interest in sociological writing follows a desire to *understand* the "frantic poverty" of urban blacks, their behavioral problems and mental illnesses (284). Likewise, he describes his early attempt at a biographical sketch of Ross, a persecuted black Communist whom Wright meets in Chicago, as an effort to bring elusive social forces into consciousness, and to bring disordered lives into graspable form (332). Wright's interest in Communism when in Chicago represents the culmination of his sociological, documentary urges to understand and make intelligible the effects of the environment on the human subject, to develop a rational and satisfying explanation of the impoverished lives of the outcast and the disinherited (317–18), and to find a coherent language that gives meaning to suffering by stressing the universal economic causes of social inequality.

As a form of hunger, then, poverty becomes not a marginal condition to be equated with illiteracy, but the empty kernel from which all desire, and thus all imaginative creativity and intellectual understanding emerge. Rather than an aesthetic luxury, literature becomes fundamentally bound up in socioeconomic suffering and the creative wants it generates. Yet Wright's theoretical explorations of the links between poverty, desire, and individual mobility provoke problems that complicate any reading in which Wright escapes racial stasis through the birth from poverty of imaginative consciousness. His time in the North, for example, challenges intellectual understanding with insurmountable degrees of bewilderment discovered in the black community itself (332), just as Wright's urge to write about representative black types derives from a "need that I did not comprehend" (284). And his sociological interpretation of the poor begins to run exactly contrary to his imaginative life: when Wright's Communist colleagues force him to research the economics of poverty by tabulating the price of groceries, it interferes directly with his ability to write fiction (356, 359). The second part of Wright's autobiography complicates the progressive narrative of hunger, and establishes how Wright's interest in poverty never fully marks the dominance of socioeconomic or individualistic reasoning over racial categories of being. We realize, in other words, how race *and* class come to hold an "artificial status" for Wright (185).

American Hunger

The material that now comprises the second part of the autobiography, "The Horror and the Glory," gained initial notoriety for its tale of Wright's break with the Communist party, a break that Wright ascribes to the party's inability to accept that even "a Negro, entrapped by ignorance and exploitation—as I had been—could, if he had the will and love of it, learn to read and understand the world in which he lived" (370).[126] Wright does not fit the ideological model of oppression and its "lumpenizing" effects. Ironically, the forces of social agency and mobility, all the forces of hunger that take Wright away from the racist South and create his interest in socialist thought, are rejected by the intellectual culture into which he has supposedly risen. For Wright, the sharpest irony lies in the fact that those who envision his poverty as an insurmountable damage are themselves "truncated and impoverished by the oppression they had suffered long before they had ever heard of Communism" (374). If Wright, the victim of racism, has managed to escape his impoverished environment by his bootstrapping energy, then the Communists—those who claim to possess understanding of the poor—remain traumatized "pris'ners of starvation" (381).

Wright reaches a similar conclusion following his increased contact with whites when first in Chicago: mainstream society, in addition to its radical opponents, seems peculiarly indigent. Wright experiences a psychological distance separating his suffering self from the "poor, ignorant white girls" (272) with whom he works in a North Side café. This breakdown of sympathy stems less from racial feeling than from the cultural and emotional need within the white world itself. Reversing the direction of the white sociologist's gaze on the black subject, Wright focuses on the tawdry dreams of these waitresses, their fear of emotion, their ignorance and thoughtlessness, their lack of insight and emotional equipment to understand themselves or others (271–72)—a bewilderment that reflects traits previously attached to Wright's father. Wright realizes that it is "not race alone, not color alone, but the daily values that give meaning to life" that stand between himself and his fellow workers, who seem shallower than blacks in striving for the "trash" of contemporary culture (273). (Echoing Agee, whites again seem psychologically worse off than their black neighbors because the ideology of white entitlement makes their indigence more reprehensible.) The irony is that blacks have been forced into poverty and isolation by whites who are themselves culturally deprived—an irony that flies in the face of the sociology of Myrdal and Frazier, who urged assimilation to white ideals as the only hope for blacks.[127] Wright had made this point earlier in "How 'Bigger' Was Born," in which the cultural poverty of African Americans pales before the "tattered rags of American 'culture,'" the absence of "rich symbols" and "colorful rituals" from this "money-grubbing, industrial civilization" (452, 461–62). These "absent things" had already been posited in the national scene by writers such as Cooper, Hawthorne, and James, and by novels such as Sinclair Lewis's *Babbitt* (1922) and Farrell's *Studs Lonigan* series (1932–35), which sharpened critiques of the spiritual poverty and the emotional bankruptcy of mainstream American life.[128] Wright signifies on these trends in white literature to establish how the poverty of blacks is not a marginal condition but is an integral part of a nation defined less by its opportunities for material wealth than by its inevitabilities of cultural impoverishment.

In Chicago Wright realizes a point that Alexis de Tocqueville theorized within an American context of purported equality: by definition, desire has no ends because it tends to deny any final state of sufficiency by setting in motion a blind spiral of ever-increasing longing.[129] Tocqueville's socially specific observations resonate with broader theories of the psychology of desire, whereby subjectivity emerges from an endless movement toward an unreachable goal.[130] Accordingly, Wright comes to realize that none of his dreams "had the barest possibility of coming true"; he is condemned to the "constant sense of wanting without having" (267). If in the South Wright had fled hungrily toward self-consciousness from the bewilderment of a racist society, then in the North he comes to dwell on the *unconscious* nature of suffering and the *meaningless* quality of pain—metaphysical unknowability outstrips material urgency. By linking poverty to desire, and by exploring hunger as a metaphysical as well as a material condition, Wright runs into a conceptual problematic that threatens to disintegrate poverty as a materially and socially bounded form of socioeconomic suffering. Wright's effort to lift poverty beyond the limits of his racial group, his effort to recognize its cross-racial, cross-class, and national significance, carries the danger of nebulizing the issue as a specific one of social injustice by blending it instead into a limitless desire that marks us all as "poor" creatures in search of impossible fulfillment.

The incursion of socioeconomic and political history into Wright's narrative of individualism, however, leads to a crucial reevaluation of poverty as a category of social being. Throughout much of *Black Boy,* Wright remains hungry because he refuses "the shame of charity" (86), but the effects of the 1929 stock-market crash force Wright to the Cook County Bureau of Public Welfare to plead for bread. The effects of the public confession of his hunger are far from what Wright expects. Instead of encountering a group of perverse and idle people who "had deliberately sought their present state of idleness" (301)—the ideological flip side of beliefs in bootstrapping—Wright experiences the beginnings of communal consciousness among the black poor specifically: "The day I begged bread from the city officials was the day that showed me I was not alone in my loneliness, society had cast millions of others with me. . . . I was slowly beginning to comprehend the meaning of my environment; a sense of direction was beginning to emerge from the conditions of my life" (301). The real social danger to the ruling class comes not from people who live in the kind of poverty that mobilizes desire—those who struggle to grab their share of wealth by force, or try to defend their property through violence—because these individuals implicitly sanction the values of the system in which they live. The revolutionary danger comes from "those who do not dream of the prizes that the nation holds forth," those who are beginning to develop a counterculture, a "new and strange way of life" (302) that rejects the materialistic desire underscoring the logic of hunger and striving. Wright's self-conscious encounter with the welfare system provides a moment of clarity ("cynicism slid from me. . . .

I wanted to know") in which *need* emerges as a special category that differs fundamentally from want or desire, as Wright realizes that his own needs give him rights to the resources of others. In effect, this moment takes desire out of poverty altogether. We are left instead with a sense of need defined by communal belonging not individual autonomy, by necessity not freedom, and by a kind of stasis that counters the restless movement of acquisition with a *delimited* focus on the essential ingredients that foreclose socioeconomic suffering.[131] Wright's return to a racial community effectively puts a lid on the endlessness of desire, just as blacks are socially bounded off from full material and cultural opportunity within the nation. The conceptual integrity of poverty becomes stabilized through its association with need. Recalling Lily Bart's encounter with Nettie Struther in Wharton's *The House of Mirth,* a shared identity is discovered in a basic (if racially motivated) acknowledgment of human lack, which sparks into life Wright's search for the powerful "something" that might bring meaning and direction to life—the needs that go beyond the level of mere subsistence to include the emotional and intellectual constituents of healthy living (301).

This welfare moment underscores how the language of want—the association of language with the desire for knowledge as a substantial thing to feed his indigence and ignorance—is balanced throughout the autobiography by the language of need. When hunger first enters Wright's life it provokes what we have seen at work throughout the first part of *Black Boy,* the dialectic of self-consciousness ("for the first time in my life I had to pause and think of what was happening to me") and collapsed selfhood ("this new hunger baffled me. . . . I would grow dizzy and my vision would dim"), which leads to a crucial lesson in the nature of language:

"Mama, I'm hungry," I complained one afternoon.
"Jump up and catch a kungry," she said, trying to make me laugh and forget.
"What's a *kungry?*"
"It's what little boys eat when they get hungry," she said.
"What does it taste like?"
"I don't know."
"Then why do you tell me to catch one?"
"Because you said that you were hungry," she said, smiling.
I sensed that she was teasing me and it made me angry. (14–15)

Wright's mother attempts to overcome her relative powerlessness to feed her suffering son by offering words instead of food. She is forced to replace the absence of nourishment with the presence of language. Yet what the young Wright realizes from this moment is exactly the incapacity of language to fill physical lack. Language betrays Wright: *kungry* does not signify any real physical possibility; it is merely a self-reflexive act of linguistic play, an arbitrary relationship between the surfaces of rhyme alone. Ironically, at the moment that hunger (the absence of something needed) is becoming physical for Wright, language (a potential physical presence) is merely exposing its own impoverishment, its inevitable signal that the described object is irreducibly missing.[132] Language is not bound here with desire, as a movement toward impossible fulfillment, but with need as that which cannot be expressed in language or held in knowledge.[133] Wright's anger is a moment of *dis*ablement as he realizes the natural relation of language to material lack, which brings this cognitive crisis into play.

Looking back, the first part of *Black Boy* is full of similar incidents in which conditions of socioeconomic suffering become moments of linguistic self-consciousness for young Richard. Needs differ from desires in their disorderly "expression of limit or spillover," writes Ruth Smith—a spillover manifested in various emetic moments, usually related to a conflict with authority, in which words slip uncontrollably from Richard's mouth, or in which he fears losing control over his own tongue.[134] Whether he is being fed alcohol and obscene language in a bar, or insulting his grandmother in the bathtub, Wright learns that words can cause upheaval despite his having acquired them unconsciously and his ignorance of their meaning.[135] He learns from his disadvantaged surroundings that language can still have tremendous force despite seeming empty of significance—a lesson that emerges most powerfully from Wright's encounter with the impoverished suffering of his mother, the agent of literacy whose role in the book subverts the correlation, in sociological literature of the period, of matrilineal families and juvenile delinquency. The suffering of Wright's mother gains symbolic value by representing a cognitive self-consciousness and overabundance of emotion that opposes the emotionless void of his father. Yet this "poverty" of "hunger-ridden days and hours" is simultaneously baffling, irrational, and meaningless, a "nameless fate" of absurd suffering that defies human justice (and hence definitions of poverty based on social injustice) and even comprehension itself (100). Wright returns to the lessons he takes from his mother's suffering—the "conviction that the meaning of living came only when one was struggling to wring a meaning out of meaningless suffering" (100)—in what seems to be a final existential promise "to create a sense of the hunger for life that gnaws in us all, to keep alive in our hearts a sense of the inexpressibly human" (384).

The end of *Black Boy* thus articulates the categorical problematics of poverty—its dynamic inclusiveness that gives it such power as a critical concept, but always threatens to move its reach beyond the bounded realms of socioeconomic suffering and material need. Wright's realization that resolution and satiation remain impossible in the culture of the North feeds a definition of human subjectivity constituted in an impossible desire for meaning, a constant struggle toward elusive knowing. Hunger here seems to refer to human incompleteness in a broad epistemological, even spiritual sense: a metaphysical lack that resonates with a Judeo-Christian perception of man as a creature of need not plentitude, and that becomes readily expressed in words that are themselves a sign of a basic absence within us all.[136] The end of *Black Boy* thus appears to gesture toward universality, with hunger being more about human identity than difference. Yet Wright's engagement with these issues of lack never disconnects fully from its foundations in material inequality. The notion of hunger being inexpressible, for example, reflects back on specific forces within Wright's sparse environment that restrict access to the tools of literacy—the forces of socioeconomic suffering that damage subjectivity and that make *need* particularly difficult to express by marking if off from literary culture. And the insatiable quality of Wright's hunger returns not to a metaphysics of subjectivity but to a politics of social identity in which the claims of race and socioeconomics finally compete and coalesce.

Delinquent Identity

In Wright's novel *Native Son* (1940), Bigger Thomas's inability to articulate his situation corresponds to what Wright terms the "chasm of emptiness" at Bigger's heart ("How 'Bigger' Was Born," 454), an incoherent realm of thoughtlessness and unintentional action that prevents the novel itself from reaching final resolution.[137] The only hunger Bigger feels is a momentary, undisciplined, chaotic vortex of instinctual emotion, a hysterical sensation that exists more in his stomach than his mind.[138] Bigger's abysmal self thus implies the segregation of his impoverishment, creating a hierarchical distinction between the representable and the unrepresentable, the literate and the nonliterary. The gaps in *Native Son,* its network of inarticulate and meaningless moments, expose the gulf between the needy and the recording consciousness. In this regard, *Native Son* can be read as a racial resignification of Depression Era fictions and documentaries in which poverty features as a process of intellectual bewilderment. For example, Algren's *Somebody in Boots* (whose initial section is titled "The Native Son") likewise represents the power of hunger specifically to destroy the intellectual self-consciousness and political agency of the poor, thus cutting them off entirely from the realm of literate culture. This sense of literary and intellectual hierarchy is what *Black Boy* both engages and works against. Wright's statements about black cultural barrenness are not solely an attempt to negate the negation, as JanMohamed phrases it, nor are they the strongest affirmation of black culture rather than its denial, as Ralph Ellison argued in his 1945 review of *Black Boy.*[139] Such arguments tend to erase problems that remain central to the book as a whole. Signifying on the cyclical explanations evident in the sociology of Frazier and Myrdal, socioeconomic suffering traumatizes Richard in ways that make him revisit self-consciously his original impoverishment, but only to explore and perpetuate the very "lack" with which this poverty emerges.[140] The barrenness and bleakness that Wright associates with black culture becomes an intensification of need that reaches across races and to the very core of national values—it is an *American* hunger in this re-gard—even as it applies more narrowly to those who remain socioeconomically marginalized and racially disenfranchised within that broader culture.[141]

Black Boy shares with Agee's *Praise* an understanding of poverty's power to cripple consciousness—a point that Wright first explores in his posthumously pub-lished early novel, *Lawd Today!* (1963).[142] In this regard, both *Praise* and *Black Boy* are integrally related to the pessimistic trend within Depression writing, which we saw running through the proletarian novel (Gold), black social realism (Petry), the literature of the marginal man (Algren), and documentary expression (Caldwell). Lifting this shared concern with the psychological and cultural damage of poverty to the level of aesthetic and linguistic theory, both *Praise* and *Black Boy* recognize that the literary potential of poverty arises not despite but because of the ethical and philosophical problems of accessing a state of material need that seems an active threat to the consciousness, emotional life, and social agency of individuals. Agee confronts the objectivism of the documentary genre by smashing together the opposing qualities that only an outsider can supposedly see in poverty—that it can be beautiful on the one hand, intellectually degenerative on the other. From the subjective perspective of autobiography, Wright confronts another central di-chotomy of poverty writing: the conflict between poverty as a pattern of cultural and psychological values that might enable the depiction of marginalized groups, and the "abysmal" sense that a confrontation with socioeconomic need has the power to undermine the very possibility of literate culture and literary representa-tion. The crucial point in Wright's autobiography is that the alleged delinquency of poverty *can* motivate the sufferer's reach toward comprehension, thus making Wright's approach to deprivation very different from the bewildering condition that horrifies Gold, frustrates Petry, and attracts Agee. If poverty is recognized in *Black Boy* as a potentially damaging condition that cannot easily be inverted by creative adaptation, then Wright also reevaluates the assumption that poverty cannot co-exist with literacy, self-consciousness, and political agency. Wright's emphasis on absence in the "bleakness" passage—the things missing in black life—makes fur-ther strategic sense as a counterpoint to Agee, whose emphasis on poverty as a physical presence, as something in the blood, creates the insurmountable differ-ence between observer and observed that Agee finds so beautiful.

Echoing Agee's *Praise*—and like all of the major works treated in this study— the complexity of poverty as a category of social being shapes the thematic con-cerns and the structural movements of Wright's autobiography. At one level, pov-erty is *metaphysical* for Wright: hunger becomes the desire that constitutes the human subject, and is thus equally the stuff of black and white consciousness, just as it motivates language and creative expression in general. In similarly cross-racial ways, poverty remains more narrowly *national* in scope, whereby a purely cultural poverty penetrates to the heart of national values, and thus makes an "escape" from poverty impossible. Poverty is a *socioeconomic* force for Wright too. A material lack of resources marks the bodies, minds, and behaviors of the poor in ways that vacillate between a degraded internalization of subservience, which is racially held, and a more individualistic if stressful drive away from stultifying dependency. A return to the black community in Chicago articulates finally the *racial* significance of poverty for Wright. The socioeconomic and political boundaries around blackness reignite a sense of need in which the restriction of social agency—the limits, in other words, on the full citizenship of African Americans—becomes strangely enabling by marking off poverty from endless desire, and by making the poor conscious of the communal necessities that define their condition.

Wright's identification of hunger at the center of his life is thus historically as well as theoretically motivated. Orlando Patterson has described the historical process whereby slavery tends to be followed by poverty because the racism and degradation of the slave system carry over into the world of relative freedom. Poverty seems such an inadequate term to describe the all-pervasive violation and dehumanization of slavery. Yet it becomes an essential term to describe the plight of emancipated blacks whose limited skills confined them to rural areas, and who were in turn limited by white competitors to the lowest-paid jobs.[143] *Black Boy* does not depict a competition between race and class as the proper lens through which to see social disadvantage, but it does isolate poverty as a dynamic force that establishes differences and similarities both within races and between them. In this regard, Wright's ideas resemble those of the sociologist William Julius Wilson, who emphasizes the singular nature of black urban poverty—social dislocation—while prioritizing its broad socioeconomic causes.[144] *Black Boy* expands Wright's sociological observations in *12 Million Black Voices,* where he traces how general economic trends and the special considerations of race combine to create a particularly black mode of destitution in which African Americans are simultaneously included in and excluded from universal structures of oppression—an ambivalent situation, Wright argues, that infuses black creative expression with the simultaneity of meaningfulness and bewilderment that is clearly demonstrated in the autobiography.[145]

Melding the metaphysical and the material, the national and the individual, as well as the socioeconomic and the racial, poverty shapes the contours of Wright's emergent subjectivity. *Black Boy* finally refuses to exploit what Roxanne Rimstead calls "the oppositional potential of autobiography" that "holds out the possibility of repairing cultural damage by enabling marginal subjects to represent identities closer to their experiences, hence decolonizing themselves as subjects of others' definitions."[146] Poverty becomes entangled with Wright's identity as a psychosocial complex that resists easy affirmation. Wright may finally reject the ideology of desire as a mode of progressive being but he refuses then to idealize need or to deny that "aching poverty" (363) does indeed contain negative behavioral and psychological effects—the results of structural impediments that compromise mobility and individual autonomy. Wright's achieved literacy and articulation thus embody the social pressures toward illiteracy and inarticulation against which they emerged. In this way, *Black Boy* holds together the dialectical movement between mobility and stasis, between enablement and disablement, that has marked the polemics and the narrative dynamics of poverty throughout this study. The important point for Wright's theory of representation is that an individual can bear the scars of social suffering yet still have the capacity to depict this traumatic situation not because poverty is comprehended rationally but because its irrationality and damage, its bewilderment, are confronted and communicated.

Here lies the source of the existential perspective that emerges in *Black Boy:* a meaninglessness that self-consciously acknowledges its own lack, whereby the presence of individual being is defined against an abyss of external significance. This existential perspective stems not solely from the dynamics of race that appear in Wright's story, "The Man Who Lived Underground," also drafted in the early 1940s.[147] Rather, it arises more specifically from a situation that sociologists have tied to the experience of poverty, in which the poor are thrust back upon the existential "me" by failing to internalize the same social structures and cultural values of *either* the dominant *or* the minority group.[148] This isolation of poverty as an ontological as much as an economic category, a psychosocial complex rooted in the experience of socioeconomic need, works in many ways to collapse the difference between Richard and Bigger, and thus to prevent the teleological progression from ignorance to intelligence, from voicelessness to articulation, which is implicit in the distinction between the narrator and Bigger in *Native Son.*[149] Wright's controversial statement on black "cultural barrenness" implies that any minority tradition of writing, if founded in substantive forces of social marginalization and institutional exclusion, must inevitably bring the intellectual, emotional, and cultural trauma of material deprivation into textual sentience.

CONCLUSION

RICHARD WRIGHT'S autobiography highlights the crucial point of my study as a whole. The exploration of poverty as a critical category is not necessarily an argument that cultural definitions of identity are simply "displacements" of class issues.[1] Poverty is such a powerful tool of inquiry—in the hands of certain writers, at least—because of its "in between-ness" as a category of social being. We saw this demonstrated in the work of Herman Melville, for whom poverty comes to fuel something like minority consciousness. Conditions of restricted agency and a material lack of resources lead to a decodable and relatively consistent pattern of behavioral values, Melville implies—values that come to seem particularly intransigent and devastating in an American context. There may be a divergence in current critical discourse between sociological approaches to social structure and a multicultural concern with identities and representations, as we saw in the introduction. For Melville, however, there is little opposition between the socioeconomic and the cultural because he uncovers poverty as a category that links them. And we can think of Melville as virtually inaugurating a certain kind of poverty writing by recognizing the literary and linguistic significance of this social category. The representational problems that have made Pierre, for example, such a rich site for critical investigation result, to a significant and largely unnoticed degree, from the specific problems of interpreting socioeconomic suffering, not from a general sense of epistemological crisis, or even from an engagement with social class,

broadly construed. Melville's work combines creative technique and social reference in ways that make abnormal material deprivation the foundation of a sophisticated mode of cultural analysis. Within this analysis, the concept of poverty rarely
escapes the dynamic of its perceptive crisis and interpretive dilemmas, its power
to taunt social observation with abysmal inaccessibility and with an inability to be
seen fully within the national culture.

In Melville's work, the ethical and literary implications of poverty are, in a sense,
aligned. Progressive social politics merges with complex formal experimentation.
Yet the nature of poverty, as a literary and social category, has tended to make this
alignment somewhat shifty. Hence the parallels and the contrasts between
Theodore Dreiser's *Sister Carrie* and Edith Wharton's *The House of Mirth.* The narrative movement of both novels is powered by a similar engagement with historically contextual notions of pauperism and poverty. Lily Bart and George Hurstwood
reveal the same collapse of time, desire for momentary pleasure, breakdown of
agency, and irrational disordering of thought. For Dreiser, pauperism becomes a
class in itself. The rhetorical forces of his book work toward a self-reflexive logic
whereby the economic dependence of purportedly mobile white men seems con-
ditional on whether the individual suffers from this disease of character to begin
with. For Wharton, however, the problem of being poor is never reduced solely to
a trait of individual being, just as the proclivity toward pauperism is not individual-
ized but universalized across an entire sex. If Dreiser's heroine has few qualms
about being financially dependent, dreading poverty alone, then Lily dreads poverty *and* pauperism, with the inevitable relation between these two states constituting Wharton's polemic and dissent. There is thus a double level of criticism in
The House of Mirth—first of pauperism itself, which is deconstructed by its partial
removal from the realms of class. A state typically seen as a disease of manhood
becomes, ironically, an inherent problematic of womanhood. And second, Wharton levels criticism at the sexist social conditions that condemn women to these
alternatives of striving misery or abysmal dependence. Pauperism as a concept is
broken down at the same time as it is used, not to explain away persistent poverty but to critique the socioeconomic foundations of gender inequity—its origins
in the absolute denial of certain types of social mobility and economic freedom for
women.

To make poverty our organizing frame, rather than race, gender, or even class
in the most general sense, inevitably provides new perspectives on literary texts
and new connections between writers. These are the very perspectives and connections to which we have been partially blinded by all the difficulties raised by
poverty as a category of critical analysis. In this regard, Wharton and Wright develop surprisingly similar theories of poverty as an underlying social condition from
which crucial elements of cultural identity are generated. For both writers, poverty
presents a fusion of cultural and sociological perspectives, wherein the class as-

pects of material deprivation and the cultural aspects of gender and race—as well as the politics of sexism and racism—naturally merge.[2] The links between these two writers suggest how difficult it is to form assumptions about the representation of poverty based on the class background of the writer, or to found treatments of social marginalization solely on a writer's cultural background. Such approaches leave us poorly equipped to acknowledge a social category that has always failed to behave within neat boundaries of class or cultural affiliation. If scholars in feminist and women's studies have emphasized, to a degree, literary representations of the disproportionate burden of poverty that has fallen on the shoulders of women, then they have often done so by prioritizing the subjective experience of poverty by lower-class women, and have thus missed exactly what Wharton acknowledges—a sense of poverty whose gender specificity makes it cross-class in kind.[3] As we have seen throughout this book, poverty is a dynamic state that people transition into and out of from many social and cultural positions, a state that even working-class writing can deemphasize by defining class as more than just exploitation and deprivation. For this reason, although a number of our texts have illustrated middle-class reactions to the poor, class itself has not been an adequate category to contain a discourse that broadly engages gender and race, and that disengages from the identity of any single class, in such textually productive ways.

This "in between-ness" of poverty defines its complexity and utility yet it is also what makes poverty such a hazardous critical category to approach, just as writers such as Rebecca Harding Davis, Henry David Thoreau, Dreiser, and James Agee become tempted by what the sociologist Kenneth Clarke calls the "cult of cultural deprivation."[4] Social pressures of individualism can flip the effects into the causes of poverty, provoking conceptions of the poor as victims of their own personal inadequacy, behavioral pathology, or even physiological disease. At times we have witnessed relativistic and progressive motivations being overwhelmed by an approach in which poverty becomes less a description of social situation than a construction of behavioral causation that reveals most about the ideological assumptions underpinning the act of representation itself. As much as this study seeks to reevaluate an emphasis on cultural identity in an unreflective, affirmative sense, it also helps us appreciate the reasons *why* a critical discourse of poverty has stumbled, particularly at moments when cultural exploration turns into pejorative rationalization. Even if writers such as Dreiser and Agee slide into essentialized views of the poor, however, they still reveal an ethical *struggle* with poverty as a polemical category, a struggle that actively structures their aesthetic theories and representational techniques. A close reading of *Let Us Now Praise Famous Men*, for example, may upset the critical framework within which Agee has been placed by revealing a vision of poverty, sprung loose from alterable socioeconomic factors, that verges on eugenic theories of dependency. Yet Agee's refiguring of the blessed-degenerate, beautiful-horrific binaries within broader conventions of poverty writing remains a fascinating maneuver from a literary perspective—the way it plays with and revises the moral and formal assumptions of the kinds of writing to which it is heir. To offer another example: *Sister Carrie* and *The House of Mirth* may move in different ethical directions but they remain two of their era's most intricate and interesting examples of poverty writing both thematically and structurally. Their plots of decline respond not to predetermined generic patterns but to dynamic and contentious political debates over the causes and effects of economic dependence at the turn of the century.

The benefit of a literary approach to poverty is a capacity to illuminate the elusive (and frequently controversial) nonmaterial effects of material situations, the cultural and psychological experiences of want amid wealth—the subjective patterns that necessarily fall beneath the radar of sociological efforts to isolate structural causes and to quantify levels of need. Poverty may lie substantially outside the discourse of identity, in the realms of social structure, institutional organization, and material conditions, but literary analysis shows its clear connections to the cultural questions of power, difference, and signifying practice that animate any discussion of social marginalization in the most basic and universal sense.[5] The writing I have analyzed remains ultimately crucial not because of the issues it acknowledges but because of the forms this acknowledgment takes. Herbert Gans and Michael Katz both argue that the language used to describe the poor has a pronounced effect on how they are viewed, and hence on how the problem of poverty is dealt with in the public sphere. Literature plays an essential part in a poverty discourse that highlights the social construction of difference; it has a social effect because it helps determine, just as it can undermine, the reigning mechanisms by which a reading public understands the root causes of, and the appropriate responses to, endemic social problems such as the persistence and widening of inequality.[6] Literary awareness of poverty as a diverse, dynamic, yet substantial category can place needed emphasis on the infrastructural forces of marginalization and exclusion that transcend identity borders, that expose divisions within "whiteness," and that simultaneously strengthen discussion of the minority and gender groups that have, throughout history, unfairly carried burdens of need.

I hope to have convinced the reader of the peculiarity of poverty as a subject of social and literary discourse. It is a subject that requires close textual attention to appreciate the complex ideological contradictions it exposes, while it needs historical contextualization to understand the social embeddedness of these literary forms. Poverty discourse changes over time, hence *Sister Carrie* reflects the conflict between environmentalist and biological reasoning in the Progressive period, just as *Black Boy* illustrates how the developing racial awareness of its era, and the "psychologizing" of poverty during the Depression, moved poverty to the center of minority consciousness. Yet there are also ways that poverty discourse

resists historical development, just as the work of Agee revisits the aesthetic dilemmas of approaching the poor explored by antebellum writers such as Melville and
Thoreau. Parallels between, say, Agee and Melville raise questions about the generic consistency and the national distinctiveness of the kind of poverty writing
treated in this book.[7] Again, the literature of poverty is complex in both of these respects. The diversity of poverty writing, in terms of the political opinions it contains
and the economic and cultural backgrounds of its writers, tends to pressure any
easy claims for a distinct genre of writing. Yet consistent stylistic practices and formal perspectives, as well as common sets of ideas and ethical debates, do seem
to emerge transhistorically from the special dynamics of poverty in an American
context—the powerful clash, for example, between ideologies of universal equality and the persistence of unequal socioeconomic barriers. Claims for the national
uniqueness of this writing are inevitably complicated by the transatlantic nature of
thinking about the poor. But I would contend, along with other critics, that reading
Agee on poverty is substantially different from reading George Orwell on the same
subject, just as Melville's approach to the poor differs profoundly from that of
Charles Dickens.[8] Both Agee and Melville view poverty as a psychological, ideological, and ethical problem that shapes a profound and sustained crisis of representation—a crisis resulting from political pressures that these two writers perceive
as peculiarly national in kind.

I hope to have established that our major texts warrant special attention because
of the complex, sustained, and historically revealing ways they open up questions
of poverty that often get overlooked or downgraded, even in works depicting the
poor. Hence, I would argue, *Pierre* exceeds Ned Buntline's *Mysteries and Miseries
of New York, Sister Carrie* outstrips Stephen Crane's *Maggie,* and *Let Us Now
Praise Famous Men* moves far beyond Erskine Caldwell's *You Have Seen Their
Faces* in the ways that ideologies of poverty impact narrative form. This literary engagement with poverty moves across periods and unsettles literary categories.
And it certainly continues to feature, with varying degrees of self-consciousness,
in texts emerging from the cultural politics and movements of the 1960s and
1970s—texts that critics have often fallen into relatively comfortable ways of reading. Take, for instance, Tomás Rivera's novel about migrant Chicano laborers in the
1940s and 1950s, . . . *y no se lo tragó la tierra* / . . . *And the Earth Did Not Devour
Him* (1971; hereafter abbreviated to *Tierra*). For good reason, perhaps, critics have
tended to place *Tierra* within a specifically Chicano cultural and historical context,
or else they have viewed Rivera's focus on class as an affirmative and counter-
hegemonic depiction of emergent class consciousness.[9] As with all of the major
works analyzed thus far, however, a full appreciation of Rivera's novel only arises
when we realize the pressures it places on poverty as a specific state of socioeconomic suffering that relates to ethnic culture and to working-class consciousness but is not completely reducible to either.

Echoing writers ranging from Melville to Wright, Rivera's understanding of poverty is material, ideological, and psychological too, as he charts the ways that children in particular become traumatized by the suffering and stigma of growing up poor.[10] Reminding us of key episodes in Wright's *Black Boy* and Melville's *Pierre,* poverty registers as both a physical and a psychological sickness, an existential nausea that compromises vision and consciousness in its extreme social dislocation.[11] If the obscurity of Melville's *Pierre* and the polemical plot movements of Wharton's *House of Mirth* both emerge directly from the recognition of poverty as a special psychosocial state, then the fractured narrative form of *Tierra* mirrors the migrancy that describes the fundamental social instability of Rivera's workers. Their vast seasonal journeys in search of agricultural labor absorb any surplus income gained from the work itself, thus keeping the migrant laborers in a state of bare subsistence and constant anxiety. This cyclical, spiraling condition, in which migrancy keeps them poor while poverty keeps them migrant, provides the philosophical denouement of the narrative—the belief, expressed in an appropriately unfinished clause, that "[a]rriving and leaving, it's the same thing because we no sooner arrive and . . ." (145). Related on one level to the theoretical tendency that Ramón Saldívar has attributed to Chicano narrative more broadly—its tendency to undermine fixed ethical conclusions and categorical definitions, particularly of polar oppositions—this "dialectics of difference" is rooted in the particular socioeconomic and geopolitical forces that shape the lives of these migrant laborers, particularly their inability to escape from the paradoxical situation in which the fruits of work can never transcend the costs of the commute.[12]

Rivera's novel makes special sense in light of the poverty discourse highlighted in this study. The novel's stress on the psychological trauma of poverty, for example, emerges from the pressures of national ideology that remain remarkably consistent over time. And the epistemological crises emerging from this confrontation with American poverty get played out—once again—in a self-conscious experimentation with literary representation. With particular conciseness and power, *Tierra* illustrates the complex contradictions and paradoxes that emerge when poverty is targeted as an autonomous and central category of social experience. On one level, *Tierra* demonstrates how impoverished conditions bring moments of class-conscious resistance and unity. Yet coherent class consciousness cannot withstand the power of socioeconomic injustice to damage subjectivity, to limit social agency, and to entrap individuals within cycles of deprivation.[13] By recognizing these rigid barriers to social mobility, *Tierra* thus explores how poverty becomes intimately associated with a particular sociocultural group of Chicano laborers, whose economic vulnerability is tied to the long history of race, colonization, and the U.S. seizure of Mexican territory. Yet poverty is also a dynamic and situational state that relates to individuals from diverse social and cultural backgrounds. Beneath the surface of *Tierra* glimmers the poverty of lower-class whites who view the spectacular poverty of Chicanos with both reassurance (it demon-strates white cultural superiority) and anxiety (it illustrates the potential for their own downward mobility within a fluid society).[14]

If recent critical debates over the categorical difference of race and class tend to oppose the inherent nature of racial identity to the situational and contingent qualities of class,[15] then Rivera's novel shows how such absolute distinctions fail to hold when poverty becomes the center of attention. The marginalized status of Rivera's characters does not arrive preformed as a Chicano identity that is au-tonomous and collective. It is described by Rivera as emerging in large part from a poverty that is socioeconomic and cross-cultural. Yet the social status of the characters is not solely reducible to their class position either: they are poor in part because of their identities as Mexican Americans, their place in a racialized situa-tion of global displacement.[16] By positioning poverty at the intersection of dis-crimination and exploitation, Rivera's novel about transnational migrants returns us to larger questions of citizenship. Poverty seems to cripple, once again, the free social agency of certain individuals and groups within the nation, limiting their ac-cess to cultural opportunity and devaluing their political liberty. Rivera's subter-ranean kinship, through poverty discourse, with the other authors considered here, also returns us to questions about the practice of literary criticism itself. By recog-nizing poverty as a critical category that effects the works of disparate writers over time, I hope to have opened a space for scholars to rethink connections between material and cultural phenomena, to envision *shared* problems of social being that cut across yet inform concerns with cultural identity, and, finally, to recover a so-cial and ethical function within a literary debate that can seem so trapped in cycles of pity and blame.

NOTES

Notes to Preface

1. Sklar quoted in Denning, "'The Special American Conditions,'" 356.
2. Wray and Newizt, *White Trash,* 8.
3. According to the official figures of the Census Bureau, 32.9 million people in the United States were living in poverty in 2001, an increase of 1.3 million on the previous year. This means that, even by conservative estimates, almost 12 percent of the population was subsisting below income thresholds deemed minimal according to family size and composition—just over $14,000 per year for a family of three (Proctor and Dalaker, *Poverty in the United States,* 1, 5).

Notes to Introduction

1. George, *Progress and Poverty,* 10; Krugman, "For Richer," 64, 142.
2. Smith argues that liberal discourse describes the poor as naturally disorderly, thus placing them beyond the boundaries of the civilizable world, because the recognition of poverty defies the terms of freedom and universality that constitute the foundation of liberal social assumptions, and raises the possibility that citizenship and the market are restrictive entities not those of freely created order ("Order and Disorder," 209–10).
3. Reed, "The 2004 Election in Perspective," 4. A recent article in the *New York Times* describes the "powerful consensus" among social scientists and state and federal policy makers, which "sees single-parent families as the dismal foundries that produced decades of child poverty, delinquency and crime" (Harden, "2-Parent Families Rise," 1, 24). Jennings argues for a tendency toward cultural rather than situational perspectives in current public and scholarly discussions of poverty ("Persistent Poverty in the United States," 14, 16). See also Zweig, *The Working Class Majority,* 89–90.

4. Franklin argues that such media images of the "black underclass" (which he estimates to be less than 1 percent of the population) impact both on the status of nonpoor blacks and on the legitimacy of welfare itself ("White Uses of the Black Underclass," 139).

5. A notable exception here is the *New York Times,* which has recently run a number of prominent articles emphasizing the impact of widening class inequalities in American society; see Entin, "Class, Culture, and the Working Body," 1212.

6. In "Did Katrina Recalibrate Attitudes Toward Poverty and Inequality?," Grusky and Ryo conclude that the journalistic attention to the problems of poverty and inequality following Katrina has not translated into public ideology changes that might bring legislative action. The "activist" class (those who favor government intervention to lessen poverty) grew only slightly after Katrina, whereas conservative responses to poverty increased because the hurricane's aftermath also served as a lesson in the inefficiency of government programs.

7. Ehrenreich, *Nickel and Dimed,* 117–18, 216–17.

8. Le Sueur, *Women on the Breadlines,* preface; Kushnick and Jennings, eds., *A New Introduction to Poverty,* 5. Kusmer notes that American homelessness has received relatively little attention from scholars, largely because the homeless themselves exist beyond traditional documentary sources (*Down and Out,* 7). Sante, *Low Life,* 319, and Thernstrom, "Poverty in Historical Perspective," 161, make similar points. See Himmelfarb, *The Idea of Poverty,* 11, and Smith, "Order and Disorder," 213, for the philosophical and historical neglect of poverty as a subject.

9. In *The Philosopher and His Poor,* Rancière argues that philosophers such as Plato, Marx, Sartre, and Bourdieu have been primarily concerned with creating and protecting their own philosophical power by excluding the poor from the privilege of free thought. "The poor" here is really a synonym for *artisans* or *servile workers,* while "poverty" remains a flat term in Rancière's thesis, defined by its largely negative function of reflecting the opposite luxury of ideas.

10. According to the editors of *Social Suffering* (Kleinman et al.), "a preoccupation with individual certainty and doubt simply seems a less interesting, less important question to ask than that of how such suffering is produced in societies and how acknowledgement of pain, as a cultural process, is given or withheld" (xiii).

11. Melville, "The Two Temples," 314. Melville's satire on American charity was published posthumously.

12. As Kerbo puts it, in *Social Stratification and Inequality,* poverty should be understood as "*relative to the society in which the poor find themselves*" (249).

13. The classic liberal account of distributive justice is, of course, Rawls, *A Theory of Justice,* which posits that the unequal distribution of resources is only fair when it is of the greatest expected benefit to the least advantaged group, and furthers the good of all sections of society.

14. On this point see especially Galbraith, *The Affluent Society,* 235.

15. Butler, "Desire," 381. Butler offers a useful introduction to theories of desire, particularly in the philosophy of Plato, in Hegelian phenomenology, and in Lacanian psychoanalysis. She also notes the rejection of the equation of desire and lack, found in the work of Gilles Deleuze and Félix Guattari (385).

16. Fleissner seeks to undermine the view of naturalism as a hypermasculine genre by re-

defining it in terms of a concern with the modern woman and the female bildungsroman. In Fleissner's discussion of Dreiser's *Sister Carrie,* for example, the character Hurstwood's decline into poverty is a function of Dreiser's manipulation of assumptions regarding sentimentalism, with Hurstwood becoming a version of the "fallen woman" of seduction fiction rather than a response to Dreiser's engagement with a social debate over the causes of poverty.

17. Cook's *Erskine Caldwell and the Fiction of Poverty* charts Caldwell's complex approach to poverty, while her earlier study, *From Tobacco Road to Route 66,* offers a broader analysis of the poor white archetype, oddly split between grotesque depravity and heroic virtue. See also Tracy, *In the Master's Eye,* which spends a couple of chapters analyzing the negative representations of poor whites, as criminal and lazy, which sanctioned the conservative, antidemocratic views of the elite southern planter class.

18. See Himmelfarb, *The Idea of Poverty* and *Poverty and Compassion.*

19. Rimstead, *Remnants of Nation,* 14, 6.

20. This is largely but not exclusively the case, even in studies of class. Zandy's *Hands,* a book concerned throughout with the exploitative impact of labor on the body, only gives "poverty" three entries in the index. In *The Syntax of Class,* Lang indexes "the poor" but not "poverty." Russo and Linkon's *New Working-Class Studies* fails to include "poverty" in its index, whereas "race" is the longest single entry, comprising twelve different subentries.

21. As bell hooks has argued passionately, class matters in American society, in some ways even more than race, yet it is the subject that makes us all nervous and that becomes so difficult to discuss (*Where We Stand,* vii, 8). See also Aronowitz, *The Politics of Identity,* chapter 1, and Katz, *The Undeserving Poor,* 8, on the traditional failure of U.S. workers to develop a language of class.

22. Griffin and Tempenis point out that social science has maintained an emphasis on class even as the field has turned to race and gender as organizing frames ("Class, Multiculturalism, and the *American Quarterly,*" 91–92). The marginalization of class has continued at recent American Studies Association meetings, according to Entin, "Class, Culture, and the Working Body," 1211.

23. Rowe, "The Writing Class," 41–43.

24. See White, "Early American Nations as Imagined Communities," 49.

25. In the realm of social theory, the most extreme example is Appadurai, *Modernity at Large,* which focuses on the global migration of imaginative forms and the processes of group identity formation, rather than on the economic or social motivations of such migrations and identities (2–6, 13–15).

26. Rimstead suggests that postcolonial modes of criticism have thus distracted us from how Western nations colonize the poor within their own borders (*Remnants of Nation,* 200, 227).

27. In "Notes on Globalization as a Philosophical Issue," Jameson argues for the importance of the nation state (72). Bérubé has also made a powerful case, against current transnationalist trends, for refocusing on how "the actions and policies of nation-states structure . . . lives in obvious and immediate ways" ("American Studies without Exceptions," 111). If the domain of economy is the world, writes Ignatieff, then "[t]he domain of polity is the nation" (*The Needs of Strangers,* 22).

28. In *The Shape of the Signifier,* Michaels argues that the rise of identities "has functioned

as the Left's way of learning to live with inequality" (17), and he outlines reasons why the subject of class difference has remained beyond approaches to the problem of the minority subject "articulated through its relation to an oppressive norm" (180). In "Class Struggle or Postmodernism?," Žižek promises to re-inject a sense of class struggle into postmodernist critical theory, but is really occupied with post-Marxist and poststructuralist theories of subjectivity and hegemony rather than with the questions of economic inequality or suffering.

29. See Mohanty, "The Epistemic Status of Cultural Identity." Mohanty's reading of Toni Morrison's *Beloved* (1987), for example, sees the novel as, in the end, an affirmative story of moral growth and communal identity, and thus ignores the contradictions, tensions, and the persistence of cultural and psychological damage present in Morrison's ending.

30. In *Chicano Narrative,* for example, Saldívar powerfully establishes how Chicano narrative has always been fundamentally concerned with issues of class, social hardship, and economic deprivation, as it seeks to oppose the dominant structures of social power by which the hegemonic culture maintains itself. Saldívar's reading of Tomás Rivera's *. . . y no se lo tragó la tierra / . . . And the Earth Did Not Devour Him* argues for a movement from ideological alienation toward "an affirmative ground for a collective cultural unity" (85) in which the working class becomes the self-emancipating subject of history (89).

31. Guillory, *Cultural Capital,* 13. "[C]lass cannot be constructed as a social identity in the *same way* as race or gender because it is not, in the current affirmative sense, a 'social identity' at all," writes Guillory (13).

32. Guillory makes a convincing case against an uncritical strain of identity politics, but his notion of "lower-class identity" could be unpacked further. Felski also tends to equate the "working class" and the "poor" throughout her essay, "Nothing to Declare."

33. Marx and Engels, *The Communist Manifesto,* 92. In *The Idea of Poverty,* Himmelfarb argues that, unlike other socialist thinkers who looked to the "dangerous class" as the bearer of revolution, Marx viewed the lumpen as a nonclass with no historical role in the class struggle (387, 391–92). See also Rancière, *The Philosopher and His Poor,* for a critique of Marx's lumpen (96), and Valentine, *Culture and Poverty,* 72, for Fanon's more revolutionary conception.

34. Rimstead, *Remnants of Nation,* 267.

35. See Smith, "Order and Disorder," 219, for an explication of this distinction. Aronowitz also clarifies the important differences, in Marxist thought, between exploitation (the condition of the working class) and domination/oppression (the state of feudal dependency); see *The Politics of Identity,* 21.

36. Williams, *Marxism and Literature,* 112. See O'Hara, "Class," 414, for a description of the Marxist perspective on poverty as the condition that laborers are always driven toward.

37. Burke occasionally mentions the awareness of poverty among social analysts who emphasized class antagonism over class harmony, though he is most interested in the perceived relation *between* classes rather than the perception or experience of material disadvantage.

38. See Fabian, "Speculation on Distress," 129. Separate studies by Templin and by Fichtelberg develop an almost identical thesis that financial panics caused a consolidation—albeit an anxious one—of middle-class consciousness, based on feminine, sentimental, and domestic ideals; see Templin, "Panic Fiction," 7–8, and Fichtelberg, *Critical Fictions,* especially chapter 6 on the "bankruptcy fictions" of the 1850s and 1860s. See Zimmerman,

"Frank Norris, Market Panic, and the Mesmeric Sublime," for a similar argument in relation to turn-of-the-century naturalism.

39. In addition to the rise of explicitly literary studies of the working class, a number of interdisciplinary studies of class have appeared, such as Russo and Linkon's *New Working-Class Studies,* as well as anthologies and introductions that emphasize class in relation to classroom practice. See Russo and Linkon's introduction for an overview of this interdisciplinary work.

40. Compare this with the stronger emphasis on the material influence of socioeconomic forces upon working-class experience, found in traditions of Marxist criticism from the 1930s; see Freeman, *Proletarian Literature,* 12, and Hicks, *The Great Tradition,* 292.

41. See Denning, *Mechanic Accents,* 56–61; 216–17, n. 1. As Entin points out in his perceptive review of Russo and Linkon, *New Working-Class Studies,* this kind of approach to class "echoes an identity-politics-based paradigm, in which social categories are assumed to be rooted in some putatively 'natural' element of existence" ("Class, Culture, and the Working Body," 1215). The essays in *New Working-Class Studies* that focus on imaginative literature make little reference to poverty; according to Lauter, the sensibility of working-class writing is defined by "class conflict over work and the control of workplaces" ("Under Construction," 68).

42. Denning, *The Cultural Front,* 4, 237–40. Denning refers to poverty as a category most frequently in chapter 6 of *The Cultural Front,* yet the crisis of representation he discovers in "ghetto pastorals" emerges most from their engagement with the category of work. At times, Denning seems to direct criticism at the very beliefs about the 1930s that would naturally encourage discussion of poverty—for example, beliefs that the Popular Front was a "documentary" culture (268), or approaches that fail to stress the importance of ethnic culture in proletarian writing (237–39).

43. Aronowitz, *The Politics of Identity,* 37; Lipsitz, *Rainbow at Midnight,* 11. Aronowitz blames the failure of U.S. class identification on the national privileging of domination over exploitation, with consumption not production becoming the social and political problematic (21); on the historical and ideological failure to challenge the hegemony of bourgeois values (70–71); and on the tendency of class-based movements themselves to weaken the class consciousness of other cultural identities by excluding them initially in their overly narrow focus on economic justice (67).

44. In *The Great Tradition,* for example, Hicks clearly values those writers, such as Dos Passos, who advocate revolutionary change through proletarian action (292). Speaking generally, these earlier critics emphasized the pain and devastation of hunger but were always primarily interested in the politics and materiality of a class struggle geared toward the eradication of poverty through socialist change.

45. Foley, *Radical Representations,* xi. Likewise, many of Hapke's textual readings, in *Labor's Text,* tend to be broad overviews.

46. In *Left Letters,* for example, Bloom attempts to erode views of radical writers Mike Gold and Joseph Freeman as "crude, reductive, partisan, and sentimental" (118) by stressing their high modernist poetics as well as their left-wing politics. In *The Revolutionary Imagination,* Wald makes an identical claim for the poetry of John Wheelright and Sherry Mangan. Shulman's *The Power of Political Art* seeks to canonize leftist writing by stressing its diver-

sity. Though the subject of poverty gets occasional mention in these studies (see Bloom's attention to Gold's psychological understanding of poverty, in *Left Letters,* 63–64), it rarely gets analyzed textually or assessed theoretically, remaining a passing reference rather than a site of detailed investigation.

47. Weinstein, *The Literature of Labor and the Labors of Literature,* does highlight the personal costs of work in a broader argument that nineteenth-century literary allegory shared a special relationship with representations of labor. Studies of work, such as Weinstein's book and Bromell, *By the Sweat of the Brow,* tend to emphasize the relationship between the understanding of manual labor and authorial self-perceptions of the practice of literary labor.

48. To offer another example, Zandy, *Hands,* considers the damaging impact of work on the human body, and treats parallel categories such as worker injury, loss, and vulnerability, though the study is more interested in understanding work as the foundation of expressive cultural identity (3).

49. Hapke, *Labor's Text,* 7, 124.

50. Dimock, "Class, Gender, and a History of Metonymy," 89–94.

51. Guillory argues that the education system, in the way it determines access to literary language, produces sociolinguistic difference and thus reproduces social inequality (*Cultural Capital,* 62–63, 54).

52. See Buell, "Downwardly Mobile for Conscience's Sake," and Michaels, *The Shape of the Signifier,* 180–81.

53. For example, Felski describes a new class formation comprising a diverse array of middle classes and a so-called underclass beneath them, "defined by longterm unemployment and poverty" ("Nothing to Declare," 34). From the opposite perspective, Zweig argues that if class is defined as a labor relation then most people in the United States are in fact working class (*The Working Class Majority,* 1–3).

54. Dimock and Gilmore, *Rethinking Class,* 6, 2–3; Dimock, "Class, Gender, and a History of Metonymy," 76. See also Kaplan, "Millennial Class," 12–14. According to Dimock and Gilmore, class is interesting "less as an instance of 'reality' than as an instance of the 'made-real'" (2).

55. Compare arguments by Janowitz, "Class and Literature," 240; Foley, *Radical Representations,* x; and Felski, "Nothing to Declare," 42.

56. "[C]lass does not have the same status as race or gender in debates over equal representations in academic culture," writes Felski, "simply because that culture inescapably alters the class identities of those who inhabit it" ("Nothing to Declare," 42). See also Foley, *Radical Representations,* x; Felski "Nothing to Declare," 38; Lang, *The Syntax of Class,* 71. In his provocative discussion of race, "Autobiography of an Ex-White Man," Michaels has challenged critics who wish to compare race and class as social constructions, arguing instead that race theorists have remained committed to essentialism.

57. Trask, *Cruising Modernism,* 3, 38–39, 41, 130. Class, for Trask, is in essence a cultural-sexual identity defined by its slipperiness and impermanence. Even when Trask does turn more explicitly to materiality, as in the chapter on Hart Crane, the "material" turns out to be the working-class male body, and labor itself becomes defined by an interest in bodily pleasure.

58. See Kerbo, *Social Stratification and Inequality,* 265, for research that the social and physical environment of poor children can harm their intellectual development. Ehrenreich has

described the impoverished as dwelling "in a place that is neither free nor in any way demo-cratic" (*Nickel and Dimed,* 210), thus placing herself in a Rawlsian tradition that associates poverty with a lack of political liberty (see, for example, Rawls, *A Theory of Justice,* 246).

59. See Miliband, "Class Analysis," 343, on criticism that class-based approaches remain unable to deal with the complexities of individuals and with the cultural importance of gen-der, race, and nation.

60. Rimstead, *Remnants of Nation,* 22.

61. Griffin and Tempenis, "Class, Multiculturalism, and the *American Quarterly,*" 91–93, 84–86.

62. Kaplan, "Millennial Class," 15. Pittenger argues that this conflation even infiltrated Bo-asian anthropology, which stressed cultural and historical over biological explanations of dif-ference—a conflation in which culture could prove just as deterministic as biology ("A World of Difference," 28).

63. Dimock and Gilmore point to a shift in recent historiography toward an interest in the middle class, whereby domesticity "emerges as the vehicle as well as the tenor of class iden-tity, and gender becomes as crucial to the making of classes as economic determinations" (*Rethinking Class,* 7).

64. Rabinowitz, *Labor and Desire,* 4, 36–37, 39, 87, 9, 135. Rabinowitz does at times admit the limitations of her argument: that these women writers verge on biological essen-tialism (123), and rely on a conventional narrative of feminine desire derived from domestic ideology (135–36). Coiner, *Better Red,* is another study of the 1930s that targets radical women writers who wrote at the intersection of feminism and class consciousness. Coiner only occasionally mentions the role of poverty in the writings of Le Sueur and Tillie Olsen (196–97).

65. In *Jews Without Money,* Gold describes how poverty sickens the female body (135) and drives women insane (265). He also emphasizes the special resilience of and commu-nity among women in poverty (158, 167). In *The Disinherited,* Conroy observes at various points the destructive effects of work and hard living on the bodies of women (225, 254–55). Le Sueur's *The Girl* is undoubtedly focused on the special ways that women suffer physically and mentally within poverty, and the ways they overcome it through collective action and emotional attachment. Yet the novel emphasizes as well how poverty cripples the bodies and minds of people, irrespective of their gender (see, for example, 17, 36, 50, 78). Le Sueur makes plentiful reference to the kind of destructive bodily hunger that Rabinowitz ascribes to male proletarian writing (see *The Girl,* 35, 36, 50, 75, 78, 97, 139, 140).

66. Hitchcock soundly criticizes the abstraction and deconstruction of class that result from recent interest in representation and in the construction of meaning ("They Must Be Represented?," 21–22, 23). Ward respects the difference of poverty in her argument that re-cent novels dealing with the abjectly poor tend to resist sympathetic reading because the no-tions by which we read in the first place—notions of perspective, representation, identifica-tion—are constructed around middle-class norms that render social "subclasses" invisible ("From the Suwanee to Egypt," 76, 79).

67. Schocket, "'Discovering Some New Race,'" 47, 48, 51; Kassanoff, "Extinction, Taxi-dermy, Tableaux Vivants," 60–61.

68. See Roediger, "'More Than Two Things,'" for a good overview and an interesting de-

fense of "whiteness studies," as employed by the poet Sterling Brown to represent the "multiple identities of working people" (38).

69. Wray and Newitz, *White Trash,* 5; Lott, *Love and Theft,* 8, 67; Glickstein, "Pressures from Below," 141–42.

70. Harrington, *The Other America,* 129. Katz argues for a continuation between nineteenth- and twentieth-century ideas of poverty in *The Undeserving Poor,* 5, and "The Urban 'Underclass,'" 3, as does Valentine in *Culture and Poverty,* 45–46.

71. Katz argues that the culture of poverty thesis originated among liberals who assumed that dependent people were helpless and needed the leadership of liberal intellectuals to break out of cycles of poverty (*The Undeserving Poor,* 17).

72. See Harvey and Reed, "Paradigms of Poverty," 278. They argue thus that Lewis should not be grouped with those who blame the victim for his or her poverty (279). In "Culture and Class in the Study of Poverty," Gans also suggests that Lewis's concept is more an effect of being poor than a cause of poverty; more a defense mechanism for dealing with social alienation (215). Valentine, however, criticizes Lewis for failing to identify community structures among the poor, and for focusing on cultural patterns above physical conditions (*Culture and Poverty,* 77, 74).

73. See Kerbo, *Social Stratification and Inequality,* for Lewis's belief that the culture of poverty was limited in the United States (267). Harvey and Reed criticize William Julius Wilson for misreading Lewis by emphasizing the autonomous characters of culture traits once they come into existence ("Paradigms of Poverty," 291), but they themselves admit that in Lewis's thesis the poor *do* play a part in the reproduction of poverty (278). On Wilson see also Ranney, "Class, Race, Gender, and Poverty," 41–42.

74. Katz, *The Undeserving Poor,* 28–35. Kushnick and Jennings argue that such myths are designed to prove the deleterious consequences of programs that benefit the poor, thus justifying policies of policing and containment, while reminding the middle classes that they have nothing in common with the worst off (*A New Introduction to Poverty,* 6). See also Jennings, "Persistent Poverty in the United States," 18, 28, 29.

75. See Moeller, "The Cultural Construction of Urban Poverty," for the argument that the very idea of poverty is nothing but a cultural construction (1).

76. Turner, "Anthropology and Multiculturalism," 410–11, 413. See also Guillory, *Cultural Capital,* 13.

77. See Gans, *The War against the Poor,* 32, 40; Katz, "The Urban 'Underclass,'" 4. For Katz, discussion of the underclass returns to the oldest themes in U.S. discussions of urban poverty (3), and distracts attention from the dynamics of power and subordination (14). See also Ranney, "Class, Race, Gender, and Poverty," 43.

78. See Katz, "The Urban 'Underclass,'" 21. Katz writes that we need a complex, nuanced understanding of how people surmount as well as succumb to their environment (21). Rimstead is also aware that the partial separation of poverty from class carries several dangers (such as cutting texts off from the positive heritage of working-class tradition), yet she believes this distinction necessary to appreciate the diversity and cross-class nature of poverty narratives—the fact that they emerge from diverse social situations, and contain a range of ideological positions (*Remnants of Nation,* 25, 27).

79. See Giddens, "Structuralism, Post-Structuralism and the Production of Culture," on

links between social theory and poststructuralist thought. Official measures of poverty draw criticism for their outdated and inflexible ways of evaluating need (see Henwood, "Trash-o-nomics," 191, n. 4), yet few social analysts would deny that significant numbers of people in the United States lack sufficient material resources for a theoretically "adequate" or "normal" standard of living.

80. See Kerbo, *Social Stratification and Inequality,* 255–56, for evidence of "rather exten-sive" movement out of poverty—even if "those who do move out of poverty seldom move very far above it, with a tendency to fall back into poverty some time in their life" (256).

81. Such views conflict with Himmelfarb's belief that relativistic ideas make poverty so protean that it is deprived of form and shape (*The Idea of Poverty,* 532).

82. As Ehrenreich establishes in *Nickel and Dimed,* low-wage work does not lift people out of poverty; indeed, hard work can even deepen poverty (217, 220).

83. On this point, see Rimstead, *Remnants of Nation,* 27, and Ehrenreich, *Fear of Falling,* 49. Rimstead notes that not all the poor are working class, and that not all the working class are poor (34).

84. In *The Working Class Majority,* Zweig estimates that over half the working class knows poverty over a ten-year period (86), and he estimates the working class at about 60 percent of the population; Henwood suggests that even suburban married couples with children—the "ideal"—have a one-in-ten chance of being poor ("Trash-o-nomics," 183). Kerbo esti-mates that 25 percent of the U.S. population experiences poverty for at least one year dur-ing a ten-year period (*Social Stratification and Inequality,* 256).

85. According to recent census figures, of the 32.9 million officially poor people, 22.7 million are white (though only 15.3 million are non-Hispanic whites), 8.1 million are black, 1.3 million Asian and Pacific Islander, and 8 million Hispanic. In terms of percentages, 9.9 percent of white people are poor (7.8 percent of non-Hispanic whites), 22.7 percent of blacks, 10.2 percent of Asian and Pacific Islanders, and 21.4 percent of Hispanics (Proctor and Dalaker, *Poverty in the United States,* 2). See Zweig, *The Working Class Majority,* 87–88, for figures outlining the disproportionate spread of poverty among nonwhites, women, and children; and see Henwood, "Trash-o-nomics," 178–79, on the extent of poverty among whites.

86. For Kushnick and Jennings, the racialization of class issues in the United States be-comes a politically effective tool for the wealthy to divide and rule the lower classes because it disguises the root economic and political causes of want (*A New Introduction to Poverty,* 2, 5–6). The main point of their essay collection is that the racialization of poverty has been a central feature in the political delegitimation and pacification of poor people in the United States (6). See also Ranney, "Class, Race, Gender, and Poverty," 53; Henwood, "Trash-o-nomics," 178, 183, 185–86; and Michaels, "Diversity's False Solace."

87. What Aronowitz says of class in the contemporary era may always have been true of poverty—that it lacks "an autonomous ideological existence among U.S. workers, but lives as a hybrid with the discourse of social movements, particularly of race and gender" (*The Politics of Identity,* 68).

88. Banta, *Failure and Success in America,* 6. See Hearn, *The American Dream in the Great Depression,* for an approach to poverty in light of success.

89. Ehrenreich, *Nickel and Dimed,* 106. Ehrenreich's book is a compelling attempt to trace

the complexity of poverty, which combines social disempowerment with physical and psychological suffering, and with a change in attitudes as the poor come to internalize their own subservience.

90. Hitchcock discusses the difficulty of maintaining the viability of the aesthetic in readings of working-class culture; the Left fears the aesthetic as evidence of bourgeois contamination, while the Right patronizingly views it as anathema to working-class expression ("They Must Be Represented?," 25). Guillory points to recent attempts to discredit the concept of the aesthetic altogether, as inherently repressive—which assumes that aesthetic values are the same as social and even economic values (*Cultural Capital,* xiii).

91. Howells, *Impressions and Experiences,* 179, 186–87, 202, 206.

92. The phrase "neutralize the disinherited" is the sociologist Lee Rainwater's; see Gans, "Culture and Class in the Study of Poverty," 202. Rainwater mentions several of these strategies: accusations that the poor are immoral, pathological, biologically inferior, culturally different, or—from another perspective—heroic.

Notes to Part One

1. Crèvecoeur, *Letters from an American Farmer,* 68–69; Rothman, *The Discovery of the Asylum,* 155–56; Kusmer, *Down and Out,* 3, 13. Kusmer writes that every city was grappling with throngs of the homeless by 1857 (13). The causes of poverty are to be found in society itself, wrote Walter Channing in 1843, an opinion emerging from a cycle of economic slumps that made people from all social classes afraid of remote forces seizing their livelihood (*An Address on the Prevention of Pauperism,* 21). See also Bremner, *From the Depths,* 14; Watterson, *An Address on Pauperism,* 7; and the various writings collected in Rothman, ed., *The Jacksonians on the Poor.*

2. Hawthorne, *The House of the Seven Gables,* 25. Although Hawthorne recognizes how poverty can become an inheritance, the conclusion to *The House of the Seven Gables* overturns the absolute poverty of the Maules, as well as the genteel poverty of Hepzibah Pyncheon, by bestowing wealth in its proper places. See Lang, *The Syntax of Class,* 29–41, for a good discussion of Hawthorne's novel.

3. Gandal suggests that poverty discourse before Jacob Riis was devoted to a small number of themes, was abstract in descriptions, and was tightly constrained by traditional moral formulas (*The Virtues of the Vicious,* 38).

4. For this recent transnational reading of Melville, see Pease, "C.L.R. James, *Moby-Dick,* and the Emergence of Transnational American Studies," an essay that positions James (and implicitly Melville) as a thinker about international issues rather than those of social class.

5. Rogin pays some attention to class issues in Melville's work, focusing in particular on "Bartleby," though Rogin argues that Melville is more interested in psychology than in society, class, or ideology (*Subversive Genealogy,* 198). James is more concerned with Melville at the macropolitical level—the crisis of world civilization, the totalitarian centralization of power (*Mariners, Renegades, and Castaways,* 16, 21–22). The recent *Cambridge Companion to Herman Melville* illustrates how class analysis is at least one part of the diverse critical

interest in Melville—or at least, it further reveals close attention to questions of work, with Weinstein's essay ("Melville, Labor, and the Discourses of Reception") supplementing Bromell's reading of Melville in *By the Sweat of the Brow.*

6. Otter, *Melville's Anatomies,* 4. I draw here from Otter's statement that "'[r]ace' is a key epistemological category for Melville, as it was for his culture and continues to be for our own. . . . Melville insists that readers acknowledge 'race' not as the abstract property of others but as the grammar book of graded meanings" that define the "world of definition, coherence, and difference" (5).

7. Colatrella, *Literature and Moral Reform,* points to a dominant trend in Melville's fiction, whereby he overturns the religious, moral, and socioeconomic principles of philanthropic reformers by demonstrating how they hurt more than they help the poor (2). See also Lewis, "'Lectures or a Little Charity.'"

8. See Ryan, *The Grammar of Good Intentions,* 1, 4, 16. Ryan argues, for example, that "frequent pronouncements that American poverty was minimal" were undercut "by the realities of slavery, Indian removal and extermination, and urban race riots" (2), not *by the realities of poverty itself.*

9. Ryan offers occasional analysis of poverty beyond a racial perspective; see, for example, her excellent analysis of the complex power dynamics within charitable giving (*The Grammar of Good Intentions,* 50–57). Yet her thesis is clearly driven by a desire to see benevolence as a "raced discourse" that both constructed whiteness and registered its vulnerability (48–49, 74–76).

10. See Rothman, *The Discovery of the Asylum,* 161–62; Bremner, *From the Depths,* 18–19; Katz, *The Undeserving Poor,* 14; and Klebaner, "Poverty and Its Relief in American Thought," 382–85.

11. See Glickstein, "Pressures from Below," for a discussion of these different opinions of poverty. Glickstein quotes William Ellery Channing in particular on the positive impact of poverty on personal character and the work incentive (125, 129–30).

12. Glickstein argues that some who wrote on behalf of skilled workers also ascribed to the view "that there were, indeed, morally and culturally inferior, even contemptible, elements of the laboring population, consisting overwhelmingly of the unskilled and dependent poor, who needed to be driven" ("Pressures from Below," 139).

13. Burroughs, *A Discourse Delivered in the Chapel of the New Alms-house,* 9; Channing, "Discourse on Tuckerman," quoted in Thernstrom, "Poverty in Historical Perspective," 163; Hartley, quoted in Bremner, *From the Depths,* 5; Brace, quoted in Katz, "The Urban 'Underclass,'" 8–9. See also Rothman, *The Discovery of the Asylum,* 171, and Klebaner, "Poverty and Its Relief in American Thought," 391.

14. Channing believed that the whole character of England was derived from its national poverty (*An Address on the Prevention of Pauperism,* 48).

15. See Glickstein, "Pressures from Below," 117.

16. Despite a desire to alleviate the suffering of the poor, Mayhew explained the apparently consistent behavioral and psychological characteristics of the poor by lapsing into absolutist, racialist reasoning: beggars and outcasts formed a distinct race with innate mental and moral natures. See Himmelfarb, *The Idea of Poverty,* 366, 369, 323–25, 329.

17. Glickstein, "Pressures from Below," 117.

18. Kusmer, *Down and Out,* 32.

19. George Fitzhugh, *Cannibals All!* (1857), is the classic criticism, by a defender of slavery, of the exploitation and curtailed freedom of the northern laborer. Glickstein describes a similar criticism of "wage slavery" in the pages of the Northhampton (Massachusetts) *Democrat*—an objection to the abolitionist cause that Glickstein describes as being made on the grounds of class not race ("Pressures from Below," 130–34).

20. Douglass, *Narrative of the Life,* 11. Douglass reveals an awareness of poverty throughout the *Narrative,* especially among whites: a result, as Douglass describes it, of the slave system on nonslaveholders (110–12). Douglass also demonstrates awareness of different levels of material discomfort within slavery (37–38, 53), even if the domination of slavery inevitably transcends the perspective of poverty—the difference between lacking property and being property (47).

21. Dickens, *American Notes,* 136–37; Foster, *New York by Gas-Light,* 140–49.

22. Kusmer, *Down and Out,* 23. Glickstein points out that Joseph Tuckerman was no less alarmed by "the number of native-born dependent poor" than by those from abroad ("Pressures from Below," 119).

23. Glickstein, "Pressures from Below," 141–42.

24. Glickstein argues that Tuckerman, for example, retained his commitment to the free-labor ethic "in the face of an evolving capitalist labor market's manifest inability to provide subsistent wages for all who sought them" ("Pressures from Below," 116–17). Glickstein describes the many "'ordinary Americans,' particularly young white males of working-class and lower middle-class backgrounds" who also equated the labor market with abundant opportunity (134).

25. Rothman, *The Discovery of the Asylum,* 158–59. Watterson comments on the extent of pauperism in America, despite "a fertile country around and thriving cities and villages on every side" (*An Address on Pauperism,* 13).

26. Tuckerman, *On the Elevation of the Poor,* 56, 58; Burroughs, *A Discourse Delivered in the Chapel of the New Alms-house,* 5; Channing, *An Address on the Prevention of Pauperism,* 46, 21; Brace, *The Dangerous Classes of New York,* 26–27.

27. Ignatieff, *The Needs of Strangers,* 27. References to primary works with multiple quotations are frequently included in parentheses in the main text, with supplemental references to primary and secondary works remaining in the notes.

28. Spooner also believed that poverty made intellectual culture an impossibility, while it suppressed the free utterance of thought (*Poverty,* 54–55).

29. Bremner discusses this antebellum literature of poverty, which grew as poverty was recognized in the 1840s as a chronic condition rather than a temporary barrier (*From the Depths,* 86–93).

30. Jameson, *The Political Unconscious,* 187–89. Hapke draws attention to the U.S. dimensions of this dichotomy, already well established by the 1840s (*Labor's Text,* 27, 30–32).

31. Denning, *Mechanic Accents,* 97. Denning argues that Buntline's world consists of the elite and the lumpen (106).

32. See Buntline, *Mysteries and Miseries of New York,* 1:47, 3:28, for occasional reference to the economic system, whereby manufacturers claim that they must sell cheap, and

thus coin "gold from the life-blood of the poor." Similarly, Foster occasionally suggests that prostitution originates in a desire to escape the suffering of poverty, caused in some instances by the exploitative practices of dressmaking establishments; see *New York by Gas-Light,* 100–103, 229, 232.

33. Lang, *The Syntax of Class,* 14–29. Lewis discusses the circumvention of class criticism in sentimental fiction; see "'Lectures or a Little Charity,'" 261.

34. Morris, "About Suffering," 37. Morris is writing about the literary depiction of human pain in general.

35. Templin, "Panic Fiction," 3; Fichtelberg, *Critical Fictions,* 203, 226. Fabian has argued that many of the era's popular, economically oriented "panic texts" resorted to recurrent images and metaphors to resolve "cultural contradictions in favor of the free expansion of nineteenth-century capitalism" ("Speculation on Distress," 129).

36. See Boucicault, *The Poor of New York,* 27, 44, for this portrayal of poverty. The "value of poverty" is that it "opens the heart" (44). According to Bremner, theatrical depictions of the poor, popular between the 1830s and 1860s, tended to treat those who were suddenly and briefly reduced to poverty (*From the Depths,* 91).

37. See Cook, *From Tobacco Road to Route 66,* 3–9, for a good account of this early "poor white tradition." Harris's tales were collected after the Civil War in *Sut Lovingood's Yarns* (1867).

38. Channing, *An Address on the Prevention of Pauperism,* 45, 72. See Woodson, "Thoreau on Poverty and Magnanimity," 21, and Bremner, *From the Depths,* 16, for discussion of Emerson's approach to poverty.

39. Buell, "Downwardly Mobile for Conscience's Sake," 664.

40. Woodson, "Thoreau on Poverty and Magnanimity," 30. Poverty sometimes led Thoreau "to the highest flights of imagination," writes Woodson, "and sometimes to involuntary contempt or disgust" (33). Woodson discusses the aesthetic potential of Thoreau's poverty in some depth. Lewis also analyzes the role of poverty in *Walden,* arguing that, in the visit to John Field, the usually iconoclastic Thoreau is overcome by the moralistic and judgmental conventions of the literary "poor visit" ("'Lectures or a Little Charity,'" 265).

41. Compare Emerson, "Self-Reliance," 150, and Thoreau, *Walden,* 73, 76–78.

42. See Burroughs, *A Discourse Delivered in the Chapel of the New Alms-house,* for the widespread identification of poverty as a foreign import (72).

43. "The Pretensions of Poverty" emphasizes instead the "dull society," "unnatural stupidity / That knows no joy or sorrow," "mediocrity," and "servile minds" of the poor (80). The virtues that Thoreau celebrates are found in the bold enterprise of international commerce (118), and in his idea of the "good man" who transforms the world unconsciously with his constant superfluity of virtue (77). In a similar vein, Thoreau encounters "an inoffensive, simple minded pauper" in *Walden,* only to discover later that his apparent simplicity "was the result of a wise policy" (151). See Woodson, "Thoreau on Poverty and Magnanimity," 24, for a different reading of "The Pretensions of Poverty."

44. See Olsen, "A Biographical Interpretation," 69, 79–80; Pfaelzer, *Parlor Radical,* 26, 29, 33; Hapke, *Labor's Text,* 77–79; Schocket, "'Discovering Some New Race,'" 47, 51; Seltzer, *Bodies and Machines,* 138–45; and Dimock, "Class, Gender, and a History of Metonymy," 95–96. "What I mean to suggest," writes Lang, "is that the project of making the contingency

of class starkly visible rendered the disinterested, the 'innocent,' sentimental narrative impossible" (*The Syntax of Class,* 71).

45. In Davis's tale, the character Mitchell refers to "this lowest deep—thieves, Magdalens, Negroes" (39), and there are other moments that stress racial intermingling not separation.

46. Harris, *Rebecca Harding Davis and American Realism,* 8. Harris's is perhaps the closest reading to mine, largely because her focus is on the genre of realism rather than on the theme of gender.

47. Here I draw from Turner, "Anthropology and Multiculturalism," 411.

48. An exception to the rejection of reform in the story is Deborah, although her solution is personal and religious rather than social and political. She must undergo years of "slow, patient Christ-love" to make her impure body and soul healthy and hopeful again (63), a process that must take place in a space absolutely disconnected from the original cultural and environmental context of impoverishment, and that requires an individual who conforms to the stabilizing idea of the goodhearted, "deserving" poor.

49. This is the general direction of Gandal's *The Virtues of the Vicious* and Giamo's *On the Bowery.* Kusmer also considers that the dark side of the success myth—the very subject of many of Melville's works—was far from prominent in antebellum literature (*Down and Out,* 32).

50. Rezneck, "The Social History of an American Depression," 665; Buntline, *Mysteries and Miseries of New York,* 3:125.

51. Ryan, *The Grammar of Good Intentions,* 47–48.

52. Tuckerman also refers to the suffering and mental desperation of this brand of sudden poverty, which stems from not being accustomed to disorder, dirt, and disadvantage (*On the Elevation of the Poor,* 72).

53. John Sergeant, "Mercantile Character" (*Hunt's Merchants' Magazine,* July 1840), quoted in Sandage, "The Gaze of Success," 184. Sandage refers to the breakdown of Melville's father.

54. See Gans, *The War against the Poor,* 5.

55. See the arguments of Templin, "Panic Fiction," and Fichtelberg, *Critical Fictions.*

56. See Himmelfarb, *The Idea of Poverty,* 131; Ignatieff, *The Needs of Strangers,* 113.

57. Rather than simply opposing the progressive vision of Smith, these ideas of Melville could be seen as a reflection of the pessimistic side of Smith's thought—his belief that without government intervention and education, the division of labor would produce the mental, spiritual, and physical deterioration of the working classes. See Himmelfarb, *The Idea of Poverty,* 55–59.

58. Hapke, *Labor's Text,* 34–35. Hapke's reading allows little room for Melville's ironic distance from his narrator. Melville's novel further resists Hapke's argument that antebellum fictions failed to embrace militant class discord, in part because they adhered to the dominant myth of upward mobility (41).

59. See Carey, *Essays on the Public Charities of Philadelphia,* for the idea—common to the period—that the horrors of poverty are beyond narration (158–59).

60. "Need is a vernacular of justification," writes Ignatieff, "specifying the claims of necessity that those who lack may rightfully address to those who have" (*The Needs of Strangers,* 27).

61. See Fabian, *The Unvarnished Truth,* 39–42.

62. Himmelfarb describes Rousseau's compassion as grounded in "the feeling of common suffering that was the great social equalizer, that made the poor the equal of the rich and gave the poor a claim on the hearts of the rich" (*The Idea of Poverty,* 37). See Staten, *Nietzsche's Voice,* 80, on the opposing Nietzschean view. Hendler has discussed this ambivalence as integral to the discourse of sympathy as a whole: "Even as it produces an affective connection between individual subjects, then, sympathy threatens to negate their individuality by confusing the *analogy* it posits between subjects with a fictional and dangerous *coincidence* between them" (*Public Sentiments,* 5).

63. Thus we have Redburn's sympathy for the expressive culture of the poor, combined with the ex-sailor beggars' purported exploitation of "sympathy with suffering among members of their own calling" (187).

64. Hence Redburn's belief that over certain scenes "a vail [*sic*] must be drawn" (286), his developing conviction that the grief of the really poor is a substantively different entity, "a gnawing reality, that eats into their vital beings" (290)—his idea, in short, that we can only "proffer our sympathy" by experiencing something like the dysphoric emotion itself (279). See Kleinman et al., eds., *Social Suffering,* on the power of suffering to ruin "the collective and the intersubjective connections of experience" (x).

65. Bezanson, "Historical Note," 204. Bezanson notes that the final chapters of *Israel Potter* are very different from Trumbull's narrative (203).

66. Melville makes a similar point in *Moby-Dick:* "There is nothing like the perils of whaling to breed this free and easy sort of genial, desperado philosophy" (247).

67. See Valentine, *Culture and Poverty,* 112–13, 115–16, 119, 120, 134; Zweig, *The Working Class Majority,* 90; and Gans, "Culture and Class in the Study of Poverty," 209–10, on this progressive type of cultural perspective.

68. Potter is described as being in a dungeon (155), pent in between dingy walls (163), while the horizon is described as coiling around the whole, like a rope (156). Melville embodies his sociology in the allegory of a brickyard kiln, whose layers of bricks represent absolute social stratification (156–57). In his references to walls and bricks, Melville seems to be playing with contemporary images to describe the social state. Spooner, for example, advocated economic reforms that would prevent fortune being represented as a wheel: "It should rather be represented by an extended surface, varied somewhat by inequalities, but still exhibiting a general level" (*Poverty,* 49).

69. Melville, *Israel Potter,* 165. This marking maintains the racial composite: the poor become "all bespattered with ebon mud, ebon mud that stuck like Jews' pitch" (159).

70. In *Remnants of Nation,* Rimstead also points to various ways that poverty can lie at the core of identity (44), in self-representations by the poor (143)—often *negative* in kind (145)—and in other forms of individual and collective identity construction (168).

71. Morris, "About Suffering," 40; Kleinman et al., eds., *Social Suffering,* xiii.

72. I am paraphrasing here Kleinman et al., eds., *Social Suffering,* xiii.

73. See Bezanson, "Historical Note," 204, n. 42.

74. Himmelfarb describes in detail these aspects of Malthus's thought; see *The Idea of Poverty,* 105–106, 118, 132.

75. Himmelfarb, *The Idea of Poverty,* 63.

76. Rimstead, *Remnants of Nation,* 54. There is at heart a conspiracy theory behind Rimstead's argument—those voices that have escaped academic attention are those capable of challenging academic views of the world (54).

77. See Newman, *A Reader's Guide,* 157–58, for an overview of the critical debate on the relationship between "Cock-A-Doodle-Doo!" and Thoreau's *A Week on the Concord and Merrimac Rivers,* "Walking," and *Walden.*

78. Melville's narrator expounds a series of Thoreauvian beliefs. He takes arguments against charity to their ridiculous extreme by violently abusing a "lean, shad-bellied wretch" of a laborer who demands payment for his services (273). He advocates the belief that the poverty of the poor stems directly from their own ignorance (276). Like the impoverished Irish emigrants in *Walden,* Merrymusk lives in a shanty beside the railroad (281). At least one critic believes that Merrymusk's hut is intended as a parody of Thoreau's cabin at Walden; see Newman, *A Reader's Guide,* 157. See Fichtelberg, *Critical Fictions,* for details of this developing pessimism over the U.S. economy (20, 205–206).

79. Rowland argues that following the repeal of the English Corn Laws, American agriculture enjoyed a sudden boom in which the poor did not share; issues of economic disparity were much written of in the years 1853–54 ("Sitting Up with a Corpse," 72).

80. See *Walden,* 256, for a moment in which the harsh elements of winter actually abet Thoreau's navigation of the forest. Marvin Fisher has suggested the influence, on Melville's sketch, of a passage from Emerson's *Nature:* "property . . . has been well compared to snow,—if it fall level today, it will be blown into drifts tomorrow" (see Newman, *A Reader's Guide,* 329).

81. Douglas compares these two texts in *The Feminization of American Culture,* 300, as does Lewis in "'Lectures or a Little Charity.'" In her advocacy of virtuous poverty, writes Lewis, Sedgwick provided material for Melville by asserting that "the poor are fortunate not to be able to afford doctors (who are mostly quacks), servants (who disappoint their masters), rich food (which weakens the digestive system), and fancy clothing" (263). Newman records that *Walden* has been suggested as an influence on Melville's "Poor Man's Pudding and Rich Man's Crumbs," as have Emerson's *Nature* and transcendentalist principles in general (*A Reader's Guide,* 329, 337).

82. Rowland, "Sitting Up with a Corpse," 73; Duban, "Transatlantic Counterparts," 275.

83. See Glickstein, "Pressures from Below," 117.

84. Several critics have noted this pun: Duban, "Transatlantic Counterparts," 276; Newman, *A Reader's Guide,* 334.

85. See Smith, "Order and Disorder," 218.

86. "'[I]f ever a Rich Man speaks prosperously to me of a Poor Man, I shall set it down as—I won't mention the word'" (296). See Newman, *A Reader's Guide,* 336, for a summary of the critical debate over whether the ending of this sketch represents clear-sightedness or cop-out. There are many other silences too, such as the one that follows Dame Coulter's rejection of the pejorative label "Poor Man's Pudding" (293).

87. In his reading of *Redburn,* for example, Bromell suggests that the unspeakability of poverty in Melville stems from a recognition that the dominant social order has successfully kept the poor silent and illegible (*By the Sweat of the Brow,* 67).

88. Thoreau is outraged at the clumsy Irish ice-cutter who strips off three pairs of pants

and two pairs of stockings after falling into the pond; he sees this as an example of the Irishman's shiftlessness (*Walden,* 75). Thoreau's claim to have detected the dissimulation of a simpleminded pauper in *Walden* (151) is repeated in Melville's *The Confidence-Man,* when the Emersonian Mark Winsome refuses to aid a seemingly insane beggar: "I take him for a cunning vagabond, who picks up a vagabond living by adroitly playing the madman" (195).

89. Arguments for a parity between the American and English halves of the diptych can be found in Rowland, "Sitting Up with a Corpse," 298, and Dillingham, *Melville's Short Fiction,* 120.

90. "The human voice was banished from the spot" (328). When the narrator tests how long the paper-making process takes, by marking a piece of paper with a name and inserting it into one end of the machine, the paper eventually emerges with the name "half faded out of it" (332).

91. Dimock argues that "The Tartarus of Maids" makes female bodily ills stand metonymically for the entire oppressions and deprivations of the working class—an example of what she calls "metonymic thinking," the tendency to abstract ideas of integral social classes from the materiality of bodily subjects ("Class, Gender, and a History of Metonymy," 85–86).

92. The narrator himself begins to be affected by this blanching world: he becomes "whitish" (334) and, moreover, he begins to lose control over his own intellect and language, as he becomes "confused and stammering" (329).

93. Newman mentions critical observations of the powerlessness and bafflement of the narrators in Melville's sketches on poverty (*A Reader's Guide,* 292, 294).

94. The narrator's charitable desire to aid Bartleby is exposed as a selfish effort to "cheaply purchase a delicious self-approval" (23); he later comes to realize that a primary motive for philanthropy is "[m]ere self-interest" (36).

95. Smith summarizes opinions that welfare gives the nonpoor an "orderly" way of thinking about those who do not work, as pathological and disorderly ("Order and Disorder," 225–26, 227). In a U.S. context, the classic account of public welfare as social control is Frances Fox Piven and Richard Cloward, *Regulating the Poor* (see Kerbo, *Social Stratification and Inequality,* 282–84).

96. For example, Dryden argues that *Pierre* is "a book about reading and writing, about the consumption and production of literary texts" ("The Entangled Text," 100).

97. See Baym, *Women's Fiction,* 184–85. Foster also cited this migration from country to city as the major cause of prostitution, as women seek an alternative to destitution and homelessness; see "The Needlewomen," in *New York by Gas-Light,* 233.

98. Compare this with Otter's argument, in "The Eden of Saddle Meadows," that *Pierre* challenges the rhetoric of an idealized, democratic, picturesque American landscape.

99. "A Wordsworthian society without beggars, or such feeble old paupers as Simon Lee, would be shorn of all its poetic beauty. Herein lies the defect we discover in his democracy" (Brownson, "Wordsworth," 435).

100. See *Pierre,* 90–91, 96, 100, for Pierre's criticisms of social vanity and the treatment of the poor.

101. The germinal plot moment in the novel is also intertwined with the theme of poverty: Pierre's visit to a local charity group, which makes shirts and gowns for the parish poor, yields a begging letter from Isabel, who claims to be Pierre's half sister, and whose dim memories

of her orphan childhood center on images of public institutions for the poor and the insane (118–21).

102. See, for example, *Pierre,* 271, 307–308, for the effects of Pierre being "suddenly translated from opulence to need" (226). Ishmael hints of his descent from "an old established family" in *Moby-Dick,* which leads to an unpleasant sensation when he becomes a common sailor (6).

103. There are clearly white people within this destitute assemblage, and English speakers as well as speakers of other languages (240).

104. See Hobsbawm, "Poverty," 402, on the difficulty of accessing these aspects of poverty.

105. Bartleby also gives up reading and writing because of a type of visual impairment: "his eyes looked dull and glazed" ("Bartleby," 32). Bartleby and Pierre are described in very similar ways.

106. *The Confidence-Man* also exposes the absurdity of applying heavenly dictates, such as "sell all thou hast and give to the poor," to earthly matters (170).

107. See Melville's 1851 letters to Hawthorne for his belief that perhaps there is no secret to the universe, that truth is ridiculous and incoherent (Melville, *Correspondence,* 186, 191, 213). Channing also describes how poverty is produced by an irrational social order (*An Address on the Prevention of Pauperism,* 34).

108. "It will be observed, that neither points of the above speculations do we, in set terms, attribute to Pierre in connection with the rag pamphlet. Possibly both might be applicable; possibly neither. Certain it is, however, that at the time, in his own heart, he seemed to think that he did not fully comprehend the strange writer's conceit in all its bearings" (*Pierre,* 109–110). The narrator further states that he can derive no satisfactory conclusion from the pamphlet, it seeming merely a restatement of the problem not its solution (210).

109. Speculating on the causes of poverty later in the century, Walker also mentions the great social and industrial law: unto those who hath shall be given, from he that hath not shall be taken away even that which he hath ("The Causes of Poverty," 216).

110. Smith, "Order and Disorder," 225, 217.

111. There are various moments in which the narrator's inability to represent is directly connected to Pierre's confrontation with poverty: "Who shall tell all the thoughts and feelings of Pierre in that desolate and shivering room, when at last the idea obtruded, that the wiser and the profounder he should grow, the more and the more he lessened the chances for bread" (305).

112. For examples of this unspeakability, see *Pierre,* 111, 134, 204, 207, 208, 282, 302, 309.

113. The down-and-outs that Pierre first encounters in New York live in "*indescribable disorder*"; they are the "*vile vomitory of some unmentionable cellar*" who fill Pierre with "*inexpressible* horror" (240–41; my italics). The ineffability of these down-and-outs is exacerbated by the fact that they speak in unrepresentable words and phrases, unknown by decent people (240).

114. Fabian, "Speculation on Distress," 127, 130. Fabian explores how panic writers sought to explain the markets and correct financial ills.

115. Morris, "About Suffering," 27. The editors of *Social Suffering* note that a "major pre-

occupation in the Western tradition has to do with the incommunicability of pain, its capacity to isolate sufferers and strip them of cultural resources, especially the resource of language" (Kleinman et al., eds., *Social Suffering,* xiii). To some extent the essays in *Social Suffering* attempt to distinguish the notion of social suffering from the broader Western discourse on pain, theorized prominently in the work of Elaine Scarry.

116. For some of the many arguments that "work" resists representation, see Bromell, *By the Sweat of the Brow,* 29; Denning, *The Cultural Front,* 244; Hapke, *Labor's Text,* 9, 14; and Scarry's chapter on work in *Resisting Representation,* 49–90.

117. Guillory, *Cultural Capital,* 18. Recent academic focus on minority identity, argues Guillory, has distracted scholars from the class-bound institutional structures that restrict access to the means of literary production in the first place (18–19).

118. Ward, "From the Suwanee to Egypt," 77. Ward refers to the paradoxical status of those who attempt to voice poverty from the inside: the very ability to articulate poverty tends to de-authorize the articulating voice itself, hence the impossibility of making the impoverished world fully intelligible (86).

119. Ward also tends at times to collapse the poor and the working class too completely, in "From the Suwanee to Egypt."

120. Some sociologists suggest that "human capital" explanations of poverty—lack of education, training, language skills, and so forth—still focus on the weakness of the individual (Jennings, "Persistent Poverty in the United States," 17).

121. Morris, "About Suffering," 31.

122. The editors of *Social Suffering* similarly describe the various ways that suffering impacts narrative, "resisting language, bending it in new directions, and distorting the received ways of expressing distress and desperation" (Kleinman et al., eds., *Social Suffering,* xiv).

123. See Fichtelberg, *Critical Fictions,* especially chapter 6.

124. Echoing *Walden,* the Emersonian disciple Egbert rejects the idea that some men are victims, forced into poverty by misfortune, because such an idea is to deny the heroic strength of the soul (206).

125. The story of Charlemont also dwells on the mental imbalance that can result from the act of giving all one has to the poor (156).

126. Ignatieff, *The Needs of Strangers,* 30.

127. Echoing Dickens's description of Five Points in *American Notes,* Melville deals with poverty among free blacks in *Redburn* (201–202) and in chapter 3 of *The Confidence-Man.*

128. Patterson argues for the usefulness of this kind of cultural perspective; see *America's Struggle Against Poverty,* 124.

129. See, for example, Valentine, *Culture and Poverty,* 115–16, 119, 120, 134.

130. See Rimstead, *Remnants of Nation,* 51, 276, 53, 92. According to Rimstead, we are unused to placing poverty and nation alongside each other, which makes it difficult to see how a national literature is complicit in an internal colonization of the poor (201). By a discursive analysis, Rimstead means one that looks at poverty in terms of ideas, images, and techniques, rather than one that tries to understand the voices of the poor as "subjects of their own stories, producers of knowledge, and agents of political change" (53).

Notes to Part Two

1. Coates quoted in Salzman, ed., *Theodore Dreiser,* 52; Kaplan, *The Social Construction of American Realism,* 147; Fleissner, *Women, Compulsion, Modernity,* chapter 4.

2. Michaels, *The Gold Standard and the Logic of Naturalism,* 35, 56, 58; Bowlby, *Just Looking,* 61, 64–65; Bell, *The Problem of American Realism,* 164–65, 153–54. Kaplan dwells on the "realistic" themes of work and deprivation but even she is finally drawn into an analysis of the aesthetics of consumption in *Sister Carrie* (*The Social Construction of American Realism,* 147, 149). See also McNamara, "The Ames of The Good Society," 233, 229, and Gelfant, "What More Can Carrie Want?," 179, 192, for similar views. There are alternatives to these views. Pizer, for example, argues that Dreiser's portrait of Hurstwood is more compelling than that of Carrie (*The Novels of Theodore Dreiser,* 72).

3. Dimock, "Debasing Exchange," 783, 789–91; Yeazell, "The Conspicuous Wasting of Lily Bart," 731; Robinson, "The Traffic in Women." Ammons's argument is summarized in Hutchinson, ed., *Edith Wharton,* 50–52.

4. Fleissner, *Women, Compulsion, Modernity,* 21, 162, 197. Fleissner's overall aim is to criticize the view that naturalism is defined by a hypermasculine determinism centered on the plot of decline (6). She argues instead that the genre foregrounds a feminized compulsion that borrows from traditions of the female bildungsroman (18). For Fleissner, *Sister Carrie* is thus not focused on Hurstwood's decline into poverty (which remains secondary and is determined by the effeminate sentimentalism of his character), but on Carrie's rise, which is read as partially successful growth rather than consumerist delusion (162, 184). Turning briefly to *The House of Mirth,* Fleissner argues that Lily Bart's trajectory represents not socioeconomic decline but a feminized form of seeking for some nondomestic purpose in life (196–97).

5. In addition to Giamo, *On the Bowery,* to which we will return, Jurca, "Dreiser, Class, and the Home," pays some attention to Hurstwood's material homelessness, for example, yet she is mostly concerned with a spiritual homelessness, an emotional alienation from middle-class domesticity. Wald, "Dreiser's Sociological Vision," focuses on female sexuality more than on class relations.

6. Fisher's classic reading of *Sister Carrie,* for example, argues that Hurstwood's decline in New York is a function of "the decisive contribution of Naturalism to the small stock of curves for human action: the plot of decline" ("Acting, Reading, Fortune's Wheel," 271). For Fisher, Hurstwood's fall results from novelistic conventions that translate broad cultural patterns—the fall of fortune's wheel, the exhaustion within Darwinian views of the individual life cycle (271–72).

7. Rather than seeing "sentimental" and "realistic" codes in opposition, Kaplan, like Bell, views sentimentalism as an essential part of realist novels, a containment of contradiction that stems from their attempt to imagine and contain social change (*The Social Construction of American Realism,* 160). See also Fleissner, *Women, Compulsion, Modernity,* 21, 165, for a similar argument.

8. In "Extinction, Taxidermy, Tableaux Vivants," Kassanoff takes the handful of racial references in the novel, and reinforces these often casual references with a wealth of circumstantial evidence and contextual inference. We are left with little sense of ambiguity—racial

or otherwise—in Wharton's sophisticated text. Ammons, "Edith Wharton and the Issue of Race," is an earlier argument for "*The House of Mirth*'s investment in white purity" (81).

9. In "*Sister Carrie,* Race, and the World's Columbian Exposition," Gair argues for an unconscious racism whereby Hurstwood's immoral and irresponsible behavior makes him "black" by association with negative stereotypes of black men in the 1890s (167–69). Gair's argument is especially questionable because it posits that Hurstwood's character is not just discursively informed by blackness, but that he actually becomes physically black as the novel progresses (169); and, moreover, Gair's thesis about racial polarities forces him to argue that Carrie is offered as an (implicitly white) "ideal."

10. The physical and emotional suffering of the working class in *The Fruit of the Tree* expands into a broader concern with bodily suffering, just as the interest in poverty and industrial working conditions is one among a host of Progressive Era social questions and problems that the novel raises.

11. Frome's terrible degree of want is caused by infertile soil, accident, and the dependence of helpless and sickly women; its effects are a loss of personal "grit" and a hopelessness that traps absolutely and cripples literally.

12. See, for example, Bremner, *From the Depths,* 124–25.

13. See Bremner, *From the Depths,* 42.

14. See Trachtenberg, *The Incorporation of America,* 87–91. By the end of the 1880s, Trachtenberg estimates that "[a]bout 45 percent of the industrial laborers barely held on above the $500-per-year poverty line; about 40 percent lived below the line of tolerable existence, surviving in shabby tenements and run-down neighborhoods by dint of income eked out by working wives and children. About a fourth of those below the poverty line lived in absolute destitution" (90).

15. Kusmer, *Down and Out,* 3. By 1880 there were 2,500 street beggars in Philadelphia alone (82), writes Kusmer, and by 1900 most Americans were affected in some way by homelessness (7). Kusmer also notes that by the end of the nineteenth century the homeless world had become overwhelmingly masculine (10).

16. Moeller, "The Cultural Construction of Urban Poverty," 10.

17. Giamo summarizes the evidence for this higher standard of living during the Gilded Age, while noting the many factors of exploitation and social degradation that offset it (*On the Bowery,* 13–14).

18. See Howells, *Impressions and Experiences,* 202, 172–73, 181. Howells wrote that poverty has become everlasting from generation to generation, with the hope of cure being laughed at even by those who cling closest to these conditions (185).

19. See especially Giamo, *On the Bowery,* 38–52.

20. See Kusmer, *Down and Out,* 32, and Cawelti, *Apostles of the Self-Made Man,* 115–17.

21. Sanborn, *Moody's Lodging House,* 1–3. Sanborn claimed not to be writing essays in sociology but offering mere transcripts from life.

22. See *The Prince and the Pauper,* 12, 105–106, for these connections between class mobility and psychological disturbance. The final "solutions" offered to the problems of inequality are charity and the education of the poor—an institutional form of social welfare that leaves the class structure intact if sweetened (181).

23. Pittenger, "A World of Difference," offers an excellent account of this ambivalence in Progressive Era cross-class representation.

24. Giamo, *On the Bowery,* 54; Gandal, *The Virtues of the Vicious,* 137–38; Howells, *Impressions and Experiences,* 186.

25. Of the former case, Flynt writes that "they have been unfortunate enough to see a picture or hear a story of some famous rascal, and it has lodged in their brains, until the temptation to 'go and do likewise' has come upon them with such overwhelming force that they simply cannot resist" (48). Flynt considers this process of seduction through storytelling to be nationally unique (56).

26. Kusmer, *Down and Out,* 8, 43–44. Kusmer describes this new image of the tramp as heroic, picturesque, and humorous, embodying a latent hostility to work under the new bureaucratic-industrial regime (177), with London's *The Road* giving a hearty affirmation of a youthful life lived outside of an effete, nervous, homogenized U.S. culture (178–79).

27. Giamo, *On the Bowery,* 85. Giamo expands on but returns to the earlier arguments of Bremner when he describes Dreiser as rejecting the romanticism of writers such as Ralph, H. C. Bunner, Richard Harding Davis, and O. Henry (101, 170–72).

28. Giamo, *On the Bowery,* 88, 32. The general direction of Giamo's argument is echoed by Gandal in *The Virtues of the Vicious.* Gandal posits that the writing of Crane and Riis was radically different from what came before in its obsession with the figure of the tough, whose character was based on self-esteem, and in its aesthetic interest in the urban poor as a spectacle not to be condemned but consumed for its own sake.

29. Crane's comments were written on a copy of *Maggie;* quoted in Bremner, *From the Depths,* 105.

30. See Horwitz, "*Maggie* and the Sociological Paradigm." In *Stephen Crane and Literary Impressionism,* Nagel offers an opposing view of Crane as an impressionist not a naturalist, whose characters seem at times to be victims of their own delusions and hypocrisies.

31. See Graham, *Half Finished Heaven,* and Curtis, *A Consuming Faith,* for thorough accounts of this important reform movement.

32. "Up the Coolly" is Garland's classic story about inequality. The successful and urbane Howard returns to confront his impoverished brother, Grant, a "dead failure" whose inner wounds place him beyond financial help (*Main-Travelled Roads,* 85, 87).

33. See Bremner, *From the Depths,* for an account of this public reaction to Markham's poem (106–107).

34. Vandover, in Norris's *Vandover and the Brute,* literally becomes a brute because of his "fatal adaptability to environment" (317), his inability to resist nature's "enormous engine, resistless, relentless" (230).

35. Markham, "The Man with the Hoe." Markham's poem was inspired by Jean-François Millet's similarly titled painting, just as Garland's "Up the Coolly" seems a response to Millet's view of the rural poor (see *Main-Travelled Roads,* 80–81).

36. See Sinclair, *The Jungle,* 94, for a Melvillean description of the ways that "the kind of anguish that comes with destitution" remains beyond "the vocabulary of poets" and the realms of "good literature" (94). *The Jungle* describes poverty in terms of physical wounding (32–33, 82, 120, 138), intellectual strain and insensibility (121, 164), environmentally determined immorality (129), reckless and indifferent attitudes (249), and insanity (276–77). Ironi-

cally, the socialist conversion at the end of the novel, which seems a solution to poverty, is also marked by craziness (374).

37. In his magazine *Ev'ry Week,* Dreiser writes that newspapers report the details of sunken cheeks and heart-weary eyes merely to increase circulation, and he criticizes Townsend's novel. See Pizer, ed., *Theodore Dreiser,* 39, 48.

38. Carrie's sentimental reading of (and about) the poor, and Hurstwood's obsession with sensationalistic journalism on economic hardship, both bring equal retreat from social action in the novel. See *Sister Carrie,* 134–35, 309, 321, 453. Unless otherwise stated, I cite from the first edition of *Sister Carrie* (1900), not from the Pennsylvania edition.

39. Kusmer points out that Hunter left social work shortly after *Poverty,* which may explain why his work received little attention from his former colleagues (*Down and Out,* 92).

40. Hunter, *Poverty,* 5. Hunter's work was controversial because he put such a high estimate on the number of the poor: some 10 million people lacked clean housing, and sufficient food and clothing to keep their bodies in good working order (*Poverty,* v–vi, 7).

41. Carrie gets sick because of her lack of winter clothes, thus losing her job (53). She is described as really hungry early in the novel, when she is unemployed (18). Employment abuses include confinement (22), miserable lighting (24), uncleanliness (37), and an "absolutely nauseating" restriction of position and repetition of movement that arise from the manufacturing process itself (36).

42. See *Sister Carrie,* 56, 88, 202, 295, 366. As the narrator puts it, Carrie's narrow lot was "almost inseparable from the early stages of this, her unfolding fate" (46). For some of the moments when Carrie makes decisions in response to the fear of poverty, see 56, 88, 202, 308–309, 340, 368, 417.

43. Looking forward to the peculiar psychological condition of Carrie Meeber, Howells argues in his essay "Glimpses of Central Park" (1894) that the self-made man is deformed by his original destitution, and prosperity is inevitably blighted by the tremendous financial insecurity of American life, with everyone being reduced to a community of anxieties (*Impressions and Experiences,* 174).

44. See the various reviews in Salzman, ed., *Theodore Dreiser,* 7–8, 15, 28, 35.

45. Bremner describes Dreiser as the first writer to look at the poor in a manner free from condescending romance (*From the Depths,* 172). Kusmer considers Dreiser fundamentally sympathetic to the homeless (*Down and Out,* 158). Giamo has made perhaps the most forceful case for the centrality of Hurstwood's decline to the novel as a whole, viewing it as key to Dreiser's interest in the "antistructural consequences of descent," the absolute destruction of social being provoked by involvement with the anonymous subculture of the Bowery (*On the Bowery,* 112–13, xv, 89). See Salzman, ed., *Theodore Dreiser,* 26, and Pizer, ed., *Theodore Dreiser,* 164, for earlier opinions—including Dreiser's—that the book's big achievement is Hurstwood's fall.

46. One of the reasons why the editors of the Pennsylvania edition prefer this earlier version of Dreiser's manuscript is because it hints at Hurstwood's early weakness and essential vulnerability prior to his meeting with Carrie, which makes his eventual decay less puzzling.

47. Haller describes *The Jukes* as the most influential American work on heredity in the nineteenth century (*Eugenics,* 21).

48. Craig, "Agencies for the Prevention of Pauperism," 339.

49. Brace quoted in Haller, *Eugenics,* 33–34.

50. Haller, *Eugenics,* 6. Sanger's call for population control was aimed, in part, at reducing poverty, and was thus targeted particularly at the families of the poor. See "The Wickedness of Creating Large Families" in *Woman and the New Race* (1920), 57–71. For a detailed discussion of Sanger, see Ordover, *American Eugenics,* 137–58.

51. The consequence of these ideas was the belief that methods of sexual selection or prevention alone could determine the fate of the race. See Haller, *Eugenics,* 104. Goddard's *The Kallikak Family* (1912) blamed poverty and immorality on feeblemindedness, writes Haller (106), while later revisions of evidence concerning the Jukes family suggested they were feebleminded too, with environmental factors taken out of the equation altogether (107).

52. See Warner, *American Charities,* 26. Warner points out how many thinkers claimed a clear connection between crime, pauperism, insanity, and vice, based on a common incapacity for self-government, which allegedly made such people unfit for social life (101). See also Ely, "Pauperism in the United States," 400, and Hunter, *Poverty,* 92.

53. Flynt writes that the children who go to the road voluntarily "seem to me to belong to that class of children which the criminologist Lombroso finds morally delinquent at birth" (*Tramping with Tramps,* 61). See also Haller, *Eugenics,* 41–42, for similar beliefs that criminals and paupers both were physically and morally degenerate.

54. See Kline, *Building a Better Race,* 27, on Goddard's use of this term; see also Rafter, *Creating Born Criminals,* 73–92, for an extensive discussion of the "moral imbecile" in relation to eugenic criminology.

55. See Clark, "The Relation of Imbecility to Pauperism and Crime," 789–91. Flynt also describes the strange wanderlust that compels many young men to wander homeless—an insane impulse that can become chronic if not properly treated in its intermittent stage (*Tramping with Tramps,* 54–55).

56. According to Dugdale, the pauper was a living embodiment of death; the pauper becomes more dangerous than the criminal because the latter at least possesses the kind of energy that can be redirected into healthy channels (*The Jukes,* 47).

57. In particular McCulloch felt that charity perpetuates the misery of children who are further condemned, as a result of charity, to the hunger, want, and exposure of a begging life (*The Tribe of Ishmael,* 7). See also Brace, *The Dangerous Classes of New York,* 389–90; Riis, *How the Other Half Lives,* 199; and Hunter, *Poverty,* 68, for similar views.

58. See Haller, *Eugenics,* 46–47. The state of Indiana, for example, prevented the marriage of imbeciles, the insane, and indigents of five years' standing, according to Warner, *American Charities,* 29.

59. McKim quoted in Haller, *Eugenics,* 42.

60. Irving's literary study, *Immigrant Mothers,* is directed at the racial fear of "mongrelization" (1). Kline, *Building a Better Race,* emphasizes race and gender by highlighting how women were made responsible for racial progress, and destruction. Berg, *Mothering the Race,* makes a similar point, even if it highlights how black writers tapped into this eugenics discourse too. Berg pays attention to class issues in Edith Summers Kelley's novel *Weeds* (1923), yet maternity is clearly a more important category than poverty (89). In *American Eugenics,* Ordover focuses mostly on immigration and homosexuality—hence again on race and sexuality. When she does call for attention to class, it is mostly viewed as a re-encoding

of racial logic (xxvi). See Doyle, "The Long Arm of Eugenics," for an overview of this recent scholarship.

61. See Rafter, ed., *White Trash,* 2–3, 12, for a discussion of this biologizing of social class. Rafter speculates that eugenics became popular as a means of professional advancement for the lower middle class, who emphasized the degeneracy of the rural poor to sanction their own social entitlement.

62. Writing in *The Century* in 1897, Walker admitted that the causes of poverty were complex, beyond any simple and single solution, yet he was sure of at least one thing: pauperism was not caused by conditions of poverty but by the base, cowardly, morally weak character of the unmanly dependant ("The Causes of Poverty," 216, 210–11). See also Haller, *Eugenics,* 35.

63. Ely may have gone too far in arguing that all specialists in sociology felt that the "morally incurable" should be removed permanently from the gene pool ("Pauperism in the United States," 407). Warner's *American Charities,* for example, recorded the clash between advocates of hereditary influences and those who absolutely denied that there was any proof of the transmission of acquired characteristics, with only environment and training having the power to affect individuals (21).

64. According to Horwitz, professional sociologists sought to institute individual agency through consciousness, thus helping the poor to transcend their controlling environment; see "*Maggie* and the Sociological Paradigm," 609–10.

65. See Warner, *American Charities,* 147, 191, 458, 465. While admitting that socioeconomic factors may push individuals below the line of self-dependence, Warner is really interested in questions of health, character, and capacity, and in the incapacity and degeneration of the individual (115).

66. Warner, *American Charities,* 150, 458. Ely follows Dugdale in offering a largely hopeful vision of eliminating abject poverty through the control of powerful environmental factors, but once again his plans for reform collide with an intractable, immoral pauper class into which individuals are born ("Pauperism in the United States," 400–402). Though Riis reduced many poverty problems to questions of race and foreignness, the pauper provided an indigenously white example of poverty, harder to deal with than the criminal because there is no "bottom to the man" (192). Flynt makes a similar distinction in *Tramping with Tramps,* 12, 5.

67. See Brace, *The Dangerous Classes of New York,* 47, and Dugdale, *The Jukes,* 55, 57–58, 61–62, 65, 66, for this environmental and educational hope.

68. One 1894 *North American Review* article argued that, because tramps lived a miserable, vicious, and wicked life, they deserved to be "severely punished, and by force exterminated—that is to say converted into working members of the community by being set to some employment more or less profitable"; quoted in Kusmer, *Down and Out,* 79.

69. See Haller, *Eugenics,* 23–24, and Pittenger, "A World of Difference," 39, on this ironic and frequently paradoxical shift between hereditary and environmental reasoning.

70. Compare Hurstwood's devious stratagems (he announces himself penniless, for example, when he still has ten dollars in hand) with Howells's candid account of the era's dominant assumptions about beggars in his sketch "Tribulations of a Cheerful Giver" (1895), collected in *Impressions and Experiences,* 111–39.

71. Hurstwood's physical degeneration is described in the language of colorlessness and shapelessness often reserved for the extremely poor: his constitution was in "no shape" to endure hard work (423), his face becomes pale, his hands white, and his body flabby (424). This erosion of physical features is matched by the deterioration of Hurstwood's own ability to see and to read (449).

72. See *Sister Carrie,* 70, 115. Carrie's face is the obvious example of inherited features determining economic plight (443).

73. For references to Hurstwood's need for comfort, see *Sister Carrie,* 43, 235; for his desire for the pleasure of the moment, see 140, 240.

74. I draw this definition of *katastates* (as well as *gemmules*) from the *Oxford English Dictionary.* Dreiser may have taken this term from the eccentric scientist Elmer Gates, who helped to feed Dreiser's interest in thought as a physiological, chemical process; see Moers, *Two Dreisers,* 159–69.

75. We discover this effect throughout the novel; see *Sister Carrie,* 306, 307, 393.

76. In *Women, Compulsion, Modernity,* Fleissner reads the trope of drift in *Sister Carrie* as a force that describes Carrie's nonlinear movement in the novel—a feminized reading of drift that is strangely out of synch with Dreiser's typical understanding of drift as an explicitly masculine force of social powerlessness.

77. See Dreiser, *Newspaper Days,* 620.

78. At least this is the time frame according to Dreiser in his foreword to *The Color of a Great City* (ix).

79. For similar statements on "the inadequate," see *The Color of a Great City,* 1, 3, 202–203.

80. Moers pays detailed attention to Dreiser's "Curious Shifts of the Poor," and to its germative influence on *Sister Carrie,* but suggests that Dreiser was not interested in the causes of poverty but in its visual spectacle (*Two Dreisers,* 60). She also mentions that Dreiser began writing *Sister Carrie* in the Fall of 1899 (57).

81. Dreiser's "The Men in the Storm" (from *The Color of a Great City*) is, more or less, "The Way of the Beaten" from *Sister Carrie,* which is the third section of "Curious Shifts of the Poor"; the ending is different in *Sister Carrie,* for this is where Hurstwood goes to take his life.

82. "For the benefit of those who have not seen it I will describe it again," writes Dreiser in "The Bread-Line," just before he gives us the scene as it appeared in *Sister Carrie,* "though the task is a wearisome one" (129).

83. These echoes are so strong that Dreiser was either plagiarizing Crane or signaling to readers his conscious rewriting of Crane's work. The closest parallel is Dreiser's echo of Crane's line, "the suggestion of hot dinners . . . was upon every hurrying face" ("The Men in the Storm," 92).

84. See "Selected Emendations in the Copy-Text" in the Pennsylvania edition of *Sister Carrie,* 635.

85. Writes Bell in *The Problem of American Realism:* "It is as if Hurstwood were somehow with *us,* regarding himself, and as if in regarding Hurstwood we were also regarding ourselves," what we would be feeling (163).

86. *The Fruit of the Tree* begins with John Amherst suggesting to the nurse Justine Brent that the family of Dillon, a worker whose right arm has been maimed by an industrial accident, would be better off if the injured man were given an overdose of morphine. Ironically,

though, toward the end of the novel the Dillons are in relatively good shape, in part because of the social reforms introduced by Amherst, whereas Amherst's first wife is "mercifully" killed by Brent after suffering a spinal injury from a riding accident.

87. Bruère, "The Perpetual Poor," 940–41.

88. See Dugdale, *The Jukes,* 38. See especially Dreiser's eugenic hints in "The Defects of Organized Charity" (1909), collected in Pizer, ed., *Theodore Dreiser,* 168–70.

89. Kusmer, *Down and Out,* 120. The homeless population remained overwhelmingly white during the industrial era, argues Kusmer (113). By 1893–94, white-collar workers became more noticeable (118), and an occasional lawyer or teacher was not unknown by the turn of the century (119).

90. See Moeller, "The Cultural Construction of Urban Poverty," 10, on these trends. Kusmer also notes that homelessness remained fairly high even during prosperous years in the last three decades of the nineteenth century (*Down and Out,* 100).

91. There was, however, a brief resurgence of hostile commentary around 1894–95, argues Kusmer in *Down and Out,* 173.

92. See *Sister Carrie,* 370. Dreiser is drawn instead to the power of a few wealthy capitalists to control the economy (a point Dreiser often returns to in his early journalism), and to the inherent powerlessness of those at the other extreme, who are forced into poverty by nothing but their personal inadequacy.

93. The captain, for example, is Christian in a vague and individualistic sense, though he is a long way from the real-life Salvation Army figure on which the character may have been based.

94. See *The Color of a Great City,* 172, 78, for these observations from Dreiser's sketches "The Beauty of Life" and "On Being Poor."

95. See *The Color of a Great City,* 78–79, 34–35.

96. Pittenger, "A World of Difference," 39, 32, 47. See also Moeller, "The Cultural Construction of Urban Poverty," 2, 12. Rafter makes this point about eugenic family studies in her introduction to *White Trash* (16).

97. See Ehrenreich, *Fear of Falling,* on this insecurity and anxiety built into the knowledge-based nature of middle-class "capital" (15). Howells mentions the psychological trauma of the once-poor in *Impressions and Experiences* (173).

98. See Giamo, *On the Bowery,* 32. In her introduction to *White Trash,* Rafter describes the genre of eugenic family studies as inherently melodramatic. My reading differs from Pizer's view that Dreiser's inclusion of Daly's play was essentially ironic (*The Novels of Theodore Dreiser,* 41).

99. In his reading of the novel, Fisher brilliantly points to a series of close parallels between the final movements of Carrie and Hurstwood, which thus locates "in two persons the prospective and retrospective phases of one life" ("Acting, Reading, Fortune's Wheel," 275). Early in the novel, Dreiser's narrator paraphrases Carrie's thoughts in a way that uncannily predicts Hurstwood's last words: "It was no use" (63).

100. Hunter does suggest that, in a decline into pauperism, the woman almost always comes first to ask aid; men resist dependence most strongly (71–72). Hunter also makes reference to the inebriate women who "may be bringing children into the world who will be debilitated, alcoholic, idiots, and imbeciles, as a result of their heritage" (92).

101. I draw here from Kusmer, *Down and Out,* 10, 110.

102. Brodhead, *Cultures of Letters,* 95–96.

103. See Kusmer, *Down and Out,* 110; Abramovitz, *Regulating the Lives of Women,* 2, 147; and Stansell, *City of Women,* 12, 18, 74.

104. Campbell studies the working poor as an interested outsider; Richardson tells her own story of falling on hard times and being forced to work or starve; and the genteel Van Vorsts attempt total class transit by disguising themselves as workers and living among the needy.

105. Pittenger also draws attention to these female class crossers like the Van Vorsts, and to their ambivalent view of the poor, though he is more concerned with the intersection of race and class than with gender itself; see "A World of Difference." Henry James's *The Bostonians* offers another fictional example of this trend. Olive Chancellor desires to know impoverished girls (31), and likes to think that Verena Tarrant had known the extremity of poverty in youth; she finds a ferocious joy in reflecting that Verena had come near "to literally going without food" (105).

106. See Stansell, *City of Women,* xii, 74–75, 219, and Abramovitz, *Regulating the Lives of Women,* 147. According to these historians, charitable ladies could only accept and help poor women to the extent that the latter conformed to a middle-class, domestic ideal of virtuous womanhood.

107. Catty's dumbness is matched in the works of Richardson and the Van Vorsts by a series of figures whose deformed voices suggest the wider incommunicability of the poor. See Richardson, *The Long Day,* 26, 53, and the Van Vorsts, *The Woman Who Toils,* 141, 211.

108. Lang, "The Syntax of Class," 274, also now in Lang's book, *The Syntax of Class.* Lang argues that Phelps's novel both demonstrates an attempt to find in gender an answer to class inequality, and illustrates the partial breakdown of this effort to move out of class altogether, thus going some way, at least, toward exposing the class origins of gender formations (*The Syntax of Class,* 87–98).

109. See Stansell, *City of Women,* 220, for a discussion of how the Progressive Era effort to domesticate the plebeian household was linked to the eradication of working-class culture.

110. See Campbell, *Prisoners of Poverty,* 43, 46, 136, and the Van Vorsts, *The Woman Who Toils,* 35, 50, 54, 120, 159, 160, 244. The Van Vorsts view female poverty as the natural result of a desire for gender equality (55, 113).

111. The Van Vorsts return repeatedly to the lack of abstraction, imagination, aesthetic sense, and thought among the working poor (*The Woman Who Toils,* 38–39, 264, 268, 273–74).

112. Richardson views women as innately unfit for labor, and female poverty as a particularly physical form of crippling; see *The Long Day,* 27–30, 138, 177, 212, 277, 282.

113. In *Twenty Years at Hull-House,* Addams ascribes her feelings of paralysis, utter futility, and hopeless pessimism to her female status (51–53). She returns to the belief that the hunger seen in the poor matches the malnourishment of her own cultural background (240, 80), while the damaged consciousness of the female laborer reflects the paralyzed self of her cultivated observer (171).

114. Like Howells before her, an encounter with Tolstoy makes Addams realize the es-

sential psychological difference between voluntary poverty and what the poor call "poverty itself" (107). This is a key moment in *Twenty Years at Hull-House* because it pushes Addams back into her social class, making her appreciate the impossibility of class transit and the necessity of cultivation to bring coherent thought to the poor (32–33, 244, 248–49, 279).

115. See Gilman, *Women and Economics,* 89, and Veblen, *The Theory of the Leisure Class,* 182, on this view of marriage. See Stansell, *City of Women,* xii, 74–75, 219, and Abramovitz, *Regulating the Lives of Women,* 147, for the bourgeois ideology at the heart of philanthropic sympathy for poor women.

116. See Henry James's notebook entry for November 26, 1892, quoted in Ziff, *The American 1890s,* 275.

117. This tradition has been thoroughly explored most recently by Lang—a tradition in which problems of poverty are cured by a natural, harmonious, and implicitly middle-class femininity; see the first chapter of *The Syntax of Class.*

118. Wharton, letter to William Crary Brownell, June 25, 1904, quoted in Ammons, ed., *The House of Mirth,* 259.

119. The view that Wharton's use of poverty is sentimental and simplistic is Hutchinson's (*Edith Wharton,* 73). For an earlier but undeveloped observation of the importance of poverty in Wharton's novel, see Tintner, "Two Novels of 'the Relatively Poor.'"

120. It remains unclear whether Wharton knew, or knew of, Hunter, though it is difficult to imagine that she was unaware of the sociological questions of poverty addressed in Hunter's work, especially given her strong interest in social problems. In 1903 Hunter married Caroline Margaretha Phelps Stokes, daughter of the New York civic leader Anson Phelps Stokes.

121. Wharton again follows Hunter in this regard; see *Poverty,* 69. Craig also compared the pauper with the idle rich ("Agencies for the Prevention of Pauperism," 340–41). Kusmer suggests that the "idle rich" were often equated with tramps (*Down and Out,* 176).

122. For Hunter's frequent use of the term *abyss,* see *Poverty,* v, 131, 327. The image of the abyss to describe extreme poverty dates back at least to the early nineteenth century, but was gaining prominence at the beginning of the twentieth: Jack London titled his 1903 study of poverty in London, for example, *The People of the Abyss.* Pittenger suggests that abyss imagery reflected belief in downward evolutionary forces ("A World of Difference," 52). See also Riis, *How the Other Half Lives,* 192, for the allegedly bottomless character of the pauper.

123. For some of the many references to Lily's poverty, see *The House of Mirth,* 7, 10, 15, 38, 39, 192, 236, 270, 318.

124. When a stock-market crash hits Lily's wealthy friends, for example, their financial problems are referred to within quotation marks—it was the season "in which everybody 'felt poor'" (120).

125. This argument is especially pronounced among critics such as Ammons and Yeazell who see Veblen's ideas as central to Wharton's novel.

126. Most recently, Fleissner has noted this oscillation, which she reads as a function of Lily's indecisiveness and a grappling with sentimental knowledge, not primarily an outcome of her material situation (*Women, Compulsion, Modernity,* 197–98).

127. These definitions are all according to the *Oxford English Dictionary.*

128. Lily enters a "slough" (168), a miry pit of depression, and Selden sees her "on the

edge of something . . . poised on the brink of a chasm" (192). See Sinclair, *The Jungle,* 86, 140, 265, for this abyss imagery.

129. For some of the many references to the edges, surfaces, and lines of Lily's life, see *The House of Mirth,* 25, 135, 191–92, 265. Poverty clearly creates "lines" of worry (40), while Lily's fear of misfortune is expressed by an anxiety that the surface of life will crack (203). There are numerous references to the void and limbo that exist just beneath, or outside, Lily's circle of life (150, 261, 274), and Lily is also described as vulnerable to overwhelming, sealike tides (53, 301). To give one example of how this subtle imagery works: when Lily contemplates returning the letters to Bertha Dorset—in effect forcing Bertha into social obligations—her thought "lit up abysses from which she shrank back ashamed" (105), abysses that suggest how Lily's action would in effect lead to a dependence on *unearned* income.

130. See *The House of Mirth,* 295, 302, 307, 320–21 for this loss of Lily's time sense.

131. Charity finally marries her adoptive father, who had rescued her as a child from the "poverty and misfortune" (169) of life in an impoverished community known as the Mountain; she settles for a culturally starved, oppressive, and sexually victimizing small-town life—a "destitution" that is inconsequential compared to the "savage misery of the Mountain farmers" (170).

132. In "The Daughter's Dilemma," Sullivan mentions the sense of a psychic void (467) and an inner emptiness of self (479) in *The House of Mirth,* which she also links to language breakdown (467)—although she relates these ideas to hysteria, from which she describes Lily as suffering.

133. See, for example, Kassanoff, "Extinction, Taxidermy, Tableaux Vivants"; Irving, *Immigrant Mothers,* 39–40; and Ammons, "Edith Wharton and the Issue of Race." In *Edith Wharton's Brave New Politics,* Bauer offers an interesting reading of Wharton's rejection of eugenic ideas, at least in later novels such as *Summer* (29). See Berg, *Mothering the Race,* 75–77, for a counterargument to Bauer.

134. See Robinson, "The Traffic in Women," 355, for the former opinion, and Restuccia, "The Name of the Lily," for the latter (416). In "The Daughter's Dilemma," Sullivan refers to interpretations, by Patricia Meyer Spacks and Cynthia Griffin Wolff, of the sentimental and regressive nature of Lily's deathbed fantasy of holding Nettie's child (472). See Hutchinson, ed., *Edith Wharton,* 62–64, for some notable exceptions to this line of argument, by Elaine Showalter and Donald Pizer.

135. See Stansell, *City of Women,* 36, 110, for discussion of this sentimental image of poverty. Wharton hints that Nettie's earlier "sickness" may have been a pregnancy, and her trip to the "sanatorium" an abortion.

136. Pizer's argument is summarized in Hutchinson, ed., *Edith Wharton,* 63–64. Pizer also suggests that the difference between Nettie and Lily is relative not absolute. See Irving, *Immigrant Mothers,* on Nettie as nativist fantasy (39).

137. Dimock, "Debasing Exchange," 790.

138. In *Summer,* when Charity Royall visits the Mountain community in which she was born, she comes to agree with her adoptive father's assessment that its poverty emerges from immorality rather than from economic forces (46); the Mountain people "seemed to be herded together in a sort of passive promiscuity in which their common misery was the strongest link," she thinks (170). The reformer Amherst in *The Fruit of the Tree* refers to the ugly and hopeless workers' colony as "sunk into blank acceptance of its isolation" (22).

139. Ignatieff, *The Needs of Strangers,* 14. Ignatieff makes this crucial distinction between "[w]hat we need in order to survive, and what we need in order to flourish" (10).

140. Peiss, *Cheap Amusements,* 52. See also Abramovitz, *Regulating the Lives of Women,* 107, 127, 147.

141. Lily's second encounter with Mrs. Haffen, for example, is clearly typed as a meeting between rich and poor (102–106). But beneath these class differences we glimpse strong parallels between the two women, verging on the suggestion of a shared psychology. Kaplan also refers to the power of the urban poor over the rich, and to the emphasis on the proximity between social classes in Wharton's novel (*The Social Construction of American Realism,* 90, 100).

142. This is true of Lily's malleable self (36, 53) and her attempt to harmonize perfectly with her surroundings (151, 192). See Papke, *Verging on the Abyss,* 6–7, and Restuccia, "The Name of the Lily," for discussions of Wharton's use of abyss imagery.

143. Selden's parents also offer some sort of ideal relationship, although this alternative is not really explored by Wharton. Like the Struthers, the Seldens live in a state of relative poverty—albeit within a different social class—which they can survive through an appreciation of high culture (151–52).

144. Buell, "Downwardly Mobile for Conscience's Sake," 662; Fleissner, *Women, Compulsion, Modernity,* 197.

145. These critics' difficulties are both cited in Hutchinson, ed., *Edith Wharton,* 29, 70.

146. Gilman, *Women and Economics,* 170; Wharton to Thayer, November 11, 1905, quoted in Ammons, ed., *The House of Mirth,* 261–62.

147. In this sense, *The House of Mirth* concurs strangely with Denning's analysis of the demise of domestic novels in the late 1860s, as part of a collapse of middle-class hegemony over women's culture, resulting from the new visibility of working women in that culture (*Mechanic Accents,* 186–200).

148. Like Lily, these toilers are "awed only by success—by the gross, tangible image of material achievement"; that Lily is a fallen star merely erases her importance (286). In effect, Lily becomes victim to her deepest-held beliefs, even feeling inferior to these girls owing to her inability to overcome a lack of early training in any trade (285).

149. Richardson enters a trance in which her memory and self-consciousness collapse, a "merciful subconscious condition of apathy, in which my soul as well as my body had taken refuge when torture grew unbearable" (*The Long Day,* 248).

150. Kaplan argues that Wharton adopted the role of professional author to distinguish herself from devalued, domestic, sentimental novelists, and from ladies of leisure and impotent genteel dilettantes, without then being reduced to the level of the common worker (*The Social Construction of American Realism,* 67–68, 71).

151. See for example the Van Vorsts, *The Woman Who Toils,* 56, 162.

152. Elaine Showalter's view that Lily is "a genuinely awakened woman, who fully recognizes her own position in the community of women workers" (cited in Hutchinson, ed., *Edith Wharton,* 62) does not quite ring true with the events of the novel. Even the fullest attempt to read *The House of Mirth* as a radically feminist text concludes that Wharton is inevitably trapped by male law (Restuccia, "The Name of the Lily," 417–18).

153. For such opinions, see Dimock, "Debasing Exchange," 790; Shulman, "Divided Selves and the Market Society," 14; and Yeazell, "The Conspicuous Wasting of Lily Bart,"

731. Wharton's reluctance to suggest answers contrasts with the tradition of female philan-thropy, which tended to call for radical social change but offered inadequately formulated ideas about how this might be achieved. See, for example, Campbell, *Prisoners of Poverty,* 255; the Van Vorsts, *The Woman Who Toils,* 303; and Richardson, *The Long Day,* 303.

154. In *Edith Wharton's Brave New Politics,* Bauer associates a self-conscious attention to the politics of culture with the second half of Wharton's career, following World War I (xi). Bauer also highlights a cross-class sensibility in Wharton (100).

155. Katha Pollitt comments on the tendency for difference feminism to look "everywhere for its explanatory force—biology, psychology, sociology, cultural identity—*except* econom-ics. The difference feminists cannot say that the differences between men and women are the result of their relative economic positions because to say that would be to move the whole discussion out of the realm of psychology and feel-good cultural pride and into the realm of a tough political struggle over the distribution of resources and justice and money" (quoted in Turner, "Anthropology and Multiculturalism," 410).

156. I draw the term "class essentialism" from Dimock and Gilmore, eds., *Rethinking Class,* 6.

Notes to Part Three

1. Pells, *Radical Visions and American Dreams,* 111, 97. Terkel's work in oral history con-curs: the Depression led to widespread bewilderment and to a private kind of shame as per-sonal guilt took over from the vague sense that outside forces were responsible for failure (*Hard Times,* 5–6).

2. According to the *Oxford English Dictionary, depression* became a specifically psychi-atric term in the early decades of the twentieth century. *Depression* was in use by the late nineteenth century to describe economic downturns, though the choice of *depression* (orig-inally intended as a euphemism) over more social terms like *panic* became particularly preva-lent in the 1930s.

3. Anderson, *Puzzled America,* 157–66. Anderson ends his chapter, "Please Let Me Ex-plain," with an anecdote about a hitchhiker who looks forward to a law being passed that would execute the poor and unemployed, and who feels that he might as well be "put out of the way" because he does not believe he will ever succeed. Anderson suspects that this is "about the average American point of view" (165–66). See Pells, *Radical Visions and Amer-ican Dreams,* 198, and Peeler, *Hope among Us Yet,* 45, 40–41, on this observed warping of the nation's psyche.

4. Kusmer, for example, points to the newfound assistance offered to the homeless dur-ing these years, which suggests a recognition that the causes of poverty lay outside the realms of personal fault (*Down and Out,* 201).

5. See Pells, *Radical Visions and American Dreams,* 100.

6. Coleman quoted in Stott, *Documentary Expression,* 276; Algren, preface to *Somebody in Boots,* 6.

7. Frederick Lewis Allen quoted in Pells, *Radical Visions and American Dreams,* 196–97. Stott records a range of observations, from magazine articles and personal reminiscences,

about the Depression being difficult to see because it consists of things *not* happening—an "invisibility" increased by official attempts to minimize the extent of the Depression by presenting inadequate facts about unemployment and hunger (*Documentary Expression,* 67–69, 71).

8. Stott, *Documentary Expression,* 73.

9. Wright's *Uncle Tom's Children* tends to generate sympathetic energies by contrasting the achievements and humanity of African Americans with the violent and abusive conditions of racism in which they are forced to live. The story "Long Black Song," for example, describes how the hopes and achievements of blacks are destroyed by power imbalance and hatred between the races.

10. Trilling, review of *Black Boy,* 28.

11. See Pells, *Radical Visions and American Dreams,* 246, 195. Pells argues that, of all writers, only Agee was able to fuse the demands of radicalism with the concerns of art into a unified statement of the decade's social, cultural, and moral ideals. For Susman, *Praise* is the great classic of the 1930s (*Culture as History,* 182). See also Stott, *Documentary Expression,* 144, and Orvell, *The Real Thing,* 272–86.

12. Agee has a culminating role for scholars such as Stott and Pells.

13. Pells, *Radical Visions and American Dreams,* 246, 248. Susman reads *Praise* as a work of passion, of commitment, of belief in the meaningfulness of the lives of such poor people—a work that achieves moral intensity without preaching (*Culture as History,* 182). For the insistence that Agee treats his tenant subjects with dignity, respect, and sensitivity, see Browder, *Rousing the Nation,* 8; Peeler, *Hope among Us Yet,* 52; Kramer, "The Consciousness of Technique," 116; Stott, *Documentary Expression,* 262; Staub, *Voices of Persuasion,* 21; and Cook, *From Tobacco Road to Route 66,* xii, 155. From the perspective of current literary theory, Reed, "Unimagined Existence," diverges little from established claims about Agee.

14. Agnew, for example, compares Agee to Clifford Geertz: both use the interpretation of the Other to question the ethnocentric apparatus customarily applied to pastoral subjects ("History and Anthropology," 34). Stott argues that *Praise* forces the reader's awareness by violating the canons of documentary (*Documentary Expression,* 265, x), as does Staub (*Voices of Persuasion,* 52–53). The outcome of Agee's methodological iconoclasm is, for most critics, a higher form of realism (Kramer); a new manner of listening to the silenced (Staub); a mystical revelation of the more complicated and less palatable truths of human existence (Cook). For Browder, as for Orvell, Agee's formal experimentation exemplifies a politically committed form of avant-garde modernism that arose in the 1930s (Browder, *Rousing the Nation,* 8, 20). Reed goes even further by reading *Praise* as a form of "postmodernist realism" that achieves a balance between aesthetic sophistication and political commitment ("Unimagined Existence," 156–57, 174).

15. Rabinowitz describes *Praise* in the end as a self-conflicted book, a paradigmatic instance of the wider problems intellectuals face when they search out and describe social Others ("Voyeurism and Class Consciousness," 166, 155–56, 150, 146). For other less positive views of Agee's representation of the tenants, see Cosgrove, "Snapshots of the Absolute," 330, 334–36, 341–42, Hoopes, "Modernist Criticism and Transcendental Literature," 464–65; and Rubin, "Trouble on the Land," 102.

16. Thaddeus gives a good account of the textual history of Wright's autobiography, in "The Metamorphosis of *Black Boy.*"

17. The book jacket had already been designed with this title before Wright changed it to *Black Boy;* see "Note on the Text" in Wright, *Black Boy,* 408. "*American Hunger*" is now included in parentheses following the primary title of the authoritative Library of America edition.

18. For Stepto's influential reading of *Black Boy,* which features in his study of African American narrative, *From Behind the Veil,* see "Literacy and Ascent." JanMohamed's article is concerned with the 1945 edition of *Black Boy.* There are some notable exceptions to this racial reading of *Black Boy,* which stress broader social and cultural concerns. See for example Cappetti, "Sociology of an Existence," and Leibowitz, "'Arise, Ye Pris'ners of Starvation.'"

19. JanMohamed, "Negating the Negation," 296, 287. *The Austinite* review is reprinted in Reilly, ed., *Richard Wright,* 145–46.

20. This conclusion added to the 1945 edition of *Black Boy* is reprinted in the notes to the Library of America edition (412–15).

21. This debate over Wright's truthfulness begins with DuBois's review, "Richard Wright Looks Back," which sees *Black Boy* as a "fictionalized biography," for the most part terribly overdrawn and unconvincing (132–33). Wright's major biographer argues that Wright exaggerated his delinquency to emphasize the harm of racial and economic oppression (Fabre, *The Unfinished Quest,* 13). See also Adams, "'I Do Believe Him Though I Know He Lies,'" for a similar argument.

22. Coleman, quoted in Stott, *Documentary Expression,* 276.

23. See Rubin, "Trouble on the Land," 97–98, on this lack of socioeconomic consciousness in southern literature during the Depression.

24. For this imagery of essentialized whiteness in *As I Lay Dying,* see especially Darl's description of Vardaman: "his mouth full and open and all color draining from his face into his mouth, as though he has by some means fleshed his own teeth in himself, sucking" (49). The Bundrens seem virtually a race apart in their interactions with shop workers toward the end of the book (199, 242).

25. See *As I Lay Dying,* 110–11, for a moment when Anse's class consciousness shades off into his desire for new teeth.

26. The merger of the human and the animal world ("My mother is a fish") and the merger of the human and the object world (the "animal magnetism" of Addie Bundren's volitional coffin) seem related to the social powerlessness of the characters, who cannot control objects, animal desires, or income. See *As I Lay Dying,* 83, 84.

27. Cook sees Faulkner as operating within the southern poor-white tradition—he is interested in its history, folklore, mythology, humor, and horror—yet he refuses to reduce poor individuals to the sum of their socioeconomic circumstances, and allows individuals an emotional and moral range that disrupts stereotype, sentimentality, and absolute class differences (*From Tobacco Road to Route 66,* 39–45).

28. See especially the description of Captain John's desertion of his sharecroppers, whom he believes would be impossible to educate in economical methods. "Co-operative and corporate farming would have saved them all," writes the narrator (63). For the operation of loan companies, see *Tobacco Road,* 16, 114–16.

29. See Cook, *From Tobacco Road to Route 66,* 65, 69, for a similar view of Caldwell.

30. For the whitening effect of McVey's marriage to Clara Butterworth, see *Poor White,* 322–25. *Poor White* is a complex novel; though McVey's social course is upward, the book is full of ambiguous moments that compromise, in part, the idea that he can "change the fact that he was at bottom poor white trash" (260), and the idea that his success is in fact personally deserved. At the end of the novel, McVey has contracted the disease of thinking; ironically, though, it brings him to doubt whether the industrialism he helps create is really progress (369).

31. Cook reads *The Grapes of Wrath* as a radical retreat from social documentary and precise political solutions through its vague philosophical resolutions and its romanticization of the poor. See *From Tobacco Road to Route 66,* 160–61, 170–71, 174.

32. Szalay, *New Deal Modernism,* 171, 176. For other descriptions of this hunger, see *The Grapes of Wrath,* 266, 315–16, 324, 386, 477. See Denning, *The Cultural Front,* 262–65, for a summary of this argument about Steinbeck's inherent conservatism.

33. Smith, *Visions of Belonging,* 74.

34. Foley, *Radical Representations,* 117. See also Pells, *Radical Visions and American Dreams,* 173, 177.

35. Gold, *Jews Without Money,* 71. In *Left Letters,* Bloom describes Gold's novel as a classic of proletarian literature (16).

36. See Pells, *Radical Visions and American Dreams,* 204–205, for an account of the individualist beliefs that lie behind the proletarian façade in novels like Cantwell's.

37. Freeman, "Introduction," 12. See also Hicks, *The Great Tradition,* 202, for this mistrust of the emotional. Smith criticized the liberal disposition to talk about social and cultural phenomena in moral and psychological terms (*Forces in American Criticism,* 316).

38. Morgan, *Rethinking Social Realism,* 244, 258, 293, 300.

39. For example Jones, the victimizing superintendent of Lutie's apartment building, becomes a "crazy" animal because of his entrapment in poverty. For Petry's analysis of resignation, see *The Street,* 197. The novel ends with Lutie's inability to understand the forces that determine her social position (436).

40. The perspective of a white schoolteacher, that it is a hopeless task to educate Harlem youth (330), is only confirmed by Lutie in the end (435), and there are various moments when she blames herself for her actions (307, 417). The novel's contemplation of white racism (see especially 323) is partly undercut by an incident, in a children's shelter, where Lutie encounters poor white women and wonders if it is poverty, not race, that harms women in particular by destroying their family relationships (409).

41. Rabinowitz, *Labor and Desire,* 40, 87.

42. Farrell, "How *Studs Lonigan* Was Written," 86. See Farrell, *Young Lonigan,* 165, for one of the many moments in which Studs cannot find words for his emotions. In *The American Dream in the Great Depression,* Hearn observes how the theme of spiritual poverty coming from the pursuit of a shabby and materialist dream was already familiar in the literature of the 1920s, but became linked to more physical forms of destitution in the 1930s (106).

43. Anderson saw hobo life as a counterculture that provokes literary expression in its great fund of experience, even if tramps often lack the grammatical and organizational ability to represent their own experience (*The Hobo,* 189). See Susman, *Culture as History,* 171,

for a description of this shift toward a literature of marginality. In *Radical Visions and American Dreams,* Pells offers a good account of Algren's unrelieved pessimism (224–25).

44. At the beginning of part 3 of *Somebody in Boots,* Algren quotes *The Communist Manifesto* on "The 'dangerous class,' the social scum (lumpenproletariat), that passively rotting mass thrown off by the lowest layers of old society" (155). The novel returns repeatedly to the "thing wholly evil" that grows in the dark minds of these impoverished characters (29–30), and becomes responsible for the gruesome violence, cruelty, and racism of their world.

45. In *The Cultural Front,* Denning argues that Dos Passos's *U.S.A.* verges on a full engagement with the lower classes, but is more interested in those who seek them out (198); the stories of Vag and the other lower-class characters thus run against Dos Passos's primary interest in the world of mass culture and in the politics of the Sacco-Vanzetti case (187–89, 191).

46. See, for example, Pells, *Radical Visions and American Dreams,* 199–200, and Stott, *Documentary Expression,* 58.

47. Peeler discusses how, for Asch, the experience of the Depression acted to disrupt a coherent perception of reality, with objectivity becoming impossible, and observations failing to fuse themselves into a clarifying whole; Adamic saw America lost in a fog, himself brought to the edge of breakdown (*Hope among Us Yet,* 18, 28).

48. See Asch, *The Road,* 217–19, and Peeler, *Hope among Us Yet,* 18–20.

49. Stott is particularly critical of Caldwell and Bourke-White in *Documentary Expression* (220). For a less critical view of Caldwell, which compares Caldwell and Agee rather than contrasting them, see Cook, *Erskine Caldwell and the Fiction of Poverty,* 282–83.

50. Reed, "Unimagined Existence," 173, 160, 174.

51. Agee criticizes Bourke-White implicitly by quoting a contemporary newspaper article that points out, apparently without irony, how this photographer of the poor is in fact one of the highest paid women in America (451). In an earlier section, Agee calls journalism "a broad and successful form of lying" (235) that cannot convey a fraction of what a moderately reflective person could describe (234).

52. This seems to be one of the purposes of the controversial "How did we get caught" section (78–82), in which Agee records a series of opinions from the general public which blame the poverty of the tenant families on their immorality, their own shiftless attitudes, their stupidity, and their lack of initiative (79–80). Agee ends this section by juxtaposing the hopeless thoughts of the tenants with the words of the Beatitudes (82), a juxtaposition that implies an ironic comment on the Christian view of the poor, which becomes merely another way of accepting and placating poverty.

53. The excerpt from the children's book that Agee quotes at the beginning of *Praise* highlights basic necessities—food, clothing, and shelter—and points toward Agee's interest in absolute levels of poverty rather than a vaguer notion of inequality; Agee implies that the tenants lack even the minimum standards for survival.

54. The tenant house is a distinct type, writes Agee, with only an occasional overlap with the homes of the poorest land-owners (206). See also *Praise,* 429.

55. Agee tries, for example, to understand the farmer's urgent egoistic and sexual need to exert full violence and domination over the mule, the symbol of work and of the whole world order of using, driving, and beating (216–17).

56. Critics have recognized this resistance to reform in Agee, but have suggested little reason for it, thus leaving us with a sense of self-contradiction, both in Agee and in these readings of him. See especially Pells, *Radical Visions and American Dreams,* 250; Staub, *Voices of Persuasion,* 35–36; Stott, *Documentary Expression,* 311–13; and Reed, "Unimagined Existence," 174–75. Hoopes's argument, in "Modernist Criticism and Transcendental Literature," is perhaps closest to mine, in that he draws attention to this darker side of Agee—his devaluing of beauty and consciousness in the tenants' lives—although Hoopes still reads Agee as self-conflicted about these questions.

57. *Praise,* 355, 211. Early in the book, Agee ironically criticizes the "well-thought-out liberal efforts to rectify the unpleasant situation down South," efforts that act to benefit the reformer (14–15). By quoting *The Communist Manifesto* at the beginning of the book, and then retracting any specific socialist agenda, Agee is again left in a kind of transcendentalist position, implying a motivation of egalitarianism while refusing to approach any kind of structural reform.

58. Agee is interested in the special effects poverty has on intelligence and behavior. Young Burt Gudger, for example, suffers from a desperate trauma in which he can only speak a "language beyond gibberish" after "he has been given the security of long and friendly attention" (302).

59. "[T]hat Ricketts is willing to work and to appear in public in a home made hat is significant of his abandonment 'beneath' the requirements of these symbologies," writes Agee (272), with poverty again seeming less economic and more of an individual behavioral condition.

60. The whole "Work 2: Cotton" section is a beautiful narrative of the cotton season, which gives sensitive attention to the plight of individuals, while relating these individuals to the wider cosmic forces of which they are part.

61. Examples of this contradiction abound. Agee suggests that circumstance alone explains the state of the tenant farmer (101, 107), yet at other times he dwells on the total incapacity of reform in the tenants (313).

62. The *Oxford English Dictionary* lists "annoyingly unperceptive or slow to understand" and "not acutely affecting the senses" as meanings of *obtuse.*

63. Agee does temper some of his absolutist statements in "Colon" (108) and in the "Education" section (307).

64. This theme becomes clear from the first paragraph of Algren's novel. Cass McKay's father "felt that he had been cheated with every breath he had ever drawn; but he did not know why, or by whom" (12).

65. The terrible work of cotton picking hardens the flesh *and* anesthetizes the nerves, the powers of reflection, and the imagination (340); consciousness itself becomes a self-protective scabbing, physically altering the mind in absolute ways. Ricketts's distinctive walk, for example, is described as a product of physical *and* mental damage, an interplay between the two: his nervous modification of walking damages his feet (271).

66. Agee's claim that the soul is still amenable to goodness (104) seems difficult to accept, given the degree to which the individual is damaged—stretching back, it seems, to the beginnings of time.

67. For other references to glands, see *Praise,* 88, 106, 208.

68. See *Praise,* 78, for a reference to feeblemindedness. Agee compares "that true-mythic natural man of racial dream" with the son of poverty, whose death is continuous and slow, and who is void of all skill (104–105). "Ivy, and her mother: what are the dreams of dogs?" (77), asks Agee. Woods has the head of a man with bird ancestors (273), and children are repeatedly compared to wild animals (363) and dogs (386). This directly contravenes Stott's belief that Agee found no animalism in the tenants' minds (*Documentary Expression,* 292).

69. See Haller, *Eugenics,* 106–107.

70. For this recent revisionist view, see, for example, Doyle, "The Long Arm of Eugenics"; Kline, *Building a Better Race;* and Ordover, *American Eugenics.*

71. By 1938 twenty-nine states and one territory had eugenics laws on the statute books, according to Sipple, "Witness [to] the Suffering of Women," 143.

72. Here I paraphrase Haller, *Eugenics,* 94, 179–80. See Ordover, *American Eugenics,* for the opposing view that, for eugenicists, the Depression only cemented anxiety over government expenditure on the poor (148).

73. The racial degeneration of the poor in *You Have Seen Their Faces* is always a product of their victimization. Caldwell mentions eugenics at one point (164), yet it is merely one among a number of solutions to inequality offered by various schools of thought.

74. Jameson, *The Political Unconscious,* 187–89.

75. Again, the *cheapness* of the materials directly yields beauty, as the grain of the wood goes into wild convulsions and ecstasies (145).

76. Hitchcock, "They Must Be Represented?," 25.

77. Despite the title of his essay, the important category for Hilgart is *use* rather than damage. He argues that Agee's aesthetic responds to the signs of a thing's use, its distance from exchange value, which directly challenges the middle-class reader's sense of value ("Valuable Damage," 103, 105).

78. Trilling, "Greatness with One Fault in It," 201.

79. Woodson, "Thoreau on Poverty and Magnanimity," 30. Stott mentions Agee's opinion, in a 1947 response to Helen Levitt's photographs of slum dwellers, that this is "the record of an ancient, primitive, transient, and immortal civilization, incomparably superior to our own" (*Documentary Expression,* 306)—an opinion that aligns Agee very closely with Thoreau's romanticization of the poor, emphasized by Woodson.

80. Hoopes also argues that Agee admired the tenants because they had been deprived of consciousness; see "Modernist Criticism and Transcendental Literature," 465.

81. The Book of Hebrews, for example, views impoverished, brutalized souls as particularly rich in faith. See Freedman, ed., *The Anchor Bible Dictionary,* 421, and the entry on poverty as a whole, for the positive assessment of humble poverty that comes to fruition in the Psalms, whereby poverty and humility dovetail as preconditions for experiencing the compassion of God—a view of the poor that remains controversial among scholars, and exists in marked contrast to the position of poverty throughout most of the Hebrew Bible (411–12). The lines Agee quotes from Ecclesiasticus, which form the poem "Let us now praise famous men" (*Praise,* 445), set Agee's work within a familiar Christian dialectic that contrasts wise and powerful men with the silent but blessed poor.

82. See the entry "Poor, Poverty" in Freedman, ed., *The Anchor Bible Dictionary,* 415–22.

83. Compare this with an earlier moment when an encounter with diseased and insect-ridden linen again brings a degree of aesthetic pleasure (174).

84. Toward the end of the book, Agee expresses hope, in future generations, for a cure and an end to an agony long begun (439), although this seems such a minor gesture in a book otherwise devoid of any sense of cure. Agee may claim there is "no open sexual desire" in his solitary exploration of the Gudger house, yet he still juxtaposes this exploration with a memory of his adolescent, masturbatory wandering around his grandfather's house (136–37). Agee admits to being healed in the Gudgers' exhaustion (418).

85. The strange scene in "Inversion," where Agee juxtaposes a memory of physical love and a vision of the tenants as war victims (390–92), also makes sense within the logic that Agee's love is provoked by the witnessing of damage, that it needs this vision of harm to exist in the first place. The refreshment and contentment at the end of this episode are clearly the subjective experience of Agee alone.

86. "The narcissistic interest of gentlemen in ragged boys," argues Lang toward the end of her reading of Alger, "stands as the motive force behind the romanticized (and romantic) marketplace in which economic transactions provide a cover for homoerotic engagement" (*The Syntax of Class,* 114). See also Trask, *Cruising Modernism.*

87. See Hoopes, "Modernist Criticism and Transcendental Literature," 462–63, for further discussion of the obvious self-contradictions in Agee's belief that the tenants have no sense of beauty.

88. Agee comments that variations in the types of body coverings are more frequent in African Americans: they have more original predilections for colors, textures, symbolisms, contrasts, while their subsequent modifications and embellishments are more free and notable (263). Yet Agee has no time to talk of black clothing, commenting merely that it is an expression of genius distributed among almost the whole race (264).

89. The Evans photograph of the Rickettses' fireplace reveals a pair of eyeglasses and what looks like a pen: signs of literacy, notably absent in Agee's description. Agee considers Ricketts's wearing of spectacles on Sunday to be only symbolic of the day (261). See Cosgrove, "Snapshots of the Absolute," for a broader reading of the ways Evans's photographs work against Agee's text.

90. In *From Tobacco Road to Route 66,* Cook explores the moral dilemma at the heart of literary depictions of the poor white: the "bad," immoral qualities associated with poverty culture—extreme violence, laziness, cunning, absurdity—became themselves valuable from a literary perspective because they generated interest, character, and sensational subject matter. See Reynolds, *Beneath the American Renaissance,* 55, Giamo, *On the Bowery,* 42–50, and Gandal, *The Virtues of the Vicious,* 71, for a similar ambivalence in earlier pieriods.

91. Reed, "Unimagined Existence," 174.

92. See the "Reversion" section of Part Three of *Praise,* especially 379–80, 385, 389, 411. The quotation from *King Lear,* with which *Praise* begins, also suggests that the experience of poverty can bring justice through personal reform, largely of the wealthy and powerful class.

93. Cook, *From Tobacco Road to Route 66,* 185.

94. Agee thus sets up a situation in which whites dominate another racial group that has definite advantages over them in several respects. African Americans have communal emo-

tional contentment (27), cultural richness (29), humor and sexual virility (28), and indeed seem materially better off than their white neighbors (36). While blacks suffer the effects of racism, they appear not to suffer from poverty *in the same way* as whites: it does not lead to the same psychological and cultural diseases.

95. See *You Have Seen Their Faces,* 51, 113, and *Blood on the Forge,* 20.

96. This point is at the heart of Melville Herskovits's criticism of Frazier, in which Herskovits argued that the prevalence of black matrilineal families was not a sign of disorganized moral failure but of the adaptation of West African social practices to an American context. My summary of Frazier's ideas, their rejection by Herskovits, and their influence on subsequent social analysts, is drawn from Williams, "E. Franklin Frazier and the African American Family." There have been some recent attempts to reconsider Frazier as a black intellectual with racial politics more radical than usually thought; see Platt, *E. Franklin Frazier Reconsidered.*

97. See *The Negro Family in the United States,* 359–68, for a good summary of Frazier's emphasis on the socioeconomic situation into which blacks were forced after slavery, and for his beliefs that urbanization in particular had stripped blacks of their cultural heritage.

98. According to Wilson in *The Truly Disadvantaged,* arguments that black poverty is caused by white racism ignore a complex set of issues, such as the widening economic inequality among blacks (11).

99. Pells, *Radical Visions and American Dreams,* 113.

100. Fabre, in *The Unfinished Quest,* describes in detail the breadth of reaction against Wright's view of black culture in *Black Boy* (279–82). Wright claimed that he had emphasized the deprivation and narrowness of black life to undermine the stereotype of the "happy Negro"; he blamed the inability of blacks to fathom his motives in writing *Black Boy* on their not being emotionally independent enough to face the naked experience of their lives (see Fabre, *The Unfinished Quest,* 279, 281). See Hakutani, "Creation of the Self," 75, and Cappetti, "Sociology of an Existence," 257, for more recent discussions of this problem in Wright's work.

101. For Wright's knowledge of and interest in Frazier's book and a number of other sociological studies (part of a program of reading provided by Louis Wirth in 1940–41), and for his later admiration of Myrdal, see Fabre, *The Unfinished Quest,* 232, 270. Wright mentions his interest in sociology in *Black Boy* (278, 284). See also Cappetti, "Sociology of an Existence."

102. *12 Million Black Voices* contains a text by Wright to accompany a series of Depression Era photographs of black life, selected from the files of the Farm Security Administration. Wright argues that slavery destroyed the personalities and folk consciousness of blacks (15), an initial trauma that has been exacerbated by the sharecropping and industrial systems, both of which thrive on a racism that serves the needs of wealthy whites (46, 120–21). For some of the many references in *12 Million Black Voices* to the ways that hunger determines black behavior, see 15, 59, 64, 118, 122, 126.

103. See Fabre, *The Unfinished Quest,* 273, for Wright's predominant sense of his own "spiritual hunger." For other references to the role of hunger in *Black Boy,* see Stepto, "Literacy and Ascent," 236–37; Thaddeus, "The Metamorphosis of *Black Boy,*" 274–75; Leibowitz, "'Arise, Ye Pris'ners of Starvation,'" 331–32; and McCall, "Wright's American Hunger," 360–61. In "Negating the Negation," JanMohamed also refers to this hunger, but he sees it as a manifestation of racially based social death (287–88).

104. For some of the many references to hunger and starvation in Conroy's *The Disinherited,* see 30, 77, 232, 259, 280. There are too many references to hunger in Algren's novel to mention them individually; as in Wright's *Black Boy,* hunger is a constant refrain, and is accompanied throughout by thirst, fatigue, and cold.

105. Wilson, *Our Nig,* 13. Indeed, Wilson's text itself is figured as an article manufactured by the author in an effort to avoid beckoning poverty (129–30); the reader becomes implicated in an economy of poverty and relief when urged to buy the book as an act of charity (139–40).

106. Douglass mentions his hunger throughout the *Narrative,* but nowhere is it more extreme than when he is the slave of Thomas Auld; it is in association with this experience that Douglass describes the failure to give a slave enough to eat as the most aggravated form of meanness (53). Douglass associates freedom with being fed both physically and intellectually (112)—an association of which slaveholders also seem to be aware, thus explaining their practice of gorging slaves with too much food and drink in an effort to disgust them with the idea of liberty (76–77). Corroborating Orlando Patterson's idea of slavery as a form of human parasitism, Douglass twice describes slavery as the consumption of black flesh (85, 106–107).

107. For a discussion of the somewhat ambiguous distinction between domination and exploitation in Marx's writings, see Aronowitz, *The Politics of Identity,* 21.

108. Patterson, *Slavery and Social Death,* 1, 4. Patterson describes the special features of the slave as a total powerlessness, an absence of independent social existence, an endless personal violation and chronic inalienable dishonor (1–13). Any move from slavery to freedom represents a crucial paradigm shift from a state of being absolutely owned to some degree of autonomy and social life, however restricted these may be.

109. To offer an example: the racist songs chanted by Wright and his young friends at neighborhood Jews are obsessively concerned with images of eating and food, thus reflecting the needs of these "poor, half-starved" children (61–62). The imagery of food in *Black Boy* often carries a racial weight, for example when Wright's young black friends talk of eating black-eyed peas and farting poison gas that kills whites (79).

110. These parallels are perhaps too close to be mere coincidence. Like Wright, Melville uses the word *whirling* to describe Pierre's poverty, which also becomes a dizzy form of vertigo that directly affects his eyes and leaves his mind "blank" and himself voiceless (*Pierre,* 339, 341). Wright's blankness and voicelessness in this episode also recall the early career of Melville's Bartleby: Wright's domination takes the form of Miss Simon forcing him to blot mechanically the envelopes she has written on (30).

111. There are many other references in *Black Boy* to this link between Wright's poverty and his "self-conscious" feeling of "stand[ing] apart" (100). See, for example, 113, 164.

112. Working to gain food to strengthen his body, for example, inevitably results in Wright falling behind with school work (150). Compare this with Douglass, *Narrative,* 41.

113. The Moss family, with whom Wright stays in Memphis, provide another example: they have plenty of food to eat, but this sufficiency means social immobility. "They had no tensions, unappeasable longings, no desire to do something to redeem themselves" (214).

114. See *Black Boy,* 196, 233. For further references to black-on-white food dependency—a kind of racialized welfare economy—see 230, 239.

115. Compare *Black Boy,* 73, 74, 191, 262, with Patterson's thesis, outlined in *Slavery and Social Death,* 1–13.

116. Bess and her mother, Mrs. Moss, reveal a similarly hungerless "peasant mentality" (214). Wright's idea of racial pauperism echoes Douglass's *Narrative,* in which slavery and education are inherently incompatible states, whereas thoughtlessness and contentment are synonymous (40, 42, 98, 102).

117. Pells describes Ruth Benedict's contemporary "feeling that deviant behavior was an illness to be treated rather than an understandable (and possibly creative) response to an intolerable situation" (*Radical Visions and American Dreams,* 114).

118. "[T]hough ties of blood made us kin," suggests Wright, "we were forever strangers, speaking a different language, living on vastly distant planes of reality" (34).

119. Wright returns to this point in the conclusion to the 1945 edition of *Black Boy.* See also 31, 127.

120. See *Black Boy,* 302, 318, for Wright's sense of how poverty can override racial and national distinctions.

121. See Glickstein, "Pressures from Below," 129–30.

122. See the reviews by Prescott and Benson for readings of *Black Boy* as a rags-to-riches success story. In another review, Campenni describes *Black Boy* as "a black Horatio Alger story" (386). Wright was an avid reader of Alger in early youth, but attacked the myth of the self-made man in a 1945 review of Alger's complete works. See Fabre, *The Unfinished Quest,* 51, 288.

123. For another example, see *Black Boy,* 341. For Wright's larger interest in juvenile delinquency, see Fabre, *The Unfinished Quest,* 267, 271.

124. This inversion recurs in *Black Boy,* for example in the moment when Wright's hunger causes his mind to drift into a fantasy about food. In this case, however, Wright ends in self-disgust at his futile daydreams (137).

125. The idea of words as a type of food is accompanied by the persistent imagery of the mouth, the site both of feeding and of language—and indeed of *taste,* which connects with Wright's interest in the values of civilization. See *Black Boy,* 7, 9, 36, 40, 103. Young Richard is repeatedly whacked across the mouth by adults (13, 39, 43, 142), a form of censorship that continues the thematic link between language and authority.

126. Sections of "The Horror and the Glory" were published in magazines and collections of the period—such as "I Tried to be a Communist," which appeared in *Atlantic Monthly* in 1944.

127. See Frazier, *The Negro Family in the United States,* 367, and Myrdal, *An American Dilemma,* 2: 928. (Myrdal did not always see the values of white society as ideal, however; like Wright, he stressed the moral conflicts within white Americans.) This irony is symbolically illustrated by Wright's encounter at the café with Tillie, the Finnish cook. If Wright's debasement is founded on malnutrition, then Tillie's stems from an excessive materialism, as she is caught spitting secretly into the food (274–77).

128. James, *Hawthorne,* 55; Cooper, *Notions of the Americans,* quoted in Hutchinson, ed., *Edith Wharton,* 17. See Pells, *Radical Visions and American Dreams,* 206, for a good account of Farrell on this issue.

129. In *Democracy in America,* Tocqueville argues that the doctrine of equality creates

men who are "ever striving toward the immense grandeur glimpsed indistinctly at the end of the long track humanity must follow" (453). See Ignatieff, *The Needs of Strangers,* 114, for a discussion of desire.

130. See Butler, "Desire," for a summary of these theories.

131. See Ignatieff, *The Needs of Strangers,* 27, for a specific discussion of the link between needs and rights; and Smith, "Order and Disorder," 211, 218, for more general consideration of the specificity of need and its conflict with the liberal notion of individual agency governed by rights and autonomy. The Moss family can also be read as such a community of need, one based not on individualistic acquisition but on a common interdependence, though here it creates a "simplicity" that Wright considers frightening (214, 217).

132. This lesson in language differs from what he learns from his encounter with race: that, while his grandmother looks white, she is not racially "white" (23). If Wright's "poverty lessons" in language revolve around an absent core of meaning, then his "race lessons" depend on the learning of a code, based on metaphor, in which the conversational surface has a submerged meaning. Significantly, Wright's interest in written words immediately follows his experience as a beggar (22–23).

133. See Butler, "Desire," 380, and Ignatieff, *The Needs of Strangers,* 11, on this point.

134. Smith, "Order and Disorder," 220. Later in the book, Wright confesses his fear that "if I clashed with whites I would lose control of my emotions and spill out words that would be my sentence of death" (200). For other moments when Richard loses linguistic control, or else is paralyzed into voicelessness, see 24–25, 25–26, 75.

135. The most obvious example comes during bath time, when Richard's grandmother attempts to scrub his anus clean: "Then, before I knew it, words—words whose meaning I did not fully know—had slipped out of my mouth. / 'When you get through, kiss back there'" (41). See also 21, 45.

136. Wright earlier describes "the thirst of the human spirit to conquer and transcend the implacable limitations of human life" (*Black Boy,* 119). See Ignatieff, *The Needs of Strangers,* 57, on these Judeo-Christian questions.

137. For the inarticulate side of Bigger, see *Native Son,* 67, 308, 421. For Bigger's thoughtlessness and inability to fathom the meaning of his life, see 12, 42, 38, 97, 136–37, 241, 418, 419. In "How 'Bigger' Was Born," Wright argues that the only difference between Bigger's hunger and that of whites is that Bigger's is as yet inarticulate (447), but we never get the sense from the novel that Bigger reveals "an objectless, timeless, spaceless element of primal fear and dread" at the heart of *all* humanity (452).

138. For some of the many references to the hysterical, nervous disease that hits Bigger in his stomach and chest, see *Native Son,* 21–22, 35, 185, 218. For Bigger's occasional moments of hunger, see 36, 247–48. In "How 'Bigger' Was Born," Wright describes Bigger as "a hot and whirling vortex of undisciplined and unchannelized impulses" (445). When Bigger attempts to explain his hunger to the lawyer Max, at the end of *Native Son,* this hunger remains essentially incoherent (425).

139. Ellison, "Richard Wright's Blues," 93. There are moments when Wright describes the transmission of culture and folk tradition among blacks, though this racial consciousness is often seen as *reactive* to the pressures of racism (*Black Boy,* 81). Wright does talk about blacks having developed their "own code of ethics, values, loyalty" at the end of the chapter

that describes Wright's experiences working in a hospital (314), though again this code seems reactive and destructive.

140. Wright echoes Myrdal when he argues that blacks are an organic part of a white culture that hates them, which thus leads to a self-hatred and emotional disorder that in turn bring an inability to function efficiently in the real world, and a confirmation of racist opinions of black inferiority (*Black Boy*, 266).

141. In *The Unfinished Quest*, 243, Fabre suggests that Wright shifted after *Native Son* from a restricted racial perspective to a more general condemnation of American values, which Fabre reads as part of Wright's veering toward existentialism (Fabre emphasizes throughout his biography how Wright attempts to merge the concerns of race and social class). Fabre also records Wright's desire to use the African American to reflect on the cultural vulgarity of the nation as a whole. Wright mentions his view that blacks are the "dark mirror" of whites in *12 Million Black Voices* (146).

142. The novel depicts the barely conscious spiritual hunger of a young black man named Jake, an emotional cripple victimized by an impoverished and racist environment. Jake's emotional tensions and longings are concentrated—like Bigger's—in the sickening hunger burning in his stomach (*Lawd Today!*, 8). Jake feels a constant hunger for something else in his life (68, 116), yet what this might be remains inarticulate and blank (142).

143. Patterson describes these typical economic conditions that follow slavery; see *Slavery and Social Death*, 246. Myrdal argues that, in limited respects, slavery was more advantageous to blacks than the precarious caste system that followed it (*An American Dilemma*, 1: 222–23).

144. See Wilson, *The Truly Disadvantaged*, for his use of the term *social dislocation* (ix). According to Harvey and Reed, Wilson considers black poverty to be rooted in the new dynamics of class, not in the impact of slavery and discrimination, yet he still sees black urban poverty as a singular type that needs more than general economic reform ("Paradigms of Poverty," 291).

145. See Wright, *12 Million Black Voices*, 128, 146.

146. Rimstead, *Remnants of Nation*, 170.

147. "The Man Who Lived Underground" (published posthumously in *Eight Men* in 1961) implies that the performative act of writing, rather than the meaning of the written words themselves, is the only value in a world that, for blacks, is unreal and irrational. This connection between race and existentialism is even clearer in another story from *Eight Men*, "The Man Who Killed a Shadow." The external world becomes an unreal realm of shadows for Saul, symbols of his deprivation (186).

148. This is a function of the stigma of poverty, argues Waxman, which forces the individual to develop identity through his or her own experiences, with the "real me" becoming the "existential me" (*The Stigma of Poverty*, 96). There are various moments in which Wright describes himself as someone who is alienated from both the black and the white communities (*Black Boy*, 196, 214).

149. Both Richard in *Black Boy* and Bigger in *Native Son* have selves that depend on the coincidence of significance and meaninglessness: the only degree of purposeful self-knowledge to which Bigger has access derives from an unintentional and meaningless act.

Notes to Conclusion

1. See Aronowitz, *The Politics of Identity,* 67, for a useful discussion of this tension between class and cultural movements.

2. Compare this with Valentine's speculation that the ethnic identity and subcultural distinctiveness of minorities may be greatest for group members who are poor (*Poverty and Culture,* 125).

3. Rimstead, *Remnants of Nation,* for example, tends to polarize class positions on the basis of the subjective experience of poverty. For another example of critical attention to women and poverty, see Sipple, "'Witness [to] the Suffering of Women.'"

4. Clarke quoted in Jennings, "Persistent Poverty in the United States," 20.

5. My aim in this respect is to find in the diverse response to poverty what Griffin and Tempenis describe as a blind spot in American studies, a sense of class as "an articulation of power and cultural difference that is historicized as materially and symbolically inscribed sets of impositions, practices, collective meanings, and identities; simultaneously constitutive of and constituted by social relations and institutional arrangements; and subject to contestation, definition, and redefinition" ("Class, Multiculturalism, and the *American Quarterly,*" 93).

6. Drawing on the work of Martha Minow, Katz suggests that the vocabulary we use to describe difference tends to naturalize constructed concepts, thereby ignoring the perspective of the powerless and reinforcing inequality (*The Undeserving Poor,* 5, 6–7). See also Gans, *The War against the Poor,* 32, 40, and Himmelfarb, *The Idea of Poverty,* 420.

7. See Agee, *Praise,* 353, for a direct if passing reference to Melville. One early reviewer claimed that Agee's prose was the most exciting since Melville's (see Stott, *Documentary Expression,* 290).

8. In a comparison of Agee's *Praise* and Orwell's *The Road to Wigan Pier* (1937), Williams argues that Orwell fails to develop a fully articulated critique of his discourse's representational techniques, thus contrasting with Agee's deconstruction of a New Deal documentary aesthetic of representation and remedy ("Post/Modern Documentary," 163, 173, 174, 177).

9. For the former approach, see Calderón, "The Novel and the Community of Readers." "[W]hile Chicano readers will be able to identify with the world depicted in *Tierra,*" writes Calderón, "many other readers may find Rivera's world remote and alien" (113). For the latter view, see Saldívar, *Chicano Narrative,* 85, 89.

10. The section "Hand in His Pocket," for example, offers a concise allegory of poverty's traumatic effect on the behavioral habits of children.

11. Melville's overworked Pierre finally suffers absolute physical exhaustion, dizziness, blackouts, and a profound loss of vision whereby the pupils of his eyes "rolled away from him in their own orbits" (*Pierre,* 341). For remarkably close echoes of this experience, see *Tierra,* 110–11, 133. See also Wright, *Black Boy,* 29.

12. Saldívar, *Chicano Narrative,* 87.

13. Despite the critical desire to see affirmative wholeness within it, much of *Tierra* remains fractured and unresolved, just as the boy is unable to maintain his contemplative stasis under the house in the final section as he is forced to move constantly by the biting fleas (148). "That poor family. First the mother now him. He must be losing his mind. He's losing

track of the years," is the final spoken comment on the boy's emergence from under the house (152), a comment that complicates any realization of ethnic *or* class consciousness by referencing once more the links between poverty, mental trauma, and disorientation that feature throughout the narrative.

14. These issues are represented with particular intensity in the episode "It's That It Hurts." Anglo dislike of the boy's Mexicanness is equivalent to a perception of his poverty, which is in turn compounded by this dislike when the stigmatized boy becomes unable to read in front of the class and is inevitably expelled from school for fighting. The key to the episode lies in the most submerged of details surrounding the origins of the fight that leads to the boy's expulsion: "There wasn't any reason, it's just that some of the older boys *who already had moustaches and who were still in the second grade* started pushing us against each other" (94; my italics). The older boys are presumably white, but the critical point is that they themselves are unable to move upward through the mainstream education system that seems to be protecting their economic interests by expelling Chicanos and thus condemning the latter to low-status work. The fight itself is a performance of social difference, though one that establishes poverty as a relational state that haunts the white as well as the Chicano community.

15. See Michaels, "Autobiography of an Ex-White Man," for a bold statement of this opposition between situational and essentialist perspectives in recent critical debate.

16. This complexity is described brilliantly when Rivera's protagonist thinks sadly that he cannot get a license to fish the creek because he and his people are from "out of state" (95). What remains at stake here is not ethnic identity but poverty—the feeling of being hungry in a context of inaccessible abundance. And what keeps these people poor is not their ethnic identity but their situational migrancy, having had to uproot themselves geographically to obtain their income. But the poverty of these migrant laborers is not simply reducible to the capitalist exploitation of workers (that is, to a class perspective), because this situation of being "out of state" is tied to an ethnic statelessness in the largest geopolitical sense.

WORKS CITED

Abramovitz, Mimi. *Regulating the Lives of Women: Social Welfare Policy from Colonial Times to the Present*. Boston, MA: South End Press, 1988.

Adams, Timothy Dow. "'I Do Believe Him Though I Know He Lies': Lying as Genre and Metaphor in *Black Boy*." *Richard Wright: Critical Perspectives Past and Present*. Edited by Henry Louis Gates, Jr., and K. A. Appiah. New York: Amistad, 1993. 302–15.

Addams, Jane. *Twenty Years at Hull-House: With Autobiographical Notes*. 1910. Harmondsworth: Penguin, 1998.

Agee, James, and Walker Evans. *Let Us Now Praise Famous Men: Three Tenant Families*. 1941. Boston, MA: Houghton Mifflin, 1988.

Agnew, Jean-Christophe. "History and Anthropology: Scenes from a Marriage." *Yale Journal of Criticism* 3.2 (1990): 29–50.

Algren, Nelson. *Somebody in Boots: A Novel*. 1935. New York: Thunder's Mouth, 1987.

Ammons, Elizabeth. "Edith Wharton and the Issue of Race." *The Cambridge Companion to Edith Wharton*. Edited by Millicent Bell. Cambridge: Cambridge University Press, 1995. 68–86.

——, ed. *The House of Mirth*. By Edith Wharton. New York: Norton, 1990.

Anderson, Nels. *The Hobo: The Sociology of the Homeless Man*. Chicago, IL: University of Chicago Press, 1923.

Anderson, Sherwood. *Poor White*. New York: B. W. Huebsch, 1920.

——. *Puzzled America*. New York: Scribner, 1935.

Appadurai, Arjun. *Modernity at Large: Cultural Dimensions of Globalization*. Minneapolis: University of Minnesota Press, 1996.

Aronowitz, Stanley. *The Politics of Identity: Class, Culture, Social Movements*. New York: Routledge, 1992.

Asch, Nathan. *The Road: In Search of America*. New York: Norton, 1937.

Attaway, William. *Blood on the Forge*. 1941. New York: New York Review Books, 2005.

WORKS CITED

Banta, Martha. *Failure and Success in America: A Literary Debate.* Princeton, NJ: Princeton University Press, 1978.

Bauer, Dale M. *Edith Wharton's Brave New Politics.* Madison: University of Wisconsin Press, 1994.

Baym, Nina. *Women's Fiction: A Guide to Novels by and about Women in America, 1820–70.* 2nd Edition. Urbana: University of Illinois Press, 1993.

Bell, Michael Davitt. *The Problem of American Realism: Studies in the Cultural History of a Literary Idea.* Chicago, IL: University of Chicago Press, 1993.

Bellamy, Edward. *Looking Backward, 2000–1887.* 1888. Harmondsworth: Penguin, 1986.

Benson, Joseph. Review of *American Hunger* by Richard Wright. *Greensboro Daily News,* June 12, 1977. Reprinted in *Richard Wright: The Critical Reception.* Edited by John M. Reilly. New York: Burt Franklin, 1978. 381–82.

Berg, Allison. *Mothering the Race: Women's Narratives on Reproduction, 1890–1930.* Urbana: University of Illinois Press, 2002.

Bérubé, Michael. "American Studies without Exceptions." *PLMA* 118.1 (January 2003): 103–113.

Bezanson, Walter E. "Historical Note." In Herman Melville. *Israel Potter: His Fifty Years of Exile.* 1855. Evanston, IL: Northwestern University Press, 1997. 173–235.

Bloom, James D. *Left Letters: The Culture Wars of Mike Gold and Joseph Freeman.* New York: Columbia University Press, 1992.

Boucicault, Dion. *The Poor of New York.* New York: Samuel French, 1857.

Bowlby, Rachel. *Just Looking: Consumer Culture in Dreiser, Gissing and Zola.* New York: Methuen, 1985.

Brace, Charles Loring. *The Dangerous Classes of New York, and Twenty Years' Work among Them.* New York: Wynkoop and Hallenbeck, 1872.

Bremner, Robert H. *From the Depths: The Discovery of Poverty in the United States.* New York: New York University Press, 1956.

Brodhead, Richard H. *Cultures of Letters: Scenes of Reading and Writing in Nineteenth-Century America.* Chicago, IL: University of Chicago Press, 1993.

Bromell, Nicholas K. *By the Sweat of the Brow: Literature and Labor in Antebellum America.* Chicago, IL: University of Chicago Press, 1993.

Browder, Laura. *Rousing the Nation: Radical Culture in Depression America.* Amherst: University of Massachusetts Press, 1998.

Brownson, Orestes A. "Wordsworth." 1839. Reprinted in Perry Miller, ed. *The Transcendentalists: An Anthology.* Cambridge, MA: Harvard University Press, 1950. 434–36.

Bruère, Robert W. "The Perpetual Poor." *Harper's Monthly Magazine* 121 (June–November 1910): 939–45.

Buell, Lawrence. "Downwardly Mobile for Conscience's Sake: Voluntary Simplicity from Thoreau to Lily Bart." *American Literary History* 17.4 (Winter 2005): 653–65.

Buntline, Ned [Edward Z. C. Judson]. *Mysteries and Miseries of New York: A Story of Real Life.* New York: Berford and Co., 1848.

Burke, Martin J. *The Conundrum of Class: Public Discourse on the Social Order in America.* Chicago, IL: University of Chicago Press, 1995.

Burroughs, Charles. *A Discourse Delivered in the Chapel of the New Alms-house, in Portsmouth, N.H.* 1835. Reprinted in David Rothman, ed. *The Jacksonians on the Poor: Col-*

lected Pamphlets. Poverty, U.S.A.: The Historical Record. New York: Arno and the New York Times, 1971.

Butler, Judith. "Desire." Critical Terms for Literary Study. Edited by Frank Lentricchia and Thomas McLaughlin. 2nd Edition. Chicago, IL: University of Chicago Press, 1995. 369–86.

Calderón, Héctor. "The Novel and the Community of Readers: Rereading Tomás Rivera's Y no se lo tragó la tierra." Criticism in the Borderlands: Studies in Chicano Literature, Culture, and Ideology. Edited by Héctor Calderón and José David Saldívar. Durham, NC: Duke University Press, 1991. 97–113.

Caldwell, Erskine. Tobacco Road. 1932. Athens: University of Georgia Press, 1995.

Caldwell, Erskine, and Margaret Bourke-White. You Have Seen Their Faces. New York: Viking, 1937.

Campbell, Helen. Prisoners of Poverty: Women Wage-Workers, Their Trades and Their Lives. 1887. Boston, MA: Roberts Brothers, 1889.

Campenni, Frank. Review of American Hunger by Richard Wright. Milwaukee Journal, July 3, 1977, Part 5, p. 5. Reprinted in Richard Wright: The Critical Reception. Edited by John M. Reilly. New York: Burt Franklin, 1978. 386–87.

Cappetti, Carla. "Sociology of an Existence: Wright and the Chicago School." Richard Wright: Critical Perspectives Past and Present. Edited by Henry Louis Gates, Jr., and K. A. Appiah. New York: Amistad, 1993. 255–71.

Carey, Mathew. Essays on the Public Charities of Philadelphia. 1828. Reprinted in David Rothman, ed. The Jacksonians on the Poor: Collected Pamphlets. Poverty, U.S.A.: The Historical Record. New York: Arno and the New York Times, 1971.

Cawelti, John G. Apostles of the Self-Made Man. Chicago, IL: University of Chicago Press, 1965.

Channing, Walter. An Address on the Prevention of Pauperism. 1843. Reprinted in David Rothman, ed. The Jacksonians on the Poor: Collected Pamphlets. Poverty, U.S.A.: The Historical Record. New York: Arno and the New York Times, 1971.

Clark, Martha Louise. "The Relation of Imbecility to Pauperism and Crime." The Arena 10 (November 1894): 788–94.

Coiner, Constance. Better Red: The Writing and Resistance of Tillie Olsen and Meridel Le Sueur. Oxford: Oxford University Press, 1995.

Colatrella, Carol. Literature and Moral Reform: Melville and the Discipline of Reading. Gainesville: University Press of Florida, 2002.

Conroy, Jack. The Disinherited. 1933. Westport, CT: Lawrence Hill, 1982.

Cook, Sylvia Jenkins. Erskine Caldwell and the Fiction of Poverty: The Flesh and the Spirit. Baton Rouge: Louisiana State University Press, 1991.

———. From Tobacco Road to Route 66: The Southern Poor White in Fiction. Chapel Hill: University of North Carolina Press, 1976.

Cosgrove, Peter. "Snapshots of the Absolute: Mediamachia in Let Us Now Praise Famous Men." American Literature 67.2 (June 1995): 329–57.

Craig, Oscar. "Agencies for the Prevention of Pauperism." The Poor in Great Cities. 1895. Robert A. Woods et al. New York: Arno Press and the New York Times, 1971. 339–69.

Crane, Stephen. "The Men in the Storm." 1894. The New York City Sketches of Stephen Crane and Related Pieces. Edited by R. W. Stallman and E. R. Hagemann. New York: New York University Press, 1966. 91–96.

Crèvecoeur, J. Hector St. John de. *Letters from an American Farmer and Sketches of Eighteenth-Century America*. 1782. Harmondsworth: Penguin, 1986.

Curtis, Susan. *A Consuming Faith: The Social Gospel and Modern American Culture*. Baltimore, MD: Johns Hopkins University Press, 1991.

Daly, Augustin. *Under the Gaslight*. 1867. *American Melodrama*. Edited by Daniel C. Gerould. New York: Performing Arts Journal Publications, 1983. 135–81.

Davis, Rebecca Harding. "Life in the Iron Mills, or the Korl Woman."1861. *Life in the Iron Mills and Other Stories*. New York: Feminist Press, 1985.

Denning, Michael. *The Cultural Front: The Laboring of American Culture in the Twentieth Century*. London: Verso, 1996.

——. *Mechanic Accents: Dime Novels and Working-Class Culture in America*. Revised Edition. London: Verso, 1998.

——. "'The Special American Conditions': Marxism and American Studies." *American Quarterly* 38 (1986): 356–80.

Dickens, Charles. *American Notes for General Circulation*. 1842. Harmondsworth: Penguin, 1985.

Dillingham, William B. *Melville's Short Fiction, 1853–1856*. Athens: University of Georgia Press, 1977.

Dimock, Wai Chee. "Class, Gender, and a History of Metonymy." *Rethinking Class: Literary Studies and Social Formations*. Edited by Wai Chee Dimock and Michael T. Gilmore. New York: Columbia University Press, 1994. 57–104.

——. "Debasing Exchange: Edith Wharton's *The House of Mirth*." *PMLA* 100.4 (September 1985): 783–92.

Dimock, Wai Chee, and Michael T. Gilmore, ed. *Rethinking Class: Literary Studies and Social Formations*. New York: Columbia University Press, 1994.

Dos Passos, John. *U.S.A.: The 42nd Parallel, 1919, The Big Money*. New York: Library of America, 1996.

Douglas, Ann. *The Feminization of American Culture*. New York: Noonday, 1998.

Douglass, Frederick. *Narrative of the Life of Frederick Douglass, An American Slave*. 1845. New York: Doubleday, 1989.

Doyle, Laura. "The Long Arm of Eugenics." *American Literary History* 16.3 (2004): 520–35.

Dreiser, Theodore. "The Bread-Line." *The Color of a Great City*. 1923. Syracuse, NY: Syracuse University Press, 1996. 129–32.

——. *The Color of a Great City*. 1923. Syracuse, NY: Syracuse University Press, 1996.

——. "Curious Shifts of the Poor." 1899. *Theodore Dreiser: A Selection of Uncollected Prose*. Edited by Donald Pizer. Detroit, MI: Wayne State University Press, 1977. 131–40.

——. *Newspaper Days*. Edited by T. D. Nostwich. Philadelphia: University of Pennsylvania Press, 1991.

——. *Sister Carrie*. The Pennsylvania Edition. Philadelphia: University of Pennsylvania Press, 1981.

——. *Sister Carrie*. 1900. World's Classics. Oxford: Oxford University Press, 1991.

Dryden, Edgar A. "The Entangled Text: Melville's *Pierre* and the Problem of Reading." *Herman Melville: A Collection of Critical Essays*. Edited by Myra Jehlen. Englewood Cliffs, NJ: Prentice Hall, 1994. 100–25.

Duban, James. "Transatlantic Counterparts: The Diptych and Social Inquiry in Melville's 'Poor

Man's Pudding and Rich Man's Crumbs.'" *New England Quarterly* 66.2 (June 1993): 274–86.

DuBois, W.E.B. "Richard Wright Looks Back." *New York Herald Tribune Weekly Book Review,* March 4, 1945, p. 2. Reprinted in *Richard Wright: The Critical Reception.* Edited by John M. Reilly. New York: Burt Franklin, 1978. 132–33.

Dugdale, Robert L. *The Jukes: A Study in Crime, Pauperism, Disease, and Heredity.* 1877. 4th Edition. New York: G. P. Putnam's Sons, 1910.

Ehrenreich, Barbara. *Fear of Falling: The Inner Life of the Middle Class.* New York: Pantheon, 1989.

———. *Nickel and Dimed: On (Not) Getting By in America.* New York: Henry Holt, 2001.

Ellison, Ralph. "Richard Wright's Blues." 1945. *Shadow and Act.* New York: Vintage, 1972. 77–94.

Ely, Richard T. "Pauperism in the United States." *North American Review* 152 (April 1891): 395–409.

Emerson, Ralph Waldo. "Self-Reliance." 1841. *Selections from Ralph Waldo Emerson.* Edited by Stephen E. Whicher. Boston, MA: Houghton Mifflin, 1960. 147–68.

Entin, Joseph. "Class, Culture, and the Working Body." *American Quarterly* 57.4 (December 2005): 1211–21.

Fabian, Ann. "Speculation on Distress: The Popular Discourse of the Panics of 1837 and 1857." *Yale Journal of Criticism* 3.1 (Fall 1989): 127–42.

———. *The Unvarnished Truth: Personal Narratives in Nineteenth-Century America.* Berkeley: University of California Press, 2000.

Fabre, Michel. *The Unfinished Quest of Richard Wright.* Translated by Isabel Barzun. 1973. 2nd Edition. Urbana: University of Illinois Press, 1993.

Farrell, James T. "How *Studs Lonigan* Was Written." *The League of Frightened Philistines, and Other Papers.* New York: Vanguard Press, 1945.

———. *Young Lonigan.* 1932. New York: Penguin, 2001.

Faulkner, William. *As I Lay Dying.* 1930. New York: Vintage, 1985.

Felski, Rita. "Nothing to Declare: Identity, Shame, and the Lower Middle Class." *PMLA* 115.1 (2000): 33–45.

Fern, Fanny. *Ruth Hall and Other Writings.* New Brunswick, NJ: Rutgers University Press, 1986.

Fichtelberg, Joseph. *Critical Fictions: Sentiment and the American Market, 1780–1870.* Athens: University of Georgia Press, 2003.

Fisher, Philip. "Acting, Reading, Fortune's Wheel: *Sister Carrie* and the Life History of Objects." *New Essays on Sister Carrie.* Edited by Donald Pizer. Cambridge: University of Cambridge Press, 1991. 259–77.

Fitzhugh, George. *Cannibals All! Or Slaves without Masters.* Cambridge, MA: Belknap Press of Harvard University Press, 1960.

Fleissner, Jennifer L. *Women, Compulsion, Modernity: The Moment of American Naturalism.* Chicago, IL: University of Chicago Press, 2004.

Flynt, Josiah. *Tramping with Tramps: Studies and Sketches of Vagabond Life.* 1899. Montclair, NJ: Patterson Smith, 1972.

Foley, Barbara. *Radical Representations: Politics and Form in U.S. Proletarian Fiction, 1929–1941.* Durham, NC: Duke University Press, 1993.

Foster, George G. *New York by Gas-Light and Other Urban Sketches.* 1850. Berkeley: University of California Press, 1990.

Franklin, Raymond S. "White Uses of the Black Underclass." *A New Introduction to Poverty: The Role of Race, Power, and Politics.* Edited by Louis Kushnick and James Jennings. New York: New York University Press, 1999. 119–45.

Frazier, E. Franklin. *The Negro Family in the United States.* 1939. Revised and Abridged Edition. Chicago, IL: University of Chicago Press, 1966.

Freedman, David Noel, ed. *The Anchor Bible Dictionary.* Volume 5. New York: Doubleday, 1992.

Freeman, Joseph. "Introduction." *Proletarian Literature in the United States: An Anthology.* Edited by Granville Hicks, Joseph North, Michael Gold, Paul Peters, Isidor Schneider, and Alan Calmer. New York: International Publishers, 1935.

Gair, Christopher. "*Sister Carrie,* Race, and the World's Columbian Exposition." *The Cambridge Companion to Theodore Dreiser.* Edited by Leonard Cassuto and Clare Virginia Eby. Cambridge: Cambridge University Press, 2004. 160–76.

Galbraith, John Kenneth. *The Affluent Society: Fortieth Anniversary Edition.* Boston, MA: Houghton Mifflin, 1998.

Gandal, Keith. *The Virtues of the Vicious: Jacob Riis, Stephen Crane, and the Spectacle of the Slum.* New York: Oxford University Press, 1997.

Gans, Herbert J. "Culture and Class in the Study of Poverty: An Approach to Anti-Poverty Research." *On Understanding Poverty: Perspectives from the Social Sciences. Perspectives on Poverty.* Edited by Daniel P. Moynihan. Vol. 1. New York: Basic, 1968. 201–28.

———. *The War against the Poor: The Underclass and Antipoverty Policy.* New York: Basic, 1995.

Garland, Hamlin. *Main-Travelled Roads.* 1891. Lincoln: University of Nebraska Press, 1995.

Gelfant, Blanche H. "What More Can Carrie Want? Naturalistic Ways of Consuming Women." *The Cambridge Companion to American Realism and Naturalism: Howells to London.* Edited by Donald Pizer. Cambridge: Cambridge University Press, 1995. 178–210.

George, Henry. *Progress and Poverty: An Inquiry into the Cause of Industrial Depressions and of Increase of Want with Increase of Wealth . . . The Remedy.* 1879. New York: Schalkenbach, 1958.

Giamo, Benedict. *On the Bowery: Confronting Homelessness in American Society.* Iowa City: University of Iowa Press, 1989.

Giddens, Anthony. "Structuralism, Post-Structuralism and the Production of Culture." *Social Theory Today.* Edited by Anthony Giddens and Jonathan H. Turner. Stanford, CA: Stanford University Press, 1987. 195–223.

Gilman, Charlotte Perkins. *Women and Economics: A Study of the Economic Relation between Men and Women as a Factor in Social Evolution.* 1898. Edited by Carl N. Degler. New York: Harper and Row, 1966.

Glickstein, Jonathan A. "Pressures from Below: Pauperism, Chattel Slavery, and the Ideological Construction of Free Market Labor Incentives in Antebellum America." *Radical History Review* 69 (Fall 1997): 114–59.

Goddard, Henry. *The Kallikak Family: A Study in the Heredity of Feeble-Mindedness.* 1912. New York: Arno, 1973.

Gold, Michael. *Jews Without Money.* 1930. New York: Carroll and Graf, 2004.

Graham, William C. *Half Finished Heaven: The Social Gospel in American Literature.* Lanham, MD: University Press of America, 1995.

Griffin, Larry J., and Maria Tempenis. "Class, Multiculturalism and the *American Quarterly.*" *American Quarterly* 54.1 (2002): 67–99.

Grusky, David, and Emily Ryo. "Did Katrina Recalibrate Attitudes toward Poverty and Inequality? A Test of the 'Dirty Little Secret' Hypothesis." *Du Bois Review* 3.1 (March 2006): 59–82.

Guillory, John. *Cultural Capital: The Problem of Literary Canon Formation.* Chicago, IL: University of Chicago Press, 1993.

Hakutani, Yoshinobu. "Creation of the Self in Richard Wright's *Black Boy.*" *The Critical Response to Richard Wright.* Edited by Robert J. Butler. Westport, CT: Greenwood Press, 1995. 71–79.

Haller, Mark H. *Eugenics: Hereditarian Attitudes in American Thought.* New Brunswick, NJ: Rutgers University Press, 1963.

Hapke, Laura. *Labor's Text: The Worker in American Fiction.* New Brunswick, NJ: Rutgers University Press, 2001.

Harden, Blaine. "2-Parent Families Rise after Change in Welfare Laws." *New York Times,* August 12, 2001: 1, 24.

Harrington, Michael. *The Other America: Poverty in the United States.* 1962. Revised Edition. Harmondsworth: Penguin, 1981.

Harris, George Washington. *Sut Lovingood's Yarns.* 1867. New Haven, CT: College and University Press, 1966.

Harris, Sharon M. *Rebecca Harding Davis and American Realism.* Philadelphia: University of Pennsylvania Press, 1991.

Harvey, David L., and Michael Reed. "Paradigms of Poverty: A Critical Assessment of Contemporary Perspectives." *International Journal of Politics, Culture and Society* 6.2 (Winter 1992): 269–97.

Hawthorne, Nathaniel. *The House of the Seven Gables.* 1851. Columbus: Ohio State University Press, 1965.

Hearn, Charles. *The American Dream in the Great Depression.* Westport, CT: Greenwood, 1977.

Hendler, Glenn. *Public Sentiments: Structures of Feeling in Nineteenth-Century American Literature.* Chapel Hill: University of North Carolina Press, 2001.

Henwood, Doug. "Trash-o-nomics." *White Trash: Race and Class in America.* Edited by Matt Wray and Annalee Newitz. New York: Routledge, 1997. 177–91.

Hicks, Granville, *The Great Tradition: An Interpretation of American Literature since the Civil War.* Revised Edition. New York: Macmillan, 1935.

Hilgart, John. "Valuable Damage: James Agee's Aesthetics of Use." *Arizona Quarterly* 52.4 (Winter 1996): 85–114.

Himmelfarb, Gertrude. *The Idea of Poverty: England in the Early Industrial Age.* New York: Knopf, 1984.

———. *Poverty and Compassion: The Moral Imagination of the Late Victorians.* New York: Knopf, 1991.

Hitchcock, Peter. "They Must Be Represented? Problems in Theories of Working-Class Representation." *PMLA* 115.1 (2000): 20–32.

Hobsbawm, E. J. "Poverty." *International Encyclopedia of the Social Sciences.* Edited by David L. Sills. Volume 12. New York: Macmillan and the Free Press, 1968. 398–404.

hooks, bell. *Where We Stand: Class Matters.* New York: Routledge, 2000.

Hoopes, James. "Modernist Criticism and Transcendental Literature." *New England Quarterly* 52.4 (December 1979): 451–66.

Horwitz, Howard. "*Maggie* and the Sociological Paradigm." *American Literary History* 10.4 (Winter 1998): 606–38.

Howells, William Dean. *A Hazard of New Fortunes.* 1890. Oxford: Oxford University Press, 1990.

———. *Impressions and Experiences.* New York: Harper, 1909.

Hunter, Robert. *Poverty: Social Conscience in the Progressive Era.* New York: Macmillan, 1904.

Hutchinson, Stuart, ed. *Edith Wharton: The House of Mirth, The Custom of the Country, The Age of Innocence.* Cambridge: Icon, 1998.

Ignatieff, Michael. *The Needs of Strangers.* New York: Picador, 1984.

Irving, Katrina. *Immigrant Mothers: Narratives of Race and Maternity, 1890–1925.* Urbana: University of Illinois Press, 2000.

James, C.L.R. *Mariners, Renegades and Castaways: The Story of Herman Melville and the World We Live In.* 1953. London: Allison and Busby, 1985.

James, Henry. *The Bostonians.* 1886. Oxford: Oxford University Press, 1990.

———. *Hawthorne.* 1879. London: Macmillan, 1967.

Jameson, Fredric. "Notes on Globalization as a Philosophical Issue." *The Cultures of Globalization.* Edited by Fredric Jameson and Masao Miyoshi. Durham, NC: Duke University Press, 1998. 54–77.

———. *The Political Unconscious: Narrative as a Socially Symbolic Act.* Ithaca, NY: Cornell University Press, 1981.

JanMohamed, Abdul R. "Negating the Negation: The Construction of Richard Wright." *Richard Wright: Critical Perspectives Past and Present.* Edited by Henry Louis Gates, Jr., and K. A. Appiah. New York: Amistad, 1993. 285–301.

Janowitz, Anne. "Class and Literature: The Case of Romantic Chartism." *Rethinking Class: Literary Studies and Social Formations.* Edited by Wai Chee Dimock and Michael T. Gilmore. New York: Columbia University Press, 1994. 239–66.

Jennings, James. "Persistent Poverty in the United States: Review of Theories and Explanations." *A New Introduction to Poverty: The Role of Race, Power, and Politics.* Edited by Louis Kushnick and James Jennings. New York: New York University Press, 1999. 13–38.

Jurca, Catherine. "Dreiser, Class, and the Home." *The Cambridge Companion to Theodore Dreiser.* Edited by Leonard Cassuto and Clare Virginia Eby. Cambridge: Cambridge University Press, 2004. 100–111.

Kaplan, Amy. *The Social Construction of American Realism.* Chicago, IL: University of Chicago Press, 1988.

Kaplan, Cora. "Millennial Class." *PMLA* 115.1 (2000): 9–19.

Kassanoff, Jennie A. "Extinction, Taxidermy, Tableaux Vivants: Staging Race and Class in *The House of Mirth.*" *PMLA* 115.1 (2000): 60–74.

Katz, Michael B. *The Undeserving Poor: From the War on Poverty to the War on Welfare.* New York: Pantheon, 1989.

——. "The Urban 'Underclass' as a Metaphor of Social Transformation." *The 'Underclass' Debate: Views from History.* Edited by Michael B. Katz. Princeton, NJ: Princeton University Press, 1993. 3–23.

Kerbo, Harold R. *Social Stratification and Inequality: Class Conflict in Historical and Comparative Perspective.* 3rd Edition. New York: McGraw-Hill, 1996.

Klebaner, Benjamin J. "Poverty and Its Relief in American Thought, 1815–1861." *Social Service Review* 38 (1964): 382–99.

Kleinman, Arthur, Veena Das, and Margaret Lock. "Introduction." *Social Suffering.* Edited by Arthur Kleinman, Veena Das, and Margaret Lock. Berkeley: University of California Press, 1997. ix–xxvii.

Kline, Wendy. *Building a Better Race: Gender, Sexuality, and Eugenics from the Turn of the Century to the Baby Boom.* Berkeley: University of California Press, 2001.

Kramer, Victor A. "The Consciousness of Technique: The Prose Method of James Agee's *Let Us Now Praise Famous Men.*" *Literature at the Barricades: The American Writer in the 1930s.* Edited by Ralph F. Bogardus and Fred Hobson. University: University of Alabama Press, 1982. 114–25.

Krugman, Paul. "For Richer." *New York Times.* Magazine Desk. October 20, 2002: 62–67, 76–77, 141–42.

Kushnick, Louis, and James Jennings, eds. *A New Introduction to Poverty: The Role of Race, Power, and Politics.* New York: New York University Press, 1999.

Kusmer, Kenneth L. *Down and Out, on the Road: The Homeless in American History.* Oxford: Oxford University Press, 2002.

Lang, Amy Schrager. "The Syntax of Class in Elizabeth Stuart Phelps's *The Silent Partner.*" *Rethinking Class: Literary Studies and Social Formations.* Edited by Wai Chee Dimock and Michael T. Gilmore. New York: Columbia University Press, 1994. 267–85.

——. *The Syntax of Class: Writing Inequality in Nineteenth-Century America.* Princeton, NJ: Princeton University Press, 2003.

Lauter, Paul. "Under Construction: Working-Class Writing." *New Working-Class Studies.* Edited by John Russo and Sherry Lee Linkon. Ithaca, NY: Cornell University Press, 2005. 63–77.

Leibowitz, Herbert. "'Arise, Ye Pris'ners of Starvation': Richard Wright's *Black Boy* and *American Hunger.*" *Richard Wright: Critical Perspectives Past and Present.* Edited by Henry Louis Gates, Jr., and K. A. Appiah. New York: Amistad, 1993. 328–58.

Le Sueur, Meridel. *The Girl.* 2nd Revised Edition. Albuquerque, NM: West End Press, 2006.

——. *Women on the Breadlines.* Revised Edition. Cambridge, MA: West End Press, 1984.

Lewis, Oscar. "The Culture of Poverty." *On Understanding Poverty: Perspectives from the Social Sciences. Perspectives on Poverty.* Edited by Daniel P. Moynihan. Vol. 1. New York: Basic, 1968. 187–200.

Lewis, Paul. "'Lectures or a Little Charity': Poor Visits in Antebellum Literature and Culture." *New England Quarterly* 73.2 (June 2000): 246–73.

Lipsitz, George. *Rainbow at Midnight: Labor and Culture in the 1940s.* Urbana: University of Illinois Press, 1994.

London, Jack. *The People of the Abyss.* 1903. London: Pluto, 1998.

Lott, Eric. *Love and Theft: Blackface Minstrelsy and the American Working Class.* New York: Oxford University Press, 1993.

Lowell, James Russell. "A Parable." 1848. *The Poetical Works of James Russell Lowell.* Boston, MA: Houghton Mifflin, 1978. 95.

Markham, Edwin. *The Man with the Hoe, and Other Poems.* Garden City, NY: Doubleday, 1929.

Marx, Karl, and Friedrich Engels. *The Communist Manifesto.* 1848. Harmondsworth: Penguin, 1967.

McCall, Dan. "Wright's American Hunger." *Richard Wright: Critical Perspectives Past and Present.* Edited by Henry Louis Gates, Jr., and K. A. Appiah. New York: Amistad, 1993. 359–68.

McCulloch, Oscar C. *The Tribe of Ishmael: A Study in Social Degeneration.* Reprinted from the Proceedings of the Fifteenth National Conference of Charities and Correction, held at Buffalo, July 1888. Indianapolis, IN: Charity Organization Society, 1891.

McNamara, Kevin R. "The Ames of The Good Society: *Sister Carrie* and Social Engineering." *Criticism* 34.2 (Spring 1992): 217–35.

Melville, Herman. "Bartleby, the Scrivener: A Story of Wall-Street." 1853. *The Piazza Tales and Other Prose Pieces, 1839–1860.* Evanston, IL: Northwestern University Press and the Newberry Library, 1987. 13–45.

——. "Cock-A-Doodle-Doo! Or, The Crowing of the Noble Cock Beneventano." 1853. *The Piazza Tales and Other Prose Pieces, 1839–1860.* Evanston, IL: Northwestern University Press and the Newberry Library, 1987. 268–88.

——. *The Confidence-Man. His Masquerade.* 1857. Evanston, IL: Northwestern University Press and the Newberry Library, 1984.

——. *Correspondence.* Evanston, IL: Northwestern University Press and the Newberry Library, 1993.

——. *Israel Potter: His Fifty Years of Exile.* 1855. Evanston, IL: Northwestern University Press, 1997.

——. "Jimmy Rose." 1855. *The Piazza Tales and Other Prose Pieces, 1839–1860.* Evanston, IL: Northwestern University Press and the Newberry Library, 1987. 336–45.

——. *Moby-Dick, or The Whale.* 1851. Harmondsworth: Penguin, 2002.

——. "The Paradise of Bachelors and the Tartarus of Maids." 1855. *The Piazza Tales and Other Prose Pieces, 1839–1860.* Evanston, IL: Northwestern University Press and the Newberry Library, 1987. 316–35.

——. *Pierre, or The Ambiguities.* 1852. Evanston, IL: Northwestern University Press, 1995.

——. "Poor Man's Pudding and Rich Man's Crumbs." 1854. *The Piazza Tales and Other Prose Pieces, 1839–1860.* Evanston, IL: Northwestern University Press and the Newberry Library, 1987. 289–302.

——. *Redburn: His First Voyage.* 1849. Evanston, IL: Northwestern University Press and the Newberry Library, 1969.

——. "The Two Temples." *The Piazza Tales and Other Prose Pieces, 1839–1860.* Evanston, IL: Northwestern University Press and the Newberry Library, 1987. 303–15.

Michaels, Walter Benn. "Autobiography of an Ex-White Man." *Transition* 73 (1997): 122–43.

——. "Diversity's False Solace." *New York Times.* Magazine Desk. April 11, 2004. Online archive.

———. *The Gold Standard and the Logic of Naturalism.* Berkeley: University of California Press, 1987.

———. *The Shape of the Signifier: 1967 to the End of History.* Princeton, NJ: Princeton University Press, 2004.

Miliband, Ralph. "Class Analysis." *Social Theory Today.* Edited by Anthony Giddens and Jonathan H. Turner. Stanford, CA: Stanford University Press, 1987. 325–46.

Moeller, Susan D. "The Cultural Construction of Urban Poverty: Images of Poverty in New York City, 1890–1917." *Journal of American Culture* 18.4 (1995): 1–16.

Moers, Ellen. *Two Dreisers.* New York: Viking, 1969.

Mohanty, Satya P. "The Epistemic Status of Cultural Identity: On *Beloved* and the Postcolonial Condition." *Reclaiming Identity: Realist Theory and the Predicament of Postmodernism.* Edited by Paula M. L. Moya and Michael R. Hames-García. Berkeley: University of California Press, 2000. 29–66.

Morgan, Stacy I. *Rethinking Social Realism: African American Art and Literature, 1930–1953.* Athens: University of Georgia Press, 2004.

Morris, David B. "About Suffering: Voice, Genre, and Moral Community." *Social Suffering.* Edited by Arthur Kleinman, Veena Das, and Margaret Lock. Berkeley: University of California Press, 1997. 25–45.

Myrdal, Gunnar. *An American Dilemma: The Negro Problem and Modern Democracy.* 2 Volumes. 1944. New York: Pantheon, 1975.

Nagel, James. *Stephen Crane and Literary Impressionism.* University Park: Pennsylvania State University Press, 1980.

Newman, Lea Bertani Vozar. *A Reader's Guide to the Short Stories of Herman Melville.* Boston, MA: G. K. Hall, 1986.

Norris, Frank. *Vandover and the Brute.* 1914. Lincoln: University of Nebraska Press, 1978.

O'Hara, Daniel T. "Class." *Critical Terms for Literary Study.* 2nd Edition. Edited by Frank Lentricchia and Thomas McLaughlin. Chicago, IL: University of Chicago Press, 1995. 406–27.

Olsen, Tillie. "A Biographical Interpretation." In Rebecca Harding Davis, *Life in the Iron Mills and Other Stories.* New York: Feminist Press, 1985. 69–174.

Ordover, Nancy. *American Eugenics: Race, Queer Anatomy, and the Science of Nationalism.* Minneapolis: University of Minnesota Press, 2003.

Orvell, Miles. *The Real Thing: Imitation and Authenticity in American Culture, 1880–1940.* Chapel Hill: University of North Carolina Press, 1989.

Otter, Samuel. "The Eden of Saddle Meadows: Landscape and Ideology in *Pierre.*" *American Literature* 66 (1994): 55–81.

———. *Melville's Anatomies.* Berkeley: University of California Press, 1999.

Papke, Mary E. *Verging on the Abyss: The Social Fiction of Kate Chopin and Edith Wharton.* New York: Greenwood, 1990.

Patterson, James T. *America's Struggle Against Poverty, 1900–1985.* Cambridge, MA: Harvard University Press, 1986.

Patterson, Orlando. *Slavery and Social Death: A Comparative Study.* Cambridge, MA: Harvard University Press, 1982.

Pease, Donald. "C.L.R. James, *Moby-Dick,* and the Emergence of Transnational American Studies." *Arizona Quarterly* 56.3 (Autumn 2000): 93–123.

Peeler, David P. *Hope among Us Yet: Social Criticism and Social Solace in Depression America.* Athens: University of Georgia Press, 1987.

Peiss, Kathy. *Cheap Amusements: Working Women and Leisure in Turn-of-the-Century New York.* Philadelphia, PA: Temple University Press, 1986.

Pells, Richard H. *Radical Visions and American Dreams: Culture and Social Thought in the Depression Years.* 1973. Middletown, CT: Wesleyan University Press, 1984.

Petry, Ann. *The Street.* 1946. Boston, MA: Houghton Mifflin, 1991.

Pfaelzer, Jean. *Parlor Radical: Rebecca Harding Davis and the Origins of American Social Realism.* Pittsburgh, PA: University of Pittsburgh Press, 1996.

Phelps, Elizabeth Stuart. *The Silent Partner: A Novel and "The Tenth of January": A Short Story.* Old Westbury, NY: Feminist Press, 1983.

Pittenger, Mark. "A World of Difference: Constructing the 'Underclass' in Progressive America." *American Quarterly* 49.1 (March 1997): 26–65.

Pizer, Donald. *The Novels of Theodore Dreiser: A Critical Study.* Minneapolis: University of Minnesota Press, 1976.

———, ed. *Theodore Dreiser: A Selection of Uncollected Prose.* Detroit, MI: Wayne State University Press, 1977.

Platt, Anthony M. *E. Franklin Frazier Reconsidered.* New Brunswick, NJ: Rutgers University Press, 1991.

Prescott, Orville. Review of *Black Boy* by Richard Wright. *New York Times,* Feb. 28, 1945, p. 21. Reprinted in *Richard Wright: The Critical Reception.* Edited by John M. Reilly. New York: Burt Franklin, 1978. 120–21.

Proctor, Bernadette D., and Joseph Dalaker. *Poverty in the United States: 2001.* US Census Bureau, Current Population Reports, P60–219. Washington, DC: US Gov., 2002.

Rabinowitz, Paula. *Labor and Desire: Women's Revolutionary Fiction in Depression America.* Chapel Hill: University of North Carolina Press, 1991.

———. "Voyeurism and Class Consciousness: James Agee and Walker Evans, *Let Us Now Praise Famous Men.*" *Cultural Critique* 21 (Spring 1992): 143–70.

Rafter, Nicole Hahn. *Creating Born Criminals.* Urbana: University of Illinois Press, 1997.

———, ed. *White Trash: The Eugenic Family Studies, 1877–1919.* Boston, MA: Northeastern University Press, 1988.

Ralph, Julian. *People We Pass: Stories of Life among the Masses of New York City.* New York: Harper, 1896.

Rancière, Jacques. *The Philosopher and His Poor.* Translated by John Drury, Corinne Oster, and Andrew Parker. Durham, NC: Duke University Press, 2003.

Ranney, David C. "Class, Race, Gender, and Poverty: A Critique of Some Contemporary Theories." *A New Introduction to Poverty: The Role of Race, Power, and Politics.* Edited by Louis Kushnick and James Jennings. New York: New York University Press, 1999. 39–56.

Rawls, John. *A Theory of Justice.* 1971. Revised Edition. Cambridge, MA: Belknap Press of Harvard University Press, 1999.

Reed, Adolph, Jr. "The 2004 Election in Perspective: The Myth of 'Cultural Divide' and the Triumph of Neoliberal Ideology." *American Quarterly* 57.1 (2005): 1–15.

Reed, T. V. "Unimagined Existence and the Fiction of the Real: Postmodernist Realism in *Let Us Now Praise Famous Men.*" *Representations* 24 (Fall 1988): 156–76.

Reilly, John M., ed. *Richard Wright: The Critical Reception.* New York: Burt Franklin, 1978.

Restuccia, Frances L. "The Name of the Lily: Edith Wharton's Feminism(s)." Shari Benstock, ed. *Edith Wharton: The House of Mirth.* Boston, MA: Bedford/St. Martin's, 1994. 404–18.

Reynolds, David S. *Beneath the American Renaissance: The Subversive Imagination in the Age of Emerson and Whitman.* Cambridge, MA: Harvard University Press, 1988.

Rezneck, Samuel. "The Social History of an American Depression, 1837–1843." *American Historical Review* 40 (1934–35): 662–87.

Richardson, Dorothy. *The Long Day: The Story of a New York Working Girl as Told by Herself.* New York: The Century, 1905.

Riis, Jacob A. *How the Other Half Lives: Studies among the Tenements of New York.* 1890. New York: Dover, 1971.

Rimstead, Roxanne. *Remnants of Nation: On Poverty Narratives by Women.* Toronto: University of Toronto Press, 2001.

Rivera, Tomás. *. . . y no se lo tragó la tierra.* With a translation into English by Evangelina Vigil-Piñón. Houston, TX: Arte Publico Press, 1992.

Robinson, Lillian S. "The Traffic in Women: A Cultural Critique of *The House of Mirth.*" Shari Benstock, ed. *Edith Wharton: The House of Mirth.* Boston, MA: Bedford/St. Martin's, 1994. 340–58.

Roediger, David. "'More Than Two Things': The State and the Art of Labor History." *New Working-Class Studies.* Edited by John Russo and Sherry Lee Linkon. Ithaca, NY: Cornell University Press, 2005. 32–41.

Rogin, Michael Paul. *Subversive Genealogy: The Politics and Art of Herman Melville.* New York: Knopf, 1983.

Rorty, James. *Where Life Is Better: An Unsentimental American Journey.* New York: Reynal and Hitchcock, 1936.

Rothman, David. J. *The Discovery of the Asylum: Social Order and Disorder in the New Republic.* Boston, MA: Little, Brown, 1971.

——, ed. *The Jacksonians on the Poor: Collected Pamphlets. Poverty, U.S.A.: The Historical Record.* New York: Arno and the New York Times, 1971.

Rowe, John Carlos. *At Emerson's Tomb: The Politics of Classic American Literature.* New York: Columbia, 1997.

——. "The Writing Class." *Politics, Theory, and Contemporary Culture.* Edited by Mark Poster. New York: Columbia University Press, 1993. 41–82.

Rowland, Beryl. "Sitting Up with a Corpse: Malthus according to Melville in 'Poor Man's Pudding and Rich Man's Crumbs.'" *Journal of American Studies* 6 (1972): 69–83.

Rubin, Louis D., Jr. "Trouble on the Land: Southern Literature and the Great Depression." *Literature at the Barricades: The American Writer in the 1930s.* Edited by Ralph F. Bogardus and Fred Hobson. University: University of Alabama Press, 1982. 96–113.

Russo, John, and Sherry Lee Linkon. *New Working-Class Studies.* Ithaca, NY: Cornell University Press, 2005.

Ryan, Susan M. *The Grammar of Good Intentions: Race and the Antebellum Culture of Benevolence.* Ithaca, NY: Cornell University Press, 2003.

Saldívar, Ramón. *Chicano Narrative: The Dialectics of Difference.* Madison: University of Wisconsin Press, 1990.

Salzman, Jack, ed. *Theodore Dreiser: The Critical Reception.* New York: David Lewis, 1972.

Sanborn, Alvan Francis. *Moody's Lodging House and Other Tenement Sketches.* Boston, MA: Copeland and Day, 1895.

Sandage, Scott A. "The Gaze of Success: Failed Men in the Sentimental Marketplace, 1873–1893." *Sentimental Men: Masculinity and the Politics of Affect in American Culture.* Edited by Mary Chapman and Glenn Hendler. Berkeley: University of California Press, 1999. 181–201.

Sanger, Margaret, *Woman and the New Race.* New York: Brentano's, 1920.

Sante, Luc. *Low Life: Lures and Snares of Old New York.* New York: Vintage, 1991.

Scarry, Elaine. *Resisting Representation.* New York: Oxford University Press, 1994.

Schocket, Eric. "'Discovering Some New Race': Rebecca Harding Davis's 'Life in the Iron Mills' and the Literary Emergence of Working-Class Whiteness." *PMLA* 115.1 (2000): 46–59.

Seltzer, Mark. *Bodies and Machines.* New York: Routledge, 1992.

Shulman, Robert. "Divided Selves and the Market Society: Politics and Psychology in *The House of Mirth.*" *Perspectives on Contemporary Literature* 11 (1985): 10–19.

——. *The Power of Political Art: The 1930s Literary Left Reconsidered.* Chapel Hill: University of North Carolina Press, 2000.

Sinclair, Upton. *The Jungle.* 1906. Harmondsworth: Penguin, 1985.

Sipple, Susan. "Witness [to] the Suffering of Women": Poverty and Sexual Transgression in Meridel Le Sueur's *Women on the Breadlines.*" *Feminism, Bakhtin, and the Dialogic.* Edited by Dale M. Bauer and Susan Jaret McKinstry. Albany: State University of New York Press, 1991. 135–53.

Smith, Bernard. *Forces in American Criticism: A Study in the History of American Literary Thought.* New York: Harcourt, Brace, 1939.

Smith, Judith E. *Visions of Belonging: Family Stories, Popular Culture, and Postwar Democracy, 1940–1960.* New York: Columbia University Press, 2004.

Smith, Ruth L. "Order and Disorder: The Naturalization of Poverty." *Cultural Critique* 14 (Winter 1989–90): 209–29.

Spooner, Lysander. *Poverty: Its Illegal Causes and Legal Cure.* 1846. New York: Da Capo, 1971.

Stansell, Christine. *City of Women: Sex and Class in New York, 1789–1860.* New York: Knopf, 1986.

Staten, Henry. *Nietzsche's Voice.* Ithaca, NY: Cornell University Press, 1990.

Staub, Michael E. *Voices of Persuasion: Politics of Representation in 1930s America.* Cambridge: Cambridge University Press, 1994.

Steinbeck, John. *The Grapes of Wrath.* 1939. New York: Penguin, 1992.

Stepto, Robert. "Literacy and Ascent: *Black Boy.*" *Richard Wright: Critical Perspectives Past and Present.* Edited by Henry Louis Gates, Jr., and K. A. Appiah. New York: Amistad, 1993. 226–54.

Stott, William. *Documentary Expression and Thirties America.* New York: Oxford University Press, 1973.

Sullivan, Ellie Ragland. "The Daughter's Dilemma: Psychoanalytic Interpretation and Edith Wharton's *The House of Mirth*." Shari Benstock, ed. *Edith Wharton: The House of Mirth*. Boston, MA: Bedford/St. Martin's, 1994. 464–81.

Susman, Warren I. *Culture as History: The Transformation of American Society in the Twentieth Century*. New York: Pantheon, 1984.

Szalay, Michael. *New Deal Modernism: American Literature and the Invention of the Welfare State*. Durham, NC: Duke University Press, 2000.

Templin, Mary. "Panic Fiction: Women's Responses to Antebellum Economic Crisis." *Legacy* 21.1 (2004): 1–16.

Terkel, Studs. *Hard Times: An Oral History of the Great Depression*. 1970. New York: Pantheon, 1986.

Thaddeus, Janice. "The Metamorphosis of *Black Boy*." *Richard Wright: Critical Perspectives Past and Present*. Edited by Henry Louis Gates, Jr., and K. A. Appiah. New York: Amistad, 1993. 272–84.

Thernstrom, Stephan. "Poverty in Historical Perspective." *On Understanding Poverty: Perspectives from the Social Sciences. Perspectives on Poverty*. Edited by Daniel P. Moynihan. Vol. 1. New York: Basic, 1968. 160–86.

Thoreau, Henry David. *Walden*. 1854. Princeton, NJ: Princeton University Press, 1971.

Tintner, Adeline R. "Two Novels of 'the Relatively Poor': *New Grub Street* and *The House of Mirth*." *Notes on Modern American Literature* 6.2 (Autumn 1982): item 12.

Tocqueville, Alexis de. *Democracy in America*. Edited by J. P. Mayer. Translated by George Lawrence. New York: Harper and Row, 1988.

Townsend, Edward W. *A Daughter of the Tenements*. 1895. New York: Street and Smith, 1900.

Trachtenberg, Alan. *The Incorporation of America: Culture and Society in the Gilded Age*. New York: Hill and Wang, 1982.

Tracy, Susan Jean. *In the Master's Eye: Representations of Women, Blacks, and Poor Whites in Antebellum Southern Literature*. Amherst: University of Massachusetts Press, 1995.

Trask, Michael. *Cruising Modernism: Class and Sexuality in American Literature and Social Thought*. Ithaca, NY: Cornell University Press, 2003.

Trilling, Lionel. "Greatness with One Fault in It." *Kenyon Review* 4.1 (Winter 1942): 99–102.

——. Review of *Black Boy* by Richard Wright. *The Nation*, April 7, 1945. Reprinted in *Richard Wright: Critical Perspectives Past and Present*. Edited by Henry Louis Gates, Jr., and K. A. Appiah. New York: Amistad, 1993. 28–30.

Tuckerman, Joseph. *On the Elevation of the Poor. A Selection from His Reports as Minister at Large in Boston*. Boston, MA: Roberts Bros., 1874.

Turner, Terrence. "Anthropology and Multiculturalism: What Is Anthropology That Multiculturalists Should Be Mindful of It?" *Multiculturalism: A Critical Reader*. Edited by David Theo Goldberg. Oxford: Blackwell, 1994. 406–25.

Twain, Mark. *The Prince and the Pauper*. 1881. Harmondsworth: Penguin, 1997.

Valentine, Charles A. *Culture and Poverty: Critique and Counter-Proposals*. Chicago, IL: University of Chicago Press, 1968.

Van Vorst, Mrs. John [Bessie], and Van Vorst, Marie. *The Woman Who Toils: Being the Experiences of Two Gentlewomen as Factory Girls*. New York: Doubleday, Page, 1903.

Veblen, Thorstein. *The Theory of the Leisure Class*. 1899. Harmondsworth: Penguin, 1994.

Wald, Alan. *The Revolutionary Imagination: The Poetry and Politics of John Wheelwright and Sherry Mangan.* Chapel Hill: University of North Carolina Press, 1983.

Wald, Priscilla. "Dreiser's Sociological Vision." *The Cambridge Companion to Theodore Dreiser.* Edited by Leonard Cassuto and Clare Virginia Eby. Cambridge: Cambridge University Press, 2004. 177–95.

Walker, Francis A. "The Causes of Poverty." *The Century* 55, n.s. 33 (November 1897–April 1898): 210–16.

Ward, Cynthia. "From the Suwanee to Egypt, There's No Place like Home." *PMLA* 115.1 (2000): 75–88.

Warner, Amos G. *American Charities: A Study in Philanthropy and Economics.* 1894. New Brunswick, NJ: Transaction Publishers, 1989.

Watterson, R. C. *An Address on Pauperism, Its Extent, Causes, and the Best Means of Prevention.* 1844. Reprinted in David Rothman, ed. *The Jacksonians on the Poor: Collected Pamphlets. Poverty, U.S.A.: The Historical Record.* New York: Arno and the New York Times, 1971.

Waxman, Chaim I. *The Stigma of Poverty: A Critique of Poverty Theories and Policies.* New York: Pergamon Press, 1977.

Weinstein, Cindy. *The Literature of Labor and the Labors of Literature: Allegory in Nineteenth-Century American Fiction.* Cambridge: Cambridge University Press, 1995.

——. "Melville, Labor, and the Discourses of Reception." *The Cambridge Companion to Herman Melville.* Edited by Robert S. Levine. Cambridge: Cambridge University Press, 1998. 202–23.

Wharton, Edith. *Ethan Frome.* 1911. Harmondsworth: Penguin, 1987.

——. *The Fruit of the Tree.* 1907. Boston, MA: Northeastern University Press, 2000.

——. *The House of Mirth.* 1905. New York: Scribner's, 1969.

——. *Summer.* 1917. New York: Penguin, 1993.

White, Ed. "Early American Nations as Imagined Communities." *American Quarterly* 56.1 (March 2004): 49–81.

Williams, Keith. "Post/Modern Documentary: Orwell, Agee and the New Reportage." *Rewriting the Thirties: Modernism and After.* Edited by Keith Williams and Steven Matthews. London: Longman, 1997. 163–81.

Williams, Raymond. *Marxism and Literature.* Oxford: Oxford University Press, 1977.

Williams, Vernon J., Jr. "E. Franklin Frazier and the African American Family in Historical Perspective." *The Western Journal of Black Studies* 23.4 (1999): 246–51.

Wilson, Harriet E. *Our Nig: or, Sketches from the Life of a Free Black.* 1859. New York: Vintage, 1983.

Wilson, William Julius. *The Truly Disadvantaged: The Inner City, the Underclass, and Public Policy.* Chicago, IL: University of Chicago Press, 1987.

Woodson, Thomas. "Thoreau on Poverty and Magnanimity." *PMLA* 85 (1970): 21–34.

Wray, Matt, and Annalee Newitz, eds. *White Trash: Race and Class in America.* New York: Routledge, 1997.

Wright, Richard. *Black Boy (American Hunger): A Record of Childhood and Youth.* 1945. New York: Harper Collins, 1998.

——. *Eight Men.* 1961. New York: Harper Collins, 1996.

——. "How 'Bigger' Was Born." 1940. *Native Son.* New York: Harper Collins, 1998. 433–62.

——. Introduction. *Black Metropolis: A Study of Negro Life in a Northern City.* By St. Clair Drake and Horace R. Cayton. 1945. Chicago, IL: University of Chicago Press, 1993. xvii–xxxiv.

——. *Lawd Today!* 1963. Boston, MA: Northeastern University Press, 1993.

——. *Native Son.* 1940. New York: Harper Collins, 1998.

——. *12 Million Black Voices.* Photo direction by Edwin Rosskam. 1941. New York: Thunder's Mouth, 1988.

——. *Uncle Tom's Children.* 1938. New York: Harper Collins, 1993.

Yeazell, Ruth Bernard. "The Conspicuous Wasting of Lily Bart." *ELH* 59 (1992): 713–34.

Zandy, Janet. *Hands: Physical Labor, Class, and Cultural Work.* New Brunswick, NJ: Rutgers University Press, 2004.

Ziff, Larzer. *The American 1890s: Life and Times of a Lost Generation.* New York: Viking, 1966.

Zimmerman, David A. "Frank Norris, Market Panic, and the Mesmeric Sublime." *American Literature* 75.1 (March 2003): 61–90.

Žižek, Slavoj. "Class Struggle or Postmodernism? Yes, please!" *Contingency, Hegemony, Universality: Contemporary Dialogues on the Left.* Edited by Judith Butler, Ernesto Laclau and Slavoj Žižek. London: Verso, 2000. 90–135.

Zweig, Michael. *The Working Class Majority: America's Best Kept Secret.* Ithaca, NY: ILR/Cornell University Press, 2000.

INDEX

DATE DUE

DISCARDED

Printed in USA

HIGHSMITH #45230